ONTARIO

BOYS

Studies in
Childhood and Family
in Canada

A broad-ranging series that publishes scholarship from various disciplines, approaches and perspectives relevant to the concepts and relations of childhood and family in Canada. Our interests also include, but are not limited to, interdisciplinary approaches and theoretical investigations of gender, race, sexuality, geography, language and culture within these categories of experience, historical and contemporary.

Series Editor:
Cynthia Comacchio
History Department
Wilfrid Laurier University

Send proposals to:
Lisa Quinn, Acquisitions Editor
Wilfrid Laurier University Press
75 University Avenue West
Waterloo, ON N2L 3C5, Canada
Phone: 519-884-0710 ext. 2843
Fax: 519-725-1399
Email: quinn@press.wlu.ca

ONTARIO
BOYS

Masculinity and the Ideas of

Boyhood in Postwar Ontario,

1945–1960

CHRISTOPHER J. GREIG

WILFRID LAURIER
UNIVERSITY PRESS

Wilfrid Laurier University Press acknowledge the support of the Canada Council for the Arts for our publishing program. We acknowledge the financial support of the Government of Canada through the Canada Book Fund for our publishing activities.

Library and Archives Canada Cataloguing in Publication

Greig, Christopher J. (Christopher John), 1965–, author
   Ontario boys : masculinity and the idea of boyhood in postwar Ontario, 1945–1960 / Christopher J. Greig.

(Studies in childhood and family in Canada)
Includes bibliographical references and index.
Issued in print and electronic formats.
ISBN 978-1-55458-900-5 (pbk.).—ISBN 978-1-55458-901-2 (pdf).—
ISBN 978-1-55458-902-9 (epub)

   1. Boys—Ontario—History—20th century. 2. Boys—Ontario—Historiography.
3. Masculinity—Social aspects—Ontario—History—20th century. 4. Ontario—
Civilization—20th century. I. Title. II. Series: Studies in childhood and family in Canada

HQ775.G74 2014   305.2308110971309'045   C2013-904771-9   C2013-904772-7

Cover design by David Drummond. Front-cover image: Body-checking instruction for young hockey players, Arnprior, Ontario, January 1956; photo from Library and Archives Canada/National Film Board of Canada/Photothèque collection/PA-111481: © Library and Archives Canada nlc-5718. Text design by Brenda Prangley.

This book is printed on FSC recycled paper and is certified Ecologo. It is made from 100% post-consumer fibre, processed chlorine free, and manufactured using biogas energy.

Printed in Canada

Every reasonable effort has been made to acquire permission for copyright material used in this text, and to acknowledge all such indebtedness accurately. Any errors and omissions called to the publisher's attention will be corrected in future printings.

Contents

Acknowledgements   vii

Introduction:
Approaching Boyhood In Postwar Ontario   ix

1   Home, Family, Citizenship:
Shaping the Boyhood Ideal   1

2   One for All:
Teamwork and the Boyhood Ideal   27

3   One above All:
The Heroic Ideal in Boyhood   55

4   Dissonant Ideas:
Other Boyhoods   75

5   Changes and Continuities:
Historic and Contemporary Boyhood Ideals   101

6   Conclusion:
Making Ontario Boys, 1945–1960   121

Notes   129

References and Sources   163

Index   173

Acknowledgements

There are a number of debts associated with this book. First and foremost, I would like to thank Rebecca Coulter who has always been a constant source of inspiration. Her continuous support and encouragement, as well as her wise, prudent, generous, and thoughtful counsel, has helped sustain me over the course of my academic life.

For helping this book on its way, I wish also to thank Cynthia Comacchio, who provided thoughtful feedback and keen insights on portions of the manuscript. I am also indebted to Cynthia for her ongoing moral and practical support that served to ensure the manuscript turned into a book. I would also like to thank others at Wilfrid Laurier University Press, including Lisa Quinn, Rob Kohlmeier, Brian Henderson, and Ryan Chynces, who have helped shepherd this book through various stages, including the production process. Finally, I would also acknowledge the support and guidance provided by Bob Gidney and Joy Parr. Of course, I alone am responsible for any weaknesses that may remain in the book.

Finally, I have also been enormously supported by my beautiful family—Leona, Jaden, Emma (my Lou), and Ashley. However, I would especially like to thank Leona, who has always supported me in my educational and intellectual pursuits over the past decade. I am incredibly grateful for her unconditional support.

Introduction

Approaching Boyhood in Postwar Ontario

The world is so full of boys.

Leamington Post and News, 28 August 1947

Today we find that the social, economic and political climate
generates intense fears, gnawing anxieties in millions of people.

Dr. Julius Schreiber, *Globe and Mail*, 28 March 1949

As these observations suggest, in country town as in burgeoning metropo-
lis, among local commentators and highly trained professionals alike,
the early post–Second World War years saw Ontarians much preoccupied with the nature and potential of boyhood. *Ontario Boys* explores these
public discourses during the so-called Baby Boom years, from roughly 1945
to 1960. In the aftermath of a second world war little more than a generation
after the first, during which a nation still reeling from the Great Depression had
again mustered its forces to contribute mightily on home front and on battle-
field, it is no surprise that many Canadians should have longed to return to "the
normal"—the familiar, in its every sense. Yet much of the Reconstruction program, as the Mackenzie King Liberal government called its postwar plan, was
an attempt to recover what two world wars and a prolonged economic depression had changed irrevocably. Among these changes were reconfigurations of
gender and familial roles, with their necessary socio-cultural implications.[1]

During these opening decades of what was seen to be a "new age"—vari-
ously the Atomic Age, the Cold War, even the TV Age—a population dealing
with "gnawing anxieties," as Dr. Julius Schreiber aptly described them in the
Globe and Mail in 1949, looked to "reconstruct" itself by means of its best
hope: children and youth. Canadians confronted a profoundly gendered insecurity, instability, and anxiety brought about by Depression era and wartime

disruptions in marital, family, and labour relations, rapid postwar economic changes, mass migration from countryside to city as well as renewed overseas immigration, the emergence of the Cold War, and the looming threat of atomic annihilation. Shaped by these historic developments, and motivated by an understandable desire for normality, stability, and security, public defenders of the traditional gender hierarchy resisted shifts in the roles and relations that underpinned it.[2] In their ongoing quest to head "back to normalcy," an assortment of public intellectuals, political leaders, psychologists, physicians, youth workers, and educators, along with concerned social commentators, projected their gendered fears about the postwar future onto discussions of boyhood development. Despite the shifts wrought by depression and war, Canadian society remained fundamentally patriarchal: "The world," a small-town newspaper columnist noted affectionately, was, after all, "so full of boys." And these boys became the focus of future-oriented postwar discourses whereby heteronormative definitions of masculinity were reasserted to define an appropriately "masculine" character formation for Ontario boys.[3]

Under the conditions of the postwar period, social commentators routinely produced public narratives that normalized boys who demonstrated a particular "ideal" of masculinity. In the decade and a half immediately following the Second World War, the "new" version of boyhood was one that harkened back, in this rapidly changing, expanding, modern urban-industrial environment, to a traditional historic form, or at least one that had been nostalgically rendered as the "norm" before the transformations of the early twentieth century. This ideal stressed teamwork, selflessness, eagerness, honesty, fearlessness, and emotional toughness. While such traits had long typified ideal boyhood, in a postwar world where, in the view of many observers, democracy was under constant threat by communist forces, and the ongoing struggle was that between freedom and tyranny, the need for all boys to develop and internalize such traits gained in importance as a vital foundation of modern democratic nationhood.

In view of the accelerated socio-cultural trends made visible in the aftermath of war, hence such pressing national and international anxieties, the traditional sources of "normal" masculine role modelling—family, school, church, community—could not be counted upon. Active public intervention to invest boys with this version of masculinity was thought essential. Such public investment would make them the kinds of citizens capable of governing, protecting, and defending the nation, and, of course, maintaining and regulating the social order. The citizen-leader of the future, like that of the past, was gender defined. Citizenship was male by nature. In contrast, girls were expected and encouraged to adopt a "special kind" of citizenship characterized by their innate maternalism.[4] In this brave new postwar world, active public citizenship and democratic participation were intended for men. Public citizenship continued to be depicted largely as a male duty, a duty best learned in boyhood. An "appropriate" boyhood in the postwar period became, if nothing else, a metaphor for the survival of the nation, but a nation whose survival was contingent on male dominance in the historic patriarchal manner.

IDEAS/IDEALS OF BOYHOOD

Boyhood is socially and historically constructed, and consequently subject to changes over time and in accordance with its specific context and culture. Despite its historically contingent nature, one association, that of biological age, remains consistent.[5] Most commentators accepted the idea that boyhood began when boys entered elementary school, usually at age six. Psychologist Leon Saul, in his 1947 work *Emotional Maturity*, saw the break from infancy and dependency to childhood and semi-independence beginning at age six and coinciding with the introduction to school.[6] Marian Breckenridge and E. Lee Vincent, two prominent psychologists of the time, noted that "the childhood cycle, which closely approximates the elementary school age, begins with the appearance of the sixth year molars and lasts until the onset of pubescence."[7] These conceptualizations, which found their basis in medicine and psychology, informed both official and popular discourses of the time. *The Report of the Royal Commission on Education in Ontario, 1950* (hereafter, *The Hope Report*) suggested that childhood was generally understood to begin at age six and coincided "with the entrance into the first grade of elementary school."[8] As to its termination, Kitchener, Ontario, writer Clayton Derstine, in his 1944 book *Paths to Noble Manhood*, observed that the development from "boyhood to manhood occurs from about eleven to fourteen years of age," when "a moustache begins to appear; the voice breaks; hair grows at various places; he becomes awkward in motions." According to the most influential postwar child care expert, the American pediatrician Dr. Benjamin Spock, boyhood ended and adolescence started with biological puberty, roughly between the ages of thirteen and fourteen.[9]

For the purposes of this work, boyhood will be bound and defined as the period between the ages of six and fourteen. Employing this age demarcation to conceptualize and frame this historic study of boyhood does not, however, render boyhood a fixed, rigid, or "natural" category. Age, like gender, race, class, and sexuality, is a socially constructed category whose multiple and complex meanings fundamentally derive from the particular ideals—"norms"—of a given society at a specific point in its history.[10]

At the outset, the "ideal" boyhood cannot be adequately considered without acknowledgement of the racialized and class-based meanings inherent to it. Despite the changing patterns of a renewed immigration that led to slowly widening racial, ethnic, and linguistic diversity in postwar Canada, the defini-tion of an "ideal" boyhood, just as it remained embedded in traditional patri-archal understandings of gender and citizenship, also remained intrinsically "white." All changes notwithstanding, and, in fact, largely in response to the perceived threat that such changes posed to "normalcy," the vast majority of positive representations of a "normal" boyhood, in professional and popular discourses alike, were as notably "white" as they had always been. Non-white identities were a key disqualifier to what constituted an ideal boyhood. Gender, power, prestige, status, and race were intimately tied together; in regard to this study's boy subjects, these were all effectively complicated by age. Attention to how these identifying categories intersect with age at the centre of this anal-ysis indicates how boys from socially disadvantaged, poor, or marginalized, working-class, non-Anglo-Protestant, non-white backgrounds, possibly from single-parent households, had a diminished claim on an "ideal" boyhood. At the same time, it helps uncover the social construction of diverse and unequal childhoods. A notable example of a specific category of non-white racialized boyhood that appeared in the popular press can be found in the consistently negative characterizations of Indigenous boys as unhealthy, intellectually inad-equate, delinquent, and in some cases criminal.[11]

The racialized representations of Indigenous boyhoods in the period's popular discourses also need to be understood in relation to the residential school system. Shaped by colonialist and racist ideologies, residential schools were established in Canada during the late nineteenth century and continued until the 1990s, funded by the federal government and administered by a number of Christian denominations. More than 150,000 Indigenous chil-dren were placed, often forcibly, in a system that left many subject to phys-ical, emotional, spiritual, and psychological violence.[12] As historians have documented, the residential school system constituted a systematic assault on Indigenous culture by means of a systematic "assault" on the children of these communities.[13] Despite the horrors that racism had unleashed during the Second World War, postwar Canada remained, literally, "a white man's country." With racism deeply institutionalized in truly separate and unequal schooling, it is not surprising that Indigenous boyhoods continued to be repre-sented as 'inferior' in postwar discourses created by, and for the benefit of, the white and predominantly middle-class majority.[14] If the boyhoods constructed and circulated through media, professional, and government discourses held up an idealized Ontario boyhood that eluded many real Ontario boys, it was that much further from realization for boys who were marginalized by race, whether Indigenous or recent immigrants, and especially for those who were classified as "visible" minorities.[15]

HISTORIOGRAPHICAL AND THEORETICAL FRAMEWORKS

Despite the recent proliferation of work on gender, children, and childhood, and the burgeoning attention in the Canadian historiography to the post–Second World War years, there is no extant sustained historical analysis of the making of boyhood in postwar Ontario. *Ontario Boys* draws from, and expands upon, the work of a number of scholars who have explored this study's principal subjects: childhood, gender, and the social construction of certain normative versions of these that are, in fact, reflections of ideals rather than norms.[16] As Franca Iacovetta and Molly-Ladd Taylor have observed, scholars such as these have demonstrated that "masculinity, like femininity, is neither a biological state of being nor a fixed and unitary set of practices and identities." Masculinity is better understood as a relational construct "forged in particular contexts and by critical forces, including class, race-ethnicity, state-power, patriarchy, and ideology, that shape such contexts."[17] It is a complex set of meanings, and like boyhood, it exists as an historical product, culturally constructed and socially organized. Moreover, masculinity intersects with the identities ascribed by class, gender, race, and sexual orientation, while also interacting with the social and institutional relations that create status differences and hierarchies. Ultimately, there is no timeless and universal definition of masculinity, no singular masculine ideal, however much dominant social groups might presume it.

To avoid conceptualizing it as an unchanging unified construct, and to account for the various, diverse, and pluralistic constructs, I have framed masculinity in terms of *masculinities*. In effect, although I employ the singular form "boyhood" for consistency, it is important to recognize that "boyhoods" is the more encompassing and appropriate term. The gender analysis employed in *Ontario Boys* draws from the work of Raewyn Connell, whose theory of multiple masculinities has had a resounding impact on the growing historical scholarship about men and masculinities.[18] Derived from Italian theorist Antonio Gramsci's concept of hegemony as an approach to class relations, Connell's work focuses on the notion of a gender hierarchy whereby competing versions of masculinity struggle for dominance within the gender order. She defines the available positions within the gender order in terms of the contest between the hegemonic or most socially, politically, and economically valued and valourized versions and those that are subordinate, marginalized, and complicit. Subordinate, marginalized, and complicit versions of masculinity compete and negotiate with the hegemonic forms for relative access to social power, privilege, and status. Because it is naturalized at the top of the hierarchy, hegemonic masculinity secures all men's systemic advantage over women.[19]

Hegemonic masculinity refers more specifically to the culturally dominant form that is constructed in relation to femininity and to various subordinated and marginalized masculinities. As noted, it is theorized to be a "cultural ideal" that is constantly promoted through the production of "exemplary masculinities." Where boys are concerned, these are exemplified in postwar newspaper images of the boy-hero. These representations of "exemplary masculinities" contribute to the continued production, reproduction, and rejuvenation of patriarchy.[20] The capacity to establish and sanction a particular definition of boyhood and to produce gender ideals was an essential part of this process. Hegemony involved persuading the greater part of the population, particularly through widely accessible print media, in ways that linked certain activities and ways of being for boys with the "natural" and "normal." Boys were often depicted in the newspapers playing hockey or baseball; "normal" boys, it was understood, actively participated in these "manly" sports. An article published in the *Globe and Mail* on 20 October 1951 described Ontario's junior male hockey players as "specimens of a perfect manhood."[21] To supplement the gendered messages of news stories, popular advertisements of the time showed boys happily playing with military or cowboy-themed toys. The ideological work done by these advertisements, whereby boys were encouraged to see themselves as warriors or soldiers who "took action" against an enemy threat, delivered the message that even very young boys could prepare to serve, protect, and defend, all traditional masculine roles that needed reinforcement in the face of contemporary threats.

METHOD AND SOURCES

Ontario Boys is based on a close reading, and layering, of a range of published materials. I have collected evidence from mass-circulation periodicals and newspapers, works of popular fiction and non-fiction, commercial advertisements, church publications, published commentaries, and men's autobiographies and memoirs, as well as from the writings of professionals and academics of the period under study in the fields of economics, education, sociology, and psychology. My purpose is straightforward: *Ontario Boys* sets out to explore and elaborate on the making of an "ideal" boyhood during the years 1945 to 1960. This analysis renders visible the ways in which an "ideal" version of boyhood was strengthened and validated through numerous acts of reiteration in the professional and public discourses of the time. As such, *Ontario Boys* considers the contours of an ideal postwar boyhood and how this ideal boyhood was produced and then disseminated in ways not yet directly addressed in the literature exploring childhood, gender, and masculinity in postwar Ontario.

I have drawn from a North American source base to support this discussion but have focused primarily on sources published in Ontario; the conclusions are thus shaped by this regional context. The largest single source of evidence for this study is Ontario's print media, and in this regard, I have examined the three most popular newspapers of the day: the *Globe and Mail*, the *Toronto Daily Star*, and the *Toronto Telegram*. In addition to these metropolitan dailies, with their province-wide readership, I have analyzed a selection of small-town and rural newspapers: the *Acton Free Press*, the *Essex County Reporter and Lakeshore News*, the *Georgetown Herald*, the *Kingsville Reporter*, the *Leamington Post and News*, the *London Free Press*, the *Newmarket Era*, and the *Stouffville Tribune*, among others. My intention has been to trace the circulation of similar ideas about boys and boyhood, in different communities, by means of the medium most likely to be accessed by the province's largest social group, of "mixed" composition in terms of class, "race," and gender. Whatever its actual social influence, the popular print media were the source most likely to reveal prevailing concerns and issues.

I have also examined a variety of popular magazines that circulated in Ontario during the period under study. These include *Saturday Night*, the most "intellectual" periodical of the time, as well as two of Canada's most popular magazines, *Maclean's* and *Chatelaine*.[22] Although *Saturday Night* did not have as large a readership as *Maclean's* or *Chatelaine*, it did become increasingly popular during the immediate postwar period, nearly doubling its circulation from 32,485 in 1945[23] to 61,750 by 1954.[24] In addition, *Ontario Boys* draws from the left-leaning *Canadian Forum* to locate possible alternative perspectives to the more conservative mainstream. Also widely read in Canada during these years were the American periodicals *Life* and *Parents' Magazine*. *Parents' Magazine* is particularly significant for the study of postwar understandings of children and childhood, as it was the foremost North American popular medium for expert advice meant to train middle-class parents in the raising of "normal" children. Even parents who did not regularly read the magazine were exposed to its ideas: throughout the late 1940s, some local newspapers, such as the *Kingsville Reporter*, regularly published a parent advice column titled "Successful Parenthood." This column was penned by the associate editor of *Parents' Magazine*, Catherine Conrad Edwards. In addition to those in the popular press, *Ontario Boys* considers relevant discourses in three popular religious publications that circulated in the province during these years: the *Church Times*, the *Canadian Baptist*, and the *United Church Observer*.[25]

Books that were promoted by adults to other adults as good reading material for their sons are also examined here. The latter include the works of popular Canadian boys fiction writer John F. Hayes, winner of the Governor General's Award for Juvenile Fiction in 1951 and 1953; and Jack Hambleton, who, with Canadian author William G. Crisp, wrote *White Gold in the Cassiar*, winner of the Boys Life–Dodd Mead Prize in 1955. Books such as these were widely recommended by established reviewers as "naturally" suited for boys, in accordance with contemporary biological and psychological understandings of masculinity. Finally, ideas about boyhood found in professional publications, including scholarly books and academic journals, are examined as well. The journals examined under this category are a mix of Canadian and American; they include *Canadian Home and School, Canadian Journal of Psychology, Journal of Educational Psychology, Journal of Educational Sociology, Journal of Education, Journal of Higher Education, Education and Psychological Assessment, Educational Review*, and *Journal of Genetic Psychology*. While many of the professional monographs and journals were published in the United States, their influence on Canadian academics and other professionals was significant, in no small measure because of the limited number of such texts written by Canadians and published in Canada at the time.

THE SOCIAL AND POLITICAL CONTEXT OF POSTWAR BOYHOOD/S

Nearly everybody is desiring a return to normalcy now that the war has ended ... normalcy with its peace and security.

Editorial, *Toronto Daily Star*, 17 September 1945

Shaped by yearnings for a "normalcy" based more on nostalgia than on actual memory, reflecting the realities of ten long years of depression followed by six of global war, the years immediately following the Second World War, as Christopher Dummitt contends, saw "a backlash against the threat of gender uncertainty and ambiguity" that these world historic events had occasioned.[26] As Dummitt and others have pointed out, postwar Canadians, by and large, "valued home life, traditional gender relations," and material security "because such things had been so endangered by international economic and political events" in their formative years as children and adolescents.[27] The Great Depression, in many ways a gender crisis, challenged men's "entitlement" to waged labour, thereby seriously undermining their power and status as family breadwinners.[28] Gender anxieties were further heightened by the significant increase in the number of women who entered the Canadian labour force during the war years, many of them in jobs that were traditionally masculine.[29] As women gained in economic independence and consequently in social status, if only "for the duration," gendered notions of work and pay began to break down.[30] Journalist Lewis Milligan, writing in the closing weeks of the war in the *Leamington Post and News*, captured postwar fears and desires in an editorial, "Should Mothers Go Out to Work?" In Milligan's view, which was echoed in rural and urban media across the land,

> the time is coming—and we are praying that it may be soon—when we shall have to return to peace-time conditions; when the men of our armed forces will return to resume their places in the home, the community and in business and industrial affairs. When that time comes the women, who have taken places of the men and turned to manual labor in order to produce the materials of war, will have to resume their normal places in the home and the community.[31]

As Milligan's writing indicates, the idealized family life, with a male breadwinner and female homemaker, was a partial focus. The social environment of wartime was thought to have bred public tolerance for brutality, "moral laxity" and ambiguity, and "loose standards of social conduct." Thus the "safety" of social conservatism appealed to many in a generation that had become too closely acquainted with insecurity and instability.[32] For many adults, reconstruction meant restabilization of social roles and relations. In this context, an ideal version of boyhood became a crucial instrument for shoring up a seemingly fragile patriarchy and the male breadwinner family that was at its heart.

Notions of an ideal boyhood were conveyed to the general public by a loose coalition of adults. The early twentieth century saw white, largely Protestant, middle-class men and women leading the child welfare movement, all the while shaping "modern" understandings of childhood that were, not surprisingly, based on their own class experiences.[33] The composition of this wide-ranging child welfare movement remained substantially the same, so that by the years examined here, these men and women—including media commentators, journalists, psychologists, physicians, educators, social workers, and "child experts" of all stripes—were working to frame, reinforce, and promulgate a consensus about what should ideally constitute an Ontario boyhood. It is evident, though, that despite the predominance of the middle class, members of the working class shared some of these emergent notions and participated in implementing new behavioural standards derived from them. For example, the Labour Council of London, a body that was exclusively comprised of male delegates from industrial unions of the Canadian Labour Congress, financed and supported local boys clubs. Their stated aim was to "assist in the leisure-time education of sons of the working classes."[34]

Class- and race-based ideas were important to public representations of masculinity, but the white middle-class "norm" was not necessarily imposed upon or rejected by working-class men, who ascribed to a number of its tenets, notably the male breadwinner-citizen model. With so much seemingly in flux in the postwar years, adults of various backgrounds shared a focus on boys as future citizens and leaders. This intensified postwar interest in boyhood is evident in other contexts as well. American feminist journalist Susan Faludi describes the postwar period in the United States as the "era of the boy." Faludi contends that postwar American culture was saturated with images of and discourses about boys and boyhood. This cultural preoccupation with boys and boyhood meant that "to grow up as a girl in this era, was to look on with envy, and to see the boy as being automatically entitled and powerful."[35] Ontario examples of this public attention on boys testify to a similar cultural focus. An editorial in the *Essex County Reporter and Lakeshore News* dated 23 August 1945 highlighted for its readers how other nations were emphasizing the social value of boyhood as the war's end approached:

> The importance of spending time and thought on a nation's boyhood was evident to the German prisoners of war in Olfag 79. A copy of *News* magazine tells that these prisoners while in camp raised $60,000 to found a new boys club in London ... The facts are an interesting commentary on what things seem important when you have plenty of time to think things through.[36]

Social commentators, experts, and the interested public consistently provided adults and children alike with abundant cues, reminders, and markers that fortified and reinforced the gendered contours of a postwar normative boyhood.

By the end of the Second World War, masculinity in general, and boyhood in particular, together formed an increasingly contested political site invested with the economic, social, and moral anxieties of an Ontario population that was greatly concerned with living in a world that seemed to be moving dangerously close to nuclear extinction. In June 1946, during a parliamentary debate on nuclear energy, one member bluntly declared that "man faces the prospect of world destruction." The threat of nuclear extinction prompted a *Toronto Star* columnist to observe that "we have ... entered an age in which it will be possible for one country to blast another off the map." "Confused and difficult" was the way Governor General Vincent Massey succinctly characterized the postwar world in 1948.[37] An editorial in the *Acton Free Press* on 21 April 1949 put the matter in psychologically unnerving terms: "Atomic war is to-day a threat so terrible that men hold the thought of it at a distance to keep it from penetrating into their minds."[38] From his perspective as a social worker, Murray Ross declared that the postwar age was one where "the uncertainty of life was proving almost overwhelming for many."[39] Joe Holliday, a popular writer of postwar children's books, wrote on the dust jacket for his *Dale of the Mounted: Dew Line Duty* that the "threat of atomic war dominates the atmosphere."[40] The testing of the hydrogen bomb by the US government in 1952 only heightened public fears generated by the use of atomic weapons to end the war with Japan in 1945.[41]

Canadian intellectuals, too, weighed in on the Cold War social anxieties that had infected the nation. In 1953, Hilda Neatby, a University of Saskatchewan professor of history and a scathing critic of progressive education, perhaps most aptly captured the prevailing feeling of the day when she described the Cold War age as "brutal and dangerous" and prophesied that students' lives would likely be "nasty, brutish and short."[42] Queen's University historian Arthur Lower envisioned a dangerous future and saw it unfolding in highly gendered terms: "The future looks as if it was going to be, not feminine and cozy, but masculine and belligerent." He contended that Canadians needed to "toughen up" if they were going to successfully navigate the postwar years: "The rough rude world will push us about and laugh at us, if we can't face up to it."[43] At stake was the nation's success, both domestically and in terms of the challenging international Cold War environment.

While Canadian politicians and diplomats attempted to forge a "middle power" identity abroad, the domestic search for stability and security manifested itself in a public desire to develop the "right kind of boy" citizen who would promote and protect democracy. Nowhere was this more clearly demonstrated than in the Boy Scout Movement. As a manifestation of early-twentieth-century concerns about boys, framed largely in terms of "the future of the race," by 1945, the international Boy Scout Movement was flourishing in Canada. Its mandate and rhetoric regarding the importance of "proper" character training in boyhood had changed little in nearly half a century; however, it now emphasized citizenship and national/international purpose more than individual development.[44] As the President of the Boy Scouts Association of Canada declared in 1945, by means of engagement with other boys, and under the leadership of worthy male role models, "scouts of today will be the responsible citizens of tomorrow" and "standing together as brothers they can help wonderfully keep the world's peace."[45] Major General Dan Spry, Chief Executive Commissioner of the Canadian Boy Scouts, acknowledged that "those things for which we have been fighting are not going to be handed to us on a platter. None wanted destruction and dissension and yet the world is full of antagonisms despite the general desire for peace." Noting that the "job of Scouting was to bring up boys, who will approach their responsibilities as citizens with the Scout background of tolerance, fellowship and service," he went on to argue that peace and security in the postwar period rested on the character of boys. At a 1946 meeting of 20,000 scouts and scout leaders in Toronto's Varsity Stadium, Lord Rowallan, Chief Scout of the British Empire, insisted that "much could be prevented in the way of saving the world if more could be persuaded to interest themselves in the Scout movement."[46]

Perhaps especially because the Cold War had been launched in Canada with the Gouzenko revelations of September 1945, Canadians were also increasingly concerned about the threat or perceived threat of communism and communist aggression. "No menace in the world tops communism," Prime Minister

William Lyon Mackenzie King told the House of Commons in the spring of 1948.[47] Externally, there was a fear of communist countries, their increasing global power, and the growing nuclear threat that they posed. Internally, there was a fear that communist agents were living in Canada—as Gouzenko had revealed—and were working assiduously to subvert and destroy the Canadian way of life. Wrote a columnist in the *Essex County Reporter* on 24 April 1947: "Hardly a day passes but what some prominent person refers to the danger of Communism in Canada, and the undercover forces at work trying to undermine our democratic way of life. The threat to democracy is more ominous than ever before."[48] In a similar vein, a columnist for the *Acton Free Press* warned readers on 12 May 1955 that communist "workers, hirelings and fellow travelers," guided by the "red light of Moscow's world-Communism movement," were "wedging" themselves into all spheres of Canadian society, from labour organizations and government offices to every area of education.[49] This sort of anxious rhetoric served to regulate and maintain the social, economic, and gender order. Anti-communist purges, most notoriously those led by Senator Joseph McCarthy in the United States, meant that, as the *Toronto Star* reported, "foreign Reds ... Communist sympathizers ... and undesirable persons" were rightly being expelled from many Canadian unions.[50] Meanwhile, under the guise of halting subversive activity, the federal government was waging a campaign against non-heterosexual identities—specifically, against male homosexuals.[51]

Postwar commentators routinely warned the reading public that communists working internally were seeking to create social division, disharmony, and disunity by exploiting race and class tensions—and by extension, tensions between men and women and consequently in families, the very basis of a healthy society. Race and class relations, along with religious differences, were, as one *Globe and Mail* letter writer offered, the "soft spot[s] in the armour of modern democracy."[52] In the *Kingsville Reporter* on 9 September 1948, a writer described for readers the methods the communists were using to achieve their goal of subverting capitalist nations:

> It is commonly understood that the prime weapons of Communism are "fire and the sword." Its belief in the class struggle and the victory of the proletariat by its very nature accepts war, bloodshed and destruction as necessary and desirable aids to its goals. Communism's methods in other countries is to promote disunity and dissension, create labour troubles, foment racial prejudice and stir up religious intolerance. By encouraging such disharmonies Communism weakens capitalistic nations and prepares to enlarge its own influence through fifth column activities.[53]

During the late 1940s and throughout the 1950s, consequently, many Canadians feared that the Soviets could destroy their country, not only by

atomic attack, but also through internal subversion. If communists and communist sympathizers were working internally to create a "spirit of unrest and of
class hatred," inciting racial prejudice and religious intolerance, bringing about
disunity and strife in Ontario, then teamwork was necessarily an important
value in the realization of an ideal Canadian boyhood.[54] Certainly a boyhood
built on the virtue of teamwork would be blind to the structural and systemic
issues surrounding class and race relations that communist agents working
inside Canada might exploit to their advantage. Or so it was believed.

Ontarians also shaped their views on boyhood in reaction to changes in
the structure of the labour market. During the 1940s and 1950s, corporations
developed in an unprecedented fashion, at once capitalizing on the buoyant
postwar prosperity and helping sustain it. In addition to bringing about the
possibility of a true "male breadwinner wage" for more men than ever before,
their expansion also created heightened demand for white-collar workers in
Ontario, where most of the corporate growth was centred. The number of
corporations in Ontario tripled from 20,000 in 1946 to just over 60,000 by 1960,
increasing at a significantly greater pace than the rate of growth of Ontario's
population.[55] A key issue in the postwar period, then, was the "personality type"
that corporations demanded of the men who worked for them. In seeking out
the ideal "company man," corporations prized conformity, the basis of a conservative, risk-averse, cooperative workplace culture that required the development of a more "domesticated" corporate male spirit emphasizing teamwork.
Capturing this particular version of masculinity, one Canadian writer described
the white-collar man in this way:

> The white collar man is generally a very stable, conscientious, hard work-
> ing, well educated and usually highly moral member of the commu-
> nity. He is seldom a good trader or an able or fortunate speculator.
> His conservative philosophy and standards prevent him from knowing
> the tricks and shifts that make money fast and easily. He is therefore
> dependent on his salary, which he works hard to earn, and to increase
> through more experience and more knowledge. He spends his hours
> away from work minding his own business and improving his home.
> He sends his kids to school and to church, well fed, well washed, de-
> cently clothed, and as well behaved as kids go. He is the backbone of
> church and community welfare effort … he is usually more community
> minded than the average.[56]

This gently melancholy portrait of the corporate white-collar man captured
his heterosexualized, middle-class, religious, collective, and seemingly diminished masculine identity. Instead of being the captain of his own ship and the
master of his own fate, reflecting an earlier, individualist, "self-made man" ideal,

the white-collar man was seemingly reduced to the bureaucratic position of a helmsmen who maintained a steady course and followed orders so that the corporate ship could move safely along in difficult waters. What was new, in what some commentators were classifying as the "age of tension," was an increased concern about men's perceived domestication and their consequently diminished vigour, independence, and individuality, all seen to be the outcome of the postwar corporate economy.[57] Real or imagined change during these years was partly generated by the giant corporate, government, and academic bureaucracies that were becoming increasingly dominant in Ontario, where a managerial, "other-directed" white-collar version of masculinity was integral to male success.[58]

Ontario's expanding corporations also desired physically healthy and robust workers who, according to the standard 1955 elementary school textbook, *Good Health,* "would start off each morning with a zest for work."[59] Corporations did not want male employees who could not work efficiently, or who needed time off from work, due to ill health. The health of workers came to be viewed as increasingly significant in the context of an expanding capitalist society.[60] Since such workers were by definition male, it was the "weaklings" who placed a burden on businesses, consumed company resources by seeking advice from company nurses, and failed to contribute their utmost to the corporate cause. Worries about communism also raised concerns over nations that possessed unhealthy populations. "Communism, breeder of world tension, thrives where health standards are low," warned Dr. Gordon Bates, the General Director of the Health League of Canada, in March 1954. To combat the spread of communism, in part by bolstering capitalist production, democratic nations would require physically and mentally healthy citizens—especially men, who were the full-time workers, leaders, and true citizens. The solution to safeguarding democracy "was better health: not the H-bomb," argued Bates. He went on to assert that "nations are great and strong because they are composed of healthy, long-lived citizens producing material wealth."[61] Thus improving and safeguarding the health of boys was urgent. Strong, healthy foot soldiers were required to wage economic war in the expanding capitalist markets in which postwar Ontario was playing a key role. Ontarians needed to commit themselves to rearing strong, competitive, aggressive boys who were also, paradoxically, dedicated to conformity and teamwork.

To a far greater extent than any other Canadian province, postwar Ontario was capitalist, industrial, and distinctly urban. By 1951, 62 percent of Canadians were urban dwellers; the figure in Ontario was 72 percent.[62] Although a continuation of an ongoing twentieth-century trend, this rapid increase raised fears among adults, who associated the urbanization process, along with the growth in "non-physical" white-collar employment for men, with increased effeminacy among boys. Such adult fears were not new to the postwar period; the growing industrialization and urbanization of the early twentieth century had seen much fretting over boys' perceived emasculation.[63] But the postwar economic boom in Ontario, which brought with it an expanded suburban, domesticated middle-class life and mass consumption, brought new emphasis to such concerns. The period's child experts promoted the idea that a key "cause" of homosexuality was the modern decline in the father's status; his daily commute from the suburbs meant that children were left to be raised, without significant paternal influence, by overbearing mothers who presided over the domesticated culture of suburban life.[64] In the Cold War context of paranoia, homosexuality, perceived in moral terms as a character flaw, was linked to espionage and treason. By extension, it was a threat the stability and security of the state.[65]

This rising social anxiety reflected and reinforced Ontarians' worries about traditional gender relations and identities, specifically those of men. The outcome, between 1945 and 1960, was a vigorous reassertion of traditional gender roles as a means to assuage fears that masculinity was in "crisis." The changing gender composition of the labour market and women's continued movement into the public sphere after the war, despite assertive government campaigns to ensure that they returned to home and family after their necessary war work, was perceived as a large part of the "problem." "Much of the male ordeal," one psychoanalyst suggested, "stems from the growing independence of working women."[66]

Fuelling the notion that masculinity was in crisis were popular writers, cultural commentators, and media critics. In 1948 a *Maclean's* writer, in an article boldly titled "Our Men Are Mice," decried the state of postwar masculinity:

> I'm getting sick of being told that Canada is a man's country. That's a colossal falsehood. If we male citizens could be said to have one characteristic in common, whether we happen to be bottle-shaped little tremble chins or tougher than the back end of a cement mixer, it's our slavish readiness to lie down flat and let women walk all over us. Except maybe for our neighbors across the border, we Canadians are the most henpecked men on earth. [67]

Similarly, in 1950, the leading Canadian women's magazine *Chatelaine* published an article provocatively titled "Man, the Vanishing Sex." The author, Fred Bodsworth, warned the magazine's female audience that men were in danger of disappearing altogether, due to the contemporary situation, which, in his view, held men in thrall to dominating and domineering females. For Bodsworth, men's emasculation and possible extinction posed a greater threat to world peace than the atom bomb.[68] Another *Chatelaine* piece, by acclaimed writer and broadcaster Gordon Sinclair, declared that the "new second sex" were men, not women.[69] Poet Irving Layton announced that postwar men were "being feminized" and subjected unfairly to the "inglorious age of the mass-woman."[70] One leading psychologist of the time, perhaps summing it up best, bemoaned that "we live in the final phase of a masculine civilization which lasted for centuries."[71]

Worries that masculinity was in "crisis" fuelled the postwar preoccupation with the state of boyhood. In this seemingly overly feminized society, both at home and in school, boys were being exposed to threats to their incipient masculinity.[72] In *Life* on 6 January 1947, one writer warned that "a matriarchy is developing." In his view, women were taking over society, especially the schools, which were the site of the formative experiences of childhood.[73] There is, of course, nothing new to the suggestion that masculinity is undermined whenever opportunities for women expand. This particular discourse has long been raised whenever threats to male status are perceived. As a number of historians have pointed out, "crises" in masculinity are recurrent expressions of social anxiety in times of rapid change. Michael Kimmel's 1996 landmark study on masculinity, *Manhood in America*, documents how a sense of crisis has plagued American men since the mid-eighteenth century.[74] As Kimmel shows, these anxieties intensify at moments when dominant forms of heteronormative masculinity are under significant threat.[75]

So these concerns about masculinity, and consequently boyhood, were not unique to the postwar years. Nonetheless, that period saw a notable and unprecedented intensification of "moral panic" regarding effeminacy in boys, one that raised the spectre of homosexuality.[76] During these years, the public perception grew that homosexuality was becoming more prevalent, and consequently more of a danger, in North America.[77] In addition to the Cold War anti-communist fears about homosexuals as spies, the groundbreaking publication of the Kinsey Report on male sexual behaviour in 1948 forcefully brought the issue into the national spotlight. In Canada, the report received much readership and publicity in both popular and professional media.[78] A *Globe and Mail* review described Kinsey's *Sexual Behavior in the Human Male* as "an epoch-marking study of sex." Perhaps alluding to the possibility of gender trouble, the reviewer went on to tell readers that "all we know or supposed about the male sex has been erroneous."[79] The most radical—and unsettling—of Kinsey's findings related to the unexpectedly high rates of same-sex male attraction and sexual relations that he documented. He cited first-person testimony from "thousands" of "homosexual males," who presented the collective idea that "most males are 'homosexual' or that they are 'partly homosexual,' or that they 'are really homosexual even though they may not be aware of it and may not have had an actual experience."[80] This discovery that a sizable portion of the male population had "at least some overt homosexual experience" ran alongside the observation that homosexuals often passed as heterosexual, raising the possibility that there were more "deviant" men in most social circles than previously thought.[81]

A 1954 Ontario provincial report on the "problems of delinquent individuals," reflected these postwar concerns about possibly high rates same-sex male attraction. Fearing a link between homosexuality and the rise in delinquency, it noted that "homosexuality exists in our society to a disturbing degree."[82] In this cultural and sexual milieu, it is not surprising that many medical and psychological experts thought that "homosexual leanings" had their origins in troubled boyhoods, a point made by the chief medical officer and psychiatrist for Johns Hopkins hospital, Dr. Manfred Guttmacher, in 1956 during a Toronto public citizens' forum on the issue of "sex perverts."[83] The idea that "homosexual leanings" were acquired during boyhood created room for experts to offer advice and guidance to parents on how to prevent their boy from becoming a "sex pervert" and thus a threat to his own success and to national stability and security.[84] A "normal" boyhood, it is evident, came to be seen as a vital instrument for preventing the decline of men, and consequently of the family and the nation itself.

The expansion of the mental hygiene movement and the role and social influence of professional psychology during the postwar period had important implications for boyhood.[85] It was during this time that mental health experts, and child psychologists in particular, came to wield significant power. As historian Elise Chenier points out, at the end of the Second World War, "psychiatrists and psychologists exerted considerably more influence in the state organization of both the war effort and reconstruction than at any time in the past." By the mid-1950s, federal and provincial governments were willingly allocating millions of dollars toward mental health research and programs across Canada, most specifically to be implemented in schools.[86] In 1948, for example, the Toronto Board of Education, the nation's largest, created a Child Guidance Clinic in order to "fight delinquency." The clinic had a particular mandate to train and help elementary schoolchildren. Along with public health nurses and educators, the clinic was staffed by a number of mental health experts, including psychologists and psychiatrists. Already, by 1948, at least according to one Toronto educator, psychologists and mental health experts had become the "Lords of Education."[87]

Ontario parents were drawn to the psychologically informed advice of child experts. In the *Kingsville Reporter*, one social commentator speculated that by 1950 almost every adult in Ontario had "read a book or two on psychology" in an effort, in part, to understand children.[88] Postwar psychologists, more than all others, promoted early childhood intervention and training in order to produce well-adjusted children—"normal" children, in short. Nineteenth-century medical and pedagogical texts had stressed the biological innate-ness of masculinity; postwar medical, psychological, and childrearing texts viewed masculinity as fundamentally grounded in behavioural habits that must be inculcated in boys from an early age. Because of the swirling anxi-eties about boys, psychologists and other child experts were publicly lauded for their crucial work in changing seemingly "deviant" boys into normal boys who would grow up to be exemplary men. In the *Globe and Mail* on 6 July 1946, columnist Frank Tumpane praised the role of Toronto's Mental Hygiene Division for salvaging "abnormal" and "maladjusted" boys by leading them gradually toward a "normal boyhood."[89] The expansion and growing public importance of the mental hygiene movement and professional psychology during the postwar years was the basis of a significant social movement, one that routinely offered up to adults an idealized heteronormative boyhood that conformed to the gendered ideals of the largely white, Canadian-born middle class—the very social group most destabilized by postwar social trends.

The expansion of the mental health movement in Canada coincided with another development that deeply influenced the character of postwar Ontario society: the renewed influx of immigrants into the province. After the restric-tions on immigration brought about by the Depression and the war, addressed by the Liberal government's revised 1950 Immigration Act, the doors opened to take in well over 1.5 million newcomers by 1960.[90] More than half of all immigrants to Canada settled in Ontario.[91] Between 1946 and 1955, more than 636,000 newcomers entered Ontario, whose entire population in 1955 stood at only 5,183,000.[92] By 1960, more than 830,000 immigrants named Ontario as their destination. The new immigration generated more anxiety among Canadians, who worried that the newcomers would undermine the "Canadian" way of life, defined narrowly as British, English-speaking, white, and Protestant.[93] Such fears prompted a loose coalition of social workers and others, often with government funding, to work toward ensuring conformity, usually represented as "integration." Programs were established to assist immigrants—particularly immigrant boys, who as future male citizens were especially problematic—to become productive, democratic citizens who would uphold and reinforce Anglo-Protestant middle-class ideals, regardless of their own origins and customs.[94]

It was in this context that rapid social, political, and economic changes created an Ontario population anxious and uncertain about the future. Fuelled by their anxieties and uncertainties, concerned adults began to cast the fate of the postwar world onto children, in particular boys.

CHAPTER ORGANIZATION AND SUMMARY

Ontario Boys focuses on the history of ideas about boyhood, and the ideals rising from these, during the early years of Cold War Ontario. As such, while the material reality of boys' lives during this period is unquestionably important, the lived experiences of boys are, for the most part, beyond the scope of this work. It is equally important to recognize, however, as pre-eminent social scientist John Porter did in his seminal study of social stratification in Canada, *The Vertical Mosaic* (1965), that "it is often difficult to effect a clean separation between the two."[95]

Chapter 1 discusses the home and family in relation to the larger social context of Atomic Age/Cold War anxieties as these manifested themselves nationally and in Ontario specifically.[96] Emerging from what was taken to be the bedrock of normalcy, the male breadwinner family, was the "normal" boy.[97] It was fancied that in such ideal environments, children in general, and boys in particular, had more opportunities to develop the prescribed good habits and attitudes. Shaped by the psychological orthodoxy of the day and bound by dominant notions of class, gender, and race, these habits and attitudes were central to the making of an idealized postwar boyhood both as a testament to ideal masculinity and as a crucial basis for nation building. In Chapter 2, I explore how adults, although still committed to some degree to the notion of individualism as a boyhood value, more aggressively promoted a version of boyhood—"the right kind of boy"—based on a deeper collective male identity. In the age of anonymous bureaucracies that were concerned more about fitting in than standing out, this version of boyhood emphasized teamwork, togetherness, group fidelity, collective identity, and loyalty. Team loyalty mattered in boyhood, just as company loyalty mattered in male adulthood. In this model of boyhood, distinctions between and among boys based on class or race were "smoothed over" as a greater sense of interchangeability between and among males was sought. This version of boyhood was classless—or, at least, organizations such as the Boy Scouts wanted it to be. [98]

While the representation of boyhood in postwar popular discourses typically pointed to cooperation and teamwork, to the loyal and obedient selflessness closely associated with the rise of postwar bureaucracies, and to the need for expanding levels of management, markers of an old-style patriarchal masculinity remained. Chapter 3 thus looks at public narratives that promoted a version of boyhood that was at odds with the dominant "manager" ideal. These alternative discourses characterized ideal boys/men as individualistic, highly competitive, and imbued with a frontier entrepreneurial masculinity bent on individual conquests. Hypermasculine narratives of the heroic entrepreneur helped ease postwar anxieties about changing gender roles, and especially about the "feminization" of society, by depicting boys as aspirants to traditional masculine virtues.[99]

Ironically, the adventurous and aggressive boy-hero shared characteristics with the postwar "demon" who was the "bad boy." Chapter 4 explores this phenomenon, a version of boyhood that stood in direct contrast to that of the normal boy. The bad boy was the problem boy. He was often imagined as the exclusive product of the "unspeakable" neighbourhood, possibly even the "broken family," and as having strong potential for delinquency.[100] Often associated with poor working-class and immigrant families, the potential bad boy was thought to pose an immediate danger to a society that was anxious about security and stability. The unsettling and at times dangerous image of the bad boy motivated many reform-minded citizens, mostly middle-class men, to volunteer time and resources to character-building organizations and boys clubs.[101]

As this brief discussion has demonstrated, public preoccupation with the making of boys into men manifests itself periodically, almost predictably, at times when intensive socio-economic changes direct attention to children and youth as future citizens, as both problems and potential solutions. Even in the twenty-first century, when commitments to patriarchy and heterosexual marriage are being openly challenged on multiple levels, worries persist regarding gender roles and how children are best socialized for adult citizenship. In the concluding chapter, I return to the main themes considered throughout this study while also giving thought to our current concerns about boyhood as expressed in contemporary public discourses. It is evident that among those now longing for a "return to normal," boyhood is once again a critical site for shoring up a traditional gender hierarchy that has consistently been undermined since the end of the Second World War.[102] This book aims to historicize these ongoing debates by returning to that starting point.

Home, Family, Citizenship:
Shaping the Boyhood Ideal

The popular and professional ideas on boyhood in the late 1940s and the 1950s took shape in a social and political context impacted by dislocations and upheavals in marital and familial relations brought on by Depression era and wartime conditions. Out of this social and political turbulence came a mixture of uncertainty and danger, fear and change, which in turn generated a search for social, political, and economic stability, security, and "normalcy." One prominent social manifestation of the search for a "healthy normalcy" was a rush to "reconstruct" the patriarchal family and its attendant "familialist ideology."[1] This point was put into sharp relief in an August 1955 article in the *Toronto Star*. Its author, Elijah Adlow, an American judge, exclaimed that "the only hope for the future lies in the resurgence of the home as the basic institution of the modern world."[2] Social commentators routinely made efforts to normalize the white, middle-class, heterosexual, nuclear family, and by extension an appropriate masculinity, as the basis upon which to safeguard and fulfill the promise of a better postwar Ontario.[3]

From this basis of familial "normalcy" and shaped by gendered concerns about a safe and secure future came a particular kind of boy. He was assumed to be white and heterosexual and to have well-adjusted, Canadian-born, happy and healthy parents whose task it was to ensure social stability by developing appropriate gender identities in their children. His masculine father was the breadwinner and was not weak, nor was he dominated by his wife, since this latter state would mean that the mother dominated the boy as she did the husband. At the same time, mothers were told not to be overprotective, the fear being that this would turn boys into "sissies" and by extension raise the postwar spectre of homosexuality. The normal boy's mother stayed at home and cared for him and as his primary caregiver handled everyday child care issues, such as communicating with teachers. There was considerable concern about families in which mothers worked outside the home or were divorced and heading fatherless, single-mother families.[4] Some commentators wondered aloud if a "return to normal" was even possible in light of the "postwar divorce epidemic" and its "deplorable" effects on children.[5] In short, shaped by efforts to reconstruct patriarchal and heterosexist relations, the boy and his family were rigidly defined, equated with normalcy, and used to fight off fears of insecurity and instability, and this ideological work was done through the rhetoric found in child care advice columns and in the psychological and academic literature.

Employing its methods of normalcy, psychological discourse helped foster the idea that normal, secure, happy, healthy boys came from good, stable homes located in good, middle-class neighborhoods. It was thought that "poor housing conditions" made the "establishing of good health habits difficult"; conversely, a clean and attractive neighbourhood with adequate space and nearby recreational facilities contributed to the development of better, happier, and "more normal individuals."[6] It was fancied that in these "purer social spaces," children, and boys in particular, would have more opportunities to develop good habits and traits such as honesty, helpfulness, teamwork, and a spirit of fair play.[7] By contrast, as one professor of psychology suggested in the May 1951 issue of *Parents' Magazine,* the home of the maladjusted boy was filled with social ills and family disunity: "You're twice as likely to find alcoholism, emotional disturbance, criminal behaviour and mental defects as in the families of the other boys who come from the same part of town. There's a double chance, too, that his parents do not get along and that his home has been or will be broken by separation, desertion or divorce."[8]

Thus, poorer neighbourhoods were viewed as threatening state security because they undermined the domestic ideal; they were also seen as delinquency-producing areas that generated maladjusted, defective boys. Franca Iacovetta has found that poor, immigrant adult males were constructed by social commentators, including psychologists, as more likely to be emotionally disturbed and to engage in criminal behaviour—tendencies that would produce abnormal boyhoods in their sons.[9] In this respect, postwar popular thought constructed and normalized the idea that normal, well-adjusted boys did not come from poverty-stricken immigrant backgrounds, nor did they have neglectful, separated, or divorced parents.[10] The inherent risks to the neglected boy were allegorized in high-profile media stories. In August 1948, when Babe Ruth, "Mr. Baseball," died of a heart attack at the age of only fifty-three, the print media in Ontario quickly pointed to his "dilapidated" and neglected boyhood as the cause of his early demise: "He [Babe Ruth] had been a poor kid in Baltimore, a tough kid and often a bitter one. He was neglected by his parents. He stole bananas from pushcarts to satisfy his hunger, and ended up in an industrial home. His prodigious appetite and reckless life after he became rich and famous, probably were a reaction to his shabby boyhood."[11]

The lesson for adult Ontario readers was that the moral degeneracy of men and by extension the potential degeneracy of the social order began with a "shabby boyhood" that was the product of poverty and neglectful, often immigrant parents. Various organizations exploited this direct link between an inferior boyhood and a problematic manhood. The Scott Mission in Toronto, for example, resorted to the notion that broken homes created the conditions for a poor boyhood, which in turn produced inadequate, fallen men. In a 1945 appeal for funds, it highlighted this theme: "A young man comes in—yes, he is a 'hobo' ... He was brought up without the care of a father or love of a mother. When he was nine he had to do chores on a farm, and only had interrupted periods in school, hence he has little education. He is restless, nervous and shiftless."[12]

The popular print media, including newspapers, presented the view that neglected boys who lacked parental love became maladjusted, effeminate, nervous, or shiftless men, who did not possess the traits of an appropriate postwar masculinity. Nor were they capable of fulfilling the responsibilities of a breadwinning manhood.

News stories touted the idea that secure, stable, privileged homes were necessary if boys were to grow into prominent, responsible men. With the traits of appropriate masculinity, such men would certainly succeed in traditional male domains, where they would ensure the continuation of the social order. This view was exemplified in "Two Fine Canadian Families," an editorial published in the *Toronto Daily Star* on 31 October 1946, which informed readers about six prominent Ontario men who came from two "wholesome" and privileged Anglo-Ontarian families:

> Perhaps no other family has contributed more to the well-being of Ontario than the six Meredith boys. Three were knighted for distinguished service to their country. Sir William Cooles Meredith was chief justice of Canada. Hon. Richard was chief justice of the court of common pleas in Ontario. Sir Henry Vincent Meredith was general manager and president of the Bank of Montreal. John S. Meredith was manager of the Merchant Bank's head office ... The richness of the contribution made by the Merediths and the Oslers to Canadian life arouses questioning as to the source of their wholesome stimulating characters and fine performances. The answer is to be found in the home ... The heads of both families set an example to their children in moral living, raised them in an atmosphere of affection and trained them to fulfill the responsibilities of manhood. Which is a reminder that when the home fails, the community suffers.[13]

Drawing on class ideologies, this item evoked notions of a healthy, normal home in which traditional values and family consciousness bred sturdy boys who grew up to conquer urban perils while becoming nation builders and pillars of the social order. It was imagined that safe, secure, "normal" nuclear families would allow parents to perform the incalculable national service of transmitting traditional values to their boys; this in turn would produce the "right" kind of men, who would fulfill the responsibilities of manhood by providing security and stability to a seemingly fragile democracy. Hence, popular and professional postwar discourse helped promote the idea that traditional middle- and upper-class nuclear families created the conditions for fostering the masculine virtues of strength, courage, and independence, and that in these families, guided by "good parents," a true national moral character built on Anglo-Protestant middle-class values would be formed. As one 1947 *Globe and Mail* headline put it, "Good Parents Make Nation Great."[14] But what was a good parent, and in particular a good father?

FATHERHOOD

By the late 1940s, cultural understandings of fatherhood had taken on new meanings. Key to this new understanding of fatherhood was the role of masculine domesticity.[15] Masculine domesticity meant that it was no longer acceptable for a father to be a distant breadwinner detached from the domestic sphere or a "grim tyrant" as was his Victorian predecessor.[16] Instead, fathers were encouraged by postwar psychologists and other experts to be kinder and gentler, as well as more engaged in family life. "A boy needs a friendly, accepting father … to be enjoyed by him, and if possible, to do things with him," Dr. Spock wrote in *Baby and Child Care*.[17] In an expanding consumer economy, the ideal postwar father was expected to engage with a variety of "home centred and family based pursuits from backyard gardener to the Scout leader or hockey coach."[18] For boys this meant, not a dictator father ruling the family with an iron hand, but rather a more open, gentle father who sought to become their son's pal.

So experts encouraged fathers to play a friendlier, more active role in their son's life. They also cautioned fathers to not be too demanding, in particular when it came to hobbies and pursuits. Dr. Spock, for example, warned fathers that being too energetic and too enthusiastic, and wanting too much for their young boy to achieve success in masculine pursuits, could come at the expense of their gender identity:

> If a father is a friendly, energetic type who loves to play touch football and if his children enjoy nothing better than to get into a game with him on a Sunday afternoon, this is wonderful … But to take another

example, if the father is overanxious to make his son an athlete, because he himself is convinced that this is the main key to manliness and success in college, his son may quickly come to dread the tense practice sessions that he is subjected to, and may even develop a distaste for all athletics.[19]

During the postwar period, a boy who developed "a distaste for all athletics" would certainly have raised concerns about his capacity to acquire a "normal" masculinity. According to Dr. Spock, then, an ideal father was one who did not impose activities or hobbies on his son; rather, an ideal father simply followed his own masculine interests, such as "fishing or watching a ball game." And by following his own masculine interests, the ideal father provided a model of masculine behaviour that his son could follow and absorb over time. Without feeling pressure or anxiety to succeed, the boy would secure an appropriate masculine identity.

An ideal father during the postwar period was also expected to build a "companionate marriage" with his wife.[20] Unlike his Victorian predecessor, the postwar father was expected to become more of a partner with his wife when it came to distributing household labour, including child care. "Parenthood is a cooperative enterprise," child expert Nancy Cleaver told readers of the *Stouffville Sun-Tribune* in a June 1954 column.[21] However, although the ideal father was expected to take on more child care responsibilities and household tasks than fathers in the past, the tasks required by fathers and mothers remained highly gendered. To some measure, the gendering of household tasks was reinforced by social commentators who warned the reading public throughout the postwar period about the consequences for families when gender boundaries were blurred. For example, a 1960 article published in *Chatelaine*, which reported research findings on "successful" families, cautioned readers about what would happen if men and women failed to accept their household roles within the family as men and women, male and female:

> It should be emphasized that dominant fathers in these [successful] families did not mean mothers who were drudges or nonentities. There was a clear division of labour: certain tasks and responsibilities belonged to the father, others to the mother. The researchers suggest that where there is a reversal or confusion of tasks, with the mother taking over some of the father's work and father doing an immoderate proportion of traditionally feminine tasks, such as housework, there will be a poorly functioning family.[22]

As the above quote indicates, emerging postwar understandings of fatherhood did not represent any real challenge to the gender order: men's position as breadwinners and household heads remained largely undisrupted. In fact, research findings of the late postwar period confirmed that the emergence of "masculine domesticity" was not in any way a real threat to masculine privilege. For example, in *Merrill-Palmer Quarterly of Behavior and Development*, a researcher reported in April 1960 that "masculine domestic involvement" throughout the postwar years was regarded by women as merely a "helping" role," with "the major responsibility for household management and child care still unquestionably the woman's job."[23] In short, shifting postwar understandings of fatherhood did not result in an elimination of the gendered division of labour, only a limited amelioration.

Popular depictions of the ideal father during the postwar era suggested that he was decidedly not poor or from an immigrant community; instead, he was "appropriately" masculine, middle class, white, Anglo, and Protestant. This conservative ideal was best embodied by postwar American TV portrayals of fathers such as Ward Cleaver (*Leave It to Beaver*, 1954–63), Jim Anderson (*Father Knows Best*, 1954–62), and Ozzie Nelson (*The Adventures of Ozzie and Harriet*, 1953–60).[24] Unlike media portrayals of the working poor, who were typically the butt of jokes, the fathers on shows such as these were typically represented as "stable, financially secure, good natured, capable breadwinners, and a source of wisdom and understanding."[25] During the postwar era, "these warm and wise men were the ultimate arbiters of rules and discipline for children while the wives ran the households."[26] Of course, the ideal father as reflected in these TV shows modelled an appropriate masculinity for their sons. And without fathers modelling an appropriate gender identity for their sons, it was widely assumed that "a boy might become delinquent, turn into a homosexual, or suffer untold mental distress."[27]

Journalists in the popular press emphasized the importance of fathers as role models in their sons' lives. For example, in *Maclean's* in 1958, Pierre Berton and C.G. Gifford advised readers that "boys growing into adults [need a] male parent whom they can like and admire, who can form their attitude to life and people."[28] Boys were encouraged to recognize their father as an understanding guide and friend, a loved and trusted parent, a model for developing their own masculine identity. Having an appropriate model of masculinity helped prepare boys to emerge successfully from an early childhood, marked by the feminine, into the rough-and-tumble world of boyhood. "Today's Father Plays a New Role," published in the *Globe and Mail* on 12 June 1958, brought this point to light: "When dolls give way to the rough and tumble of school age, the boy is again preparing for a man's role in the world. Here, too, he will take the cue of mature, masculine adjustment from his father."[29]

In a climate of gender uncertainty and ambiguity, normalcy as expressed through popular channels such as magazines quickly became linked with stable gender identities, and it was engaged fathers who were thought to provide both boys and girls with a clear sense of "normalcy": "Fathers have an important part to play, in helping sons to be manly, daughters feminine," advised one commentator in *Parents' Magazine* in March 1949.[30] Of course, a caring and engaged father had not always been equated with an appropriate masculinity. In this regard, a little nudge by an expert was needed. Being a real father was not "sissy business," argued psychiatrist Edward Strecker in *Parents' Magazine* in 1947; postwar fathers could take a masculine interest in raising their children.[31] Similarly, postwar childrearing guru Dr. Spock reassured fathers in *Baby and Child Care* that "you can be a warm father and a real man at the same time."[32] The striving within popular discourse to normalize clear and unambiguous gender roles, to rejuvenate a sense of gender certainty, meant that normal boys had a masculine father who took an active, masculine interest in the boy's growth and development and who inspired respect for an appropriate masculinity by being a worthy father himself. Certainly, it was assumed that to acquire a successful heterosexual masculinity, a boy could not have a weak, emasculated, or immature father. "Father should be the wise, kindly and understanding, but reasonably firm, authority for his sons, and his grave responsibility of being the original object of their early hero worship. If he has clay feet—because he is immature—his children will know it." So asserted Norman Kelman, an American psychoanalyst in *Parents' Magazine* in March 1949.[33]

According to postwar thought, an appropriate father was one who epitomized a masculine identity and who took pride in the power and strength of his own primary maleness. Here again, Kelman described for readers the perceived importance of an "appropriately masculine" father to the stability of his children:

> A father must, first of all esteem his own maleness. This is another way of saying he should have self-respect, pride in being a man. A daughter of such a man will see that her mother respects her father and is respected by him. Consequently she will not feel the need either to fear or belittle men ... Her father will be the measure of all men. The son of such a man, on the other hand, was thought to have a similar experience. He will respect and admire his father and will have a relationship with him that is not confined to an occasional bull session. Through his regard for his father he will be enabled to grow towards a healthy regard for himself as a boy, and gradually to become a truly mature man.[34]

This passage reveals the importance attached to the father–son relationship within prevailing postwar thought. It was imagined that the father, by modelling an appropriate "primary maleness," supplied the boy with a sense of security and stability within the family structure by providing a concrete and material example of what was appropriately masculine. It was believed the boy would emulate his male role model, and imitation would lead to the boy's own stable, secure and primary masculinity.

Mothers were designated and valued as chief caregivers of infant boys; fathers were highly valued for their masculine qualities such as strength, physical toughness, and unconquerable rugged individualism. Boys, as they grew older, were supposed to admire and eventually emulate such traits. In a child advice column on 21 July 1945, Angelo Patri[35] made this point clear:

> Boys look up to their fathers and are proud of them. Proud of their strength, their ability to hold their own anywhere. They want to be associated with them so that they can feel the reflected glory of manhood and leadership. When a boy does not get this thought and care and affection from his father, he feels an emptiness that he has no words for, but which makes him uneasy, restless and jumpy. He resents his Mother's constant oversight and longs for the freer broader guidance of the man who is his father.[36]

In a similar way, one professor of psychiatry accentuated the need for a father to be present in a boy's life. O. Spurgeon English told readers of *Parents' Magazine* in June 1950 that during grade school, a boy needed plenty of his father's attention on the boy's games and hobbies. The closer the relationship between the two at this time, the easier it would be to inculcate important masculine standards. The psychiatrist suggested that "over a bottle of soda pop at a ball park or over a lathe, a boy learns unconsciously to absorb his father's views, attitudes and values."[37] Within this understanding of gender, fathers modelled masculine qualities for boys in order for them to learn what it meant to be a man, a father, and a husband. In Patri's example, the father's masculine qualities counterpoised the feminine and overprotective traits of the mother. There was a reliance on gender role models of behaviour that supported fixed notions that linked differences between masculinity and femininity to biology. The masculinizing of the boy was the key message. Patri's version of masculinity promoted an older style of masculinity that valued taking an unwavering stand—a virtue often learned in conflict and expressed through masculine deeds. In this sense, boys were encouraged to become confident, self-reliant, individual men capable of asserting themselves.

Postwar era advertisements exploited the idea that fathers were central to a boy's life. Fathers were believed to be best able to grant boys the needed security, strength, and wisdom to navigate successfully the masculine world they would inherit. This was crucial, since boys were viewed as inheriting an unstable, turbulent, and ever-changing postwar world and thus needing a steady and solid masculine presence to guide them into a successful manhood. Expressing this notion was a 1959 Seagram's advertisement, published to coincide with Father's Day:

> For where does a boy look ... For light which will lead to sure places for young feet to stand? For guidance through the great continent of the mind? For strength of will and love of goodness? For those words and teachings that will open up wisdom's way? For a held-out hand, a haven in every sudden storm? Where else but to a father, who knows that every son is a miracle, like daily light.[38]

In a social and political milieu increasingly filled with anxiety over gender roles, the father offered a psychological fortress, a buffer against threats both internal and external. Undergirded by a mix of biological essentialism and postwar psychology, this ad asserted that without a father, or an appropriate male role model, boys would feel lost emotionally and psychologically. It was assumed that fathers taught boys how to navigate the changes they would experience. A boy who was mentored by his father would gain infinite knowledge about the broader world, knowledge assumed to exist outside the female domain. Texts such as this promoted the idea that boys without the strong and steady hand of a male were literally and figuratively in danger.

Anticipating what has become a standard theme in twenty-first-century boy crisis rhetoric, postwar public commentators elevated a father's relationship with his son above the boy's relationship with his mother. As such, fathers were portrayed as having something singular to offer their sons. One *Globe and Mail* columnist discussed this dimension of boyhood: "Boys over 10, these especially need their fathers. They are coming out of childhood into boyhood, preparing for adolescence. They need to be touched by the masculine point of view. Mother is necessary always, but at this stage and henceforward father should come first in the boys' lives, not as a disciplinary force, but as a leading, guiding, sustaining force."[39] Similarly, in *Baby and Child Care*, Dr. Spock advised parents that the thing that makes a boy feel and act like a man is being able to "copy" himself after his father.[40] While effectively dismissing mothers and positioning their importance as secondary, both writers conveyed that in order for a boy to march to an acceptable masculine identity, he was required to release his mother's apron strings and distance himself from her feminine influence, while orienting himself to the "masculine" embodiment that was his father.

Popular discourse added credence to the idea that a boy was disadvantaged by his mother, who was thought bereft of the masculine traits that were necessary to provide her son with suitable guidance or proper recreation, due to her biological makeup and despite being a competent parent. This view was made explicit by one writer in *Parent's Magazine* in 1945: "Competent as any mother may be to direct her child's energies and activities, there is simply no escaping the fact that when a man takes a hand in the youngster's games a sort of rough and ready wholesome masculinity adds to the fun."[41] Mothers, unlike fathers, could not engage in the rough and rugged play assumed to be the natural state of boyhood. The mother was useful, but it was the father's "wholesome masculinity" that made the real difference in a growing boy's normal development. Some experts thought that most boys between six and twelve years old rarely had access to any "wholesome masculinity," as they were subjected to exclusively feminine influences and female domination. O. Spurgeon English, for example, described for readers how very young boys were situated in a female-dominated world, which he argued would have long-term consequences for them as men:

> Teachers from the first grade up to junior high are almost all women. At home there is Mother deciding, ordering and maintaining discipline. Perhaps there is Grandma, a few aunts and a female houseworker to scold when a fellow tracks in mud ... Children growing up under feminine domination ... This makes boys inclined to be too passive when they grow up or unconsciously hostile toward their wives and eager to escape from them for a night out with the boys.[42]

The fear of the social feminization of boys that permeates this account reflected postwar concerns that boys were disadvantaged in almost every domain—including home and school—by overexposure to female influences. For this reason, it was assumed that fathers, or father substitutes such as male teachers, would provide boys with the necessary masculine presence to offset the corrupting womanly influence of females, particularly mothers.

For children, learning their appropriate sex role was thought to be closely tied to strong emotional attachment, a boy to his father, a girl to her mother. A boy was required to set aside any attachment to his mother and focus his identity on his father. That is, an important challenge for the boy was to emancipate himself from the dependent relationship with his mother and learn to develop the "we" feeling (as it was termed by sociologist Frederick Elkin) with his father and other males.[43] In *The Child and Society*, Elkin viewed mothers as having little or no value for a growing boy's life. It was the father who would influence the son, guiding him into a successful masculinity; meanwhile, the mother was denigrated and no longer viewed as vital to her son's development. Other child experts agreed with this view. "Since, the mother obviously cannot be the model for this, her role in her son's acquisition of masculine characteristics cannot be as vital as the father's," two psychologists declared in a 1960 issue of *Child*

Development.[44] The establishment of a strong father–son relationship did more than supply the boy with the desired masculine interests. Drawing on a misogynist discourse that viewed all things feminine as toxic to the development of a successful boyhood, child experts Ilg and Ames suggested that the father's close relationship to his son would serve as a patriarchal barrier for preventing and withstanding the threats posed by feminine influences: "Children now share real interests with their fathers; and boys and their fathers may group together against feminine interests."[45]

Boys, however, were not the only ones imagined to benefit from fathers who embodied an appropriate model of masculinity. An appropriately masculine father was also thought to supply a stable sex role identity for girls. Writing in *Parents' Magazine* in February 1950, psychiatrist Herschel Alt put the matter this way: "In a myriad ways—to his son as a model of adult manhood, as the first 'man in her life' to his daughter—the father inevitably plays an all-important part in the lives of his children."[46] This view was reiterated in other popular media. In *Chatelaine* in April 1960, Joan Morris wrote that "the dominant father does provide a more satisfactory identification model for the male children and by clearly fulfilling the masculine role within the family he makes the task of sexual identification much clearer for the children—both male and female."[47] Within this psychological discourse, the boy's sister was seen as in need of an appropriate heterosexual model of masculinity because she would be "looking to father for help in defining her particular role of approaching womanhood," at least according to one expert from the University of Toronto's Institute of Child Study.[48] Girls, then, were assumed to require a model of an appropriate masculinity in order to develop a "normal" heterosexual identity. Edward Strecker, an eminent psychiatrist in his day, put the matter this way in *Parents' Magazine* in May 1947: "For his daughters, only he [father] can be the foil which parries the necessarily strong feminine influence of the mother, and it is he who sets the pattern for his daughter's budding male romance."[49] Popular discourse structured the patriarchal father figure as a good provider and as the ultimate source of knowledge and authority; it was he, as well, who provided a strong masculine character and a feeling of security and stability, financial and emotional, literally and figuratively, to his wife and children.

WEAK FATHERS

An age obsessed with security and stability is necessarily an age haunted by a fear of weakness, to paraphrase Whitaker and Marcuse.[50] In the postwar period, boys who did not have a father and who did not have access to a father substitute were viewed as at risk and as a source of state weakness in the future. A boy's lack of a father led to what became known as the absentee father syndrome. As already noted, in psychological discourse it was considered essential for boys to have access to a father to ensure a proper masculine identity. In the popular discourse, parents were told that it was the father who balanced the mother's feminizing influences so to protect the boy's masculinity. In this context, the fatherless boy was a cause for concern. Without a father to shore up gender identity, boys were thought to be without an anchor. A fundamental question in postwar discourse was: Without a father, who would guide the boy safely and securely into a successful masculinity?

Social psychologist Joseph Pleck notes that in the 1950s and 1960s the father "became a dominant figure, not by his presence, but by his absence."[51] Some Canadian novelists such as Hugh MacLennan used the plight of fatherless boys as a theme in their work, and academic studies concluded that fatherless boys were disadvantaged socially.[52] A study published in *Educational Review* in June 1957 presupposed that boys deprived of their fathers by death (as opposed to divorce or desertion) tended to be overprotected by their mothers and were likely to be antisocial or to show other abnormal behaviour. The researcher concluded that "normal boys" raised with a father at home "under normal family conditions" were more likely to possess traits associated with "appropriate" masculinity such as "Self-Confidence, Persistence, Assertiveness and Strength of Self Regard." Boys from fatherless families, the researcher contended, appeared to be more "sensitive" and often demonstrated emotional difficulties caused by their mothers' "overprotection."[53]

The researcher's conclusions were not original; they also accorded well with the dominant gender ideology of the time, which assumed that boys in care of their mothers were more likely to be rendered feminized and to fail to meet the standards of normative masculinity. In this sense, the research seemed to suggest that all sons who lacked fathers were deficient both socially and psychologically. For instance, in his bestselling book, *Baby and Child Care*, Dr. Spock warned millions of postwar parents that fatherless boys were at risk, for a mother as sole or primary parent might be tempted to make her boy her "spiritual companion," getting him interested in "clothes and interior decoration" and other stereo-typical feminine pursuits. Based on supposed gender differences between males and females, Spock went on to warn that if the mother succeeded in making her world more appealing to the boy and easier to get along in than the "world of boys," the boy would most likely grow up abnormal, a boy "with feminine interests."[54] Clearly, Spock's language was a coded warning to parents that a boy who became too involved with his mother faced the threat of homosexuality.

In the postwar period, fathers who lacked proper hegemonic mascu-linity were perceived as a source of weakness for the state, for the family, and in particular for boys. This was linked to the rising number of bureaucratic, white-collar male occupations that did not require physical strength, as well as to the intense care that mothers provided to modern urban boys, who were separated from their fathers because the latter spent long hours at the office. A 1956 article in *Life* drew on the postwar cultural overlay of gender ideologies to raise just such concerns. Its author considered how boys' "basic maleness" was imagined to become warped: "The mother probably [is] the dominant personality in the household, with the father a somewhat shadowy figure in the minds of the children—shadowy because he [is] unassertive or uninterested or, more likely, simply because his job keeps him away all day and brings him home at night too late and too tired to spend time with them."[55]

Such changes in work and family life led some psychiatrists to claim that weak, passive, feminized fathers and domineering, aggressive mothers were failing their sons. In November 1958, Dr. Alastair Macleod, an assistant professor of psychiatry at McGill University, speaking to a group gathered for a conference on the theme of "Man and Industry," argued that lost masculine opportunities in Ontario's industrial sector were disturbing traditional gender roles, causing fathers to become passive: "Father no longer has opportunities for pursuing aggressive competitive goals openly at work. Some of his basic masculine needs remain unmet. Mother no longer feels she has a real man for a husband and becomes openly aggressive and competitive herself." The inverted gender roles generated a decrease in the father's masculinity, Macleod noted: "Father becomes even more passive and retiring when faced with an increasingly discontented and demanding wife."[56] In postwar thought, it was imagined that the passive, feminized father, deficient in his masculinity, who could not provide balance and stability to the family's gender relations failed his son, who became vulnerable to the aggressive and predatory mother: "the son, deprived of father as a model of masculinity, has no one to turn to when mother moves aggressively toward him."[57]

Weak fathers were blamed for undermining the stability of the nuclear family by abdicating their masculine role, and this, according to psychologists, led mothers to become unfit because they had to assume the "unnatural role of leadership" in the family. An American psychoanalyst, Dr. Harry Tashman, expressed his views about this in the *Globe and Mail* on 25 March 1960:

> This abdication forces the wife to assume an unnatural role of leadership and command ... Unable to handle it with the sureness she brings to bear in traditional feminine areas such a wife asserts her new-found authority in a high-handed manner. In the process she loses her femininity and becomes an unsatisfactory mother and wife. Why does a man become passive and submissive? Why does he relinquish his masculine role?[58]

Regarding the discourse of the weak father, perhaps most troubling for postwar adults was the link it forged between weak fathers and homosexuality in their sons. In a 1960 issue of the *Pacific Sociological Review,* one academic made this point clear: "Men with weak fathers or no fathers at all are more inclined to become homosexual." According to this academic, the fear that sons of weak fathers would develop a "deviant sexual behaviour" was based on the notion that emasculated fathers were not strong enough to prevent a boy's identification with his hostile, aggressive mother.[59] In *The Psychoanalytical Theory of Neurosis* (1945), Otto Fenichel helped put into play the nefarious mother-raises-homosexual-boy discourse: "In quite a number of male homosexuals, the decisive identification with the mother was made as an 'identification with an aggressor,' that is, in boys who were very much afraid of their mothers."[60] In the midst of the Cold War paranoia, boys who displayed homosexual tendencies and men who were homosexual were to be cast as deviant, depraved, or—as some senior RCMP officials of the time called them—"practicing criminals."[61]

Homosexuals, then, were thought to pose a particular threat to the traditional Canadian nuclear family. According to Whitaker and Marcuse, by the mid- to late 1950s Canadian security experts also viewed them as particular threats to state security, in large part because "homosexuals" were thought to have especially weak, immoral characters "prone to blackmail."[62] One study submitted to the federal cabinet's security panel during the postwar period, for example, warned that homosexuals "often appear to believe that the accepted ethical code which governs normal human relations does not apply to them."[63] Another study, funded by the Canadian Social Science Research Council and published in *Social Problems* in April 1956, noted that the homosexual "deviant" sought out homosexual communities in order to exist in a context where his abnormal, immoral behaviour was seen as normal and moral.[64] The Canadian government took the issue of homosexuality seriously. By the late 1950s the RCMP, for example, had formed a separate unit to deal with the "homosexual issue" and had implemented "anti-homosexual campaigns" in order to root out homosexuals from federal offices, efforts "that advanced far beyond a security rationale and into outright homophobia."[65]

Postwar popular discourse produced the view that fathers who were shiftless or incompetent, albeit present, represented a potential threat to national strength and to the security and stability of a normal and well-adjusted boyhood. James C. Anderson's short story "Father Was a Gambler," published in *Maclean's* on 1 January 1949, emphasized this theme.[66] Continually late for supper, a father of two boys is cast as a stupid, lazy, bumbling fool, a gambling addict, and socially and morally irresponsible. At the outset, readers learn that he has squandered the family's entire savings on gambling, reducing them all to poverty. Contrary to an appropriate postwar masculinity and undermining efforts to establish a stable social order, this failed breadwinner has forced his family to live "where dingy houses elbowed each other for space." The son narrates: "It seemed the only thing about Father that changed was his jobs and we were always on the move from one house to another. And the houses got smaller, and the districts dirtier, and Father's jobs got worse, and Mother's clothes got more made-over looking, and her eyes became tired. There were always bills, always people asking for money."[67]

The financial and social degradation wrought by the failed father weighs heavily on the boy, who wants to make amends to his mother for his father's failure at masculinity. In a small gesture of affection, he aspires, like his father, to buy mother a present—a fond although minuscule compensation for a life in the slums. The boy works and saves money, but ultimately his project fails because he, too, has turned to gambling like his father. He relates: "I ran upstairs then. I threw myself on my bed and cried bitterly for mother ... but mostly for Father because I knew how he felt. I had almost a present for mother, too. I almost had a whole dollar for it."[68] The inadequate father, whose inability to be a proper breadwinner offers a model of deficient masculinity, has deeply influenced his son. The boy, emulating his father, has become a gambler.

But for some commentators, weak or absent fathers were not the only cause for concern. Aggressive, hypermasculine fathers, who lacked emotional and physical self-control, were also thought to undermine the security and stability of a "normal" boy's childhood. An article published in *Life* on 7 October 1957 presented the idea that a father who treated his son with brutality caused him short- and long-term emotional and psychological harm: "Many delinquents have domineering and often cruel fathers of whom they are terribly afraid. Their unexpressed, unresolved hostility toward the father floats through their personalities like a mine in the ocean, ready to explode at the first object it touches."[69] A boy in an unstable home, where he is dominated and rejected by his hypermasculine father, never experiences "normal love and affection" and becomes maladjusted.

Even as the postwar period was coming to a close, there remained concern over the absence of a father in a boy's life and the perceived impact of this on his development into a "normal" heterosexuality. In the summer of 1960 in *American Scholar*, medical doctor and psychoanalyst Norman Kelman warned that a boy who was cut off from his father was likely to become feminized, and by extension turn into a homosexual:

> But the harmful effects of being cut off from the father are still more striking. I think of a patient who was homosexual, whose touching of life was delicate, shallow, concerned with appearances, whose life was parasitic, taking the form of a quest for some older woman who would

> sponsor his aesthetic interests. We are often led to emphasize the effect
> of domineering, castrating mother as decisive in life history. In this
> instance features of the father seem to call for attention, however.[70]

At the beginning of the 1960s, Kelman and other scholars continued to promote psychological arguments suggesting that great damage could be done to a boy's essential heterosexual masculine core in his early years, not only through being raised by a domineering mother, but also because of the lack of adequate access to a father.[71] Unfortunately, we still encounter these arguments today (see Chapter 5).

In the context of the Cold War and the gender anxiety it generated, the "ideal" father was neither effeminate nor weak nor hypermasculine. A father who was any of these, so the argument ran, was incapable of providing his son with an appropriate model of masculinity. Popular psychological advice encouraged fathers to become pals with their sons, to share sports and hobbies with them, and to serve as models of masculine maturity. Hearty doses of an "appropriate" heterosexual masculinity in men—a masculinity that was characterized in part by emotional and physical discipline and self-control—was seen as desirable in fathers in order to produce "normal" heterosexual sons and by extension contribute to the support of patriarchal and heterosexist relations. But it was also the case that fathers and mothers together had to play their gendered parts as ideal citizens in order to secure the safety and future of the nation. So, what of mothers?

MOTHERHOOD AND BOYHOOD

Postwar familialist ideology reinforced conservative ideas about gender relations, calling for the demobilization of women from war work and encouraging them to embrace domestic roles.[72] In a 1950 letter to the editor of the *Globe and Mail*, one male writer put the matter this way: "What this tired old world needs more than anything else right now is a strong injection of good old common sense ... We must once again come to realize the importance of the housekeeper, and women must realize how vital their natural position as a wife and mother really is, before we can hope for healthy normalcy."[73]

Within this moral regulatory discourse, it was imagined that women as homemakers and stay-at-home mothers were responsible for the rearing and education of healthy, normal, and productive boys as future citizens. Sons without adequate fathers were thought likely to become delinquent or homosexual and thus threats to the social order; in the same vein, working mothers and women who led families were typically denigrated, not only as a threat to the political stability of capitalism, but also as inadequate to the task of raising healthy, normal boys.

During the postwar period, the media constantly reaffirmed the nation-building virtues of a stable family, with women back in the home as dutiful wives and mothers.[74] One male letter writer from Collingwood, Ontario, argued in the *Globe and Mail* on 4 July 1947 that "career women" undermined the stability of society. According to this writer, stay-at-home mothers "give this troubled world a family that is developed normally, both physically and mentally," and in so doing, contributed "more to advance the progress of humanity than all other agencies and services combined."[75] Certainly, public commentators taught that it was the stay-at-home mother who provided a "happy home" that was the "vanguard of a stable postwar social order," and it was this kind of mother who became the standard for a healthy boyhood.[76]

Postwar discourse routinely conveyed the message that mothers who failed to remain in the home caused harm to boys. In the *Toronto Star* in 1955, one court official argued that "the desire of women to retain their place in industry since the war is not without sinister implications." The implication here was that boys left unsupervised and "unprotected" would "go so tragically wrong."[77] A healthy boyhood was conflated with a healthy, secure, and stable state, which required that mothers stay at home. The psychoanalytic discourse maintained that working mothers contributed to problems with boys. This ideological thread positioned working mothers as selfish, greedy, and often materialistic—a theme that permeated a news item in the *Toronto Evening Telegram* titled "Parent's Greed for Money Seen Boy's Downfall." Nine boys, all less than 13 years old, appeared in juvenile court on criminal charges resulting from damage caused to a local office building. The story made careful mention that "in three of the families the mother is working and in a fourth the mother is dead and two boys are unsupervised all day." The judge castigated the mothers, asserting in patriarchal and condescending tones that "you care too much for money … It's your greed for money that has brought this about." To remove any doubt about whose fault the boys' delinquency was, the judge scolded the parents, strongly suggesting that "the mother … give up her job or work part time" so that "she can supervise her children when they are home."[78] During the postwar period, professional and popular commentators routinely reinforced the idea that good mothers did not work outside the home, and that the good mother, by staying home, would prevent boys from becoming delinquent.

Popular and professional discourse routinely blamed mothers for a variety of problems, including delinquency and homosexuality; it also blamed them for wars. In *Chatelaine* in July 1948, in a provocative article titled "Do Women Make Wars?", well-known Canadian psychologist Brock Chisholm argued that women played a larger role than men in creating the conditions for war. "Women carry the major responsibility for the development of character of children," he argued. "Therefore we cannot avoid the conclusion that women are at least as, and probably more, responsible for wars than men." For Chisholm, women were responsible for war because, as the child's primary caregiver, it was they who established the "excessive aggressive pressures" in their sons: "The sources of excessive aggressive necessities are well known. They are found commonly in people who have experienced 'rejection' in childhood. The experience of 'rejection' does not necessarily mean that a child was not loved or wanted by the mother. The child feels not loved, not wanted, rejected, if at an early age his natural behavior is too strongly disapproved by his mother."

Foreshadowing his modern-day counterparts such as *Globe* columnist Margaret Wente, who trades in essentialist arguments about gender, Chisholm then asserted that a boy whose "basic boyness" was not valued or celebrated by his mother would become filled with fear, guilt, inferiorities, and excessive pressures. And, he continued, boys who developed "excessive pressures" provided the "Hitlers of the world" with the support and the "raw materials of war." There was a vital need to raise "normal" boys in such a way as to ensure postwar security. "Mothers, grandmothers, aunts, sisters, teachers and all other women" must decide "whether to design a world for the living ... or the dead."[79]

In the postwar context, there was a growing belief that improper mothering in the form of overprotection could have significant negative consequences for boys' emotional and psychological well-being. In 1946, in an address to seventy-five delegates attending the United Church Chaplain's Conference in London, Ontario, Major B.H. McNeel, a psychiatrist with the Ontario Hospital, remarked that "the possessive mother is often a contributing factor to her child's mental deficiency since she keeps him in bonds and he is never allowed to be an independent being."[80] McNeel was far from alone in condemning mothers for improper parenting: psychologists routinely blamed possessive, overprotective mothers and their strong emotional attachment to their sons for a variety of supposed social ills. This included blaming mothers for converting "normal" boys into emasculated boys who lacked the necessary amount of masculinity to engage successfully in military combat. In 1946, for example, the chief of neuropsychiatry for the British Army claimed that mothers were to blame for men's wartime mental and physical breakdowns: "In the English-speaking countries there has been, perhaps, some over emphasis on mother dominance in family life, and we are not without evidence that the dependent attitude which is developed in those families where the mother's influence is felt too much has played some part in producing maladjustments and breakdowns of which we have had so many in the services during the war."[81]

One year later, in a 1947 article in the *Globe and Mail*, Dr. John Griffin expressed his concern that improper parenting of boys by mothers during the fragile years of boyhood directly caused masculine decline: "During the war it was common to find vigorous, healthy young men who—as a result of inhibiting crippling dependence on their mothers—were incapable of participating in the defense of their country." Continuing on from this indictment of mothers, Griffin warned of the imminent danger that overprotective mothers still posed to boys: "the over-solicitous parent and mother who pampers, dominates and controls her son, interferes with his mature development into young manhood."[82] A 1947 article in the *Globe and Mail* again expressed the view that ambitious career mothers were "sacrificing something which is far beyond any fame a career may bring, something eternal and imperishable." What was imagined by the writer as being sacrificed was a boy's eternal masculinity. This writer, citing his own Second World War experiences, said that men from homes where mothers stayed at home "were generally the bravest and manliest of his men."[83] Similarly, eight years later, on 24 December 1956, an article in *Life* presented a psychologist who emphasized for readers the perceived damage inflicted on men's masculinity by an "overwhelming mother." For this psychologist, the "overwhelming mother" was responsible for the emasculation of boys, which had led to a generation of passive, emotionally immature soldiers: "Of all the men turned down at induction centres, 38% were sent home because of 'emotional inadaptability' to military life and many medical discharges were for the same reason. Most of them were emasculated males ... They wanted to depend on somebody else. Instead of giving and protecting, they wanted to be protected ... Somewhere they had lost the male image."[84]

The cultural concerns embodied in the above texts reveal the postwar preoccupation with the masculinizing of boys, who were expected to reject their mothers, physically and emotionally, in order to achieve an "appropriate" masculinity. To some degree, the effort to separate boys from their mothers served both directly and indirectly the interests of the state and postwar corporations, which needed men who were aggressive, capable of some violence, unemotional, patriotic, and distanced from family.

Mothers in postwar discourses about boyhood were reprimanded and often vilified for being overprotective of their boys and too emotionally attached to them, thus turning them into sissies. In the literature of the normal child, the normal boy was the psychological ideal. What, then, was a "sissy"? According to Janet Power, writing in *Maclean's* in May 1946, a "sissy" was a boy raised "in a downy nest," who broke the masculine agreement, had no masculine connections, shied away from the aggressive play of "normal" boys, was afraid of getting hurt, did not fight, avoided all rugged competitive sports, and was likely to turn into a homosexual.[85] The "sissy" was the boy who from the beginning preferred feminine activities—or, as two popular postwar psychologists, Ilg and

Ames, put it, who "shuns anything rough and tumble. He prefers to play with girls. He favours such activities as painting, singing, play-acting, dressing dolls. He himself loves to dress up in girls' clothes."[86] "Normal" boys seemed destined to have a good chance of developing the necessary masculinity as adult men; by contrast, the "sissy" was a deviant in the making who undermined postwar stability and security. One child advice columnist, perhaps summing up postwar fears about boys and boyhood, told parents in the *Newmarket Era* on 4 January 1951 that "no real boy wants to be a sissy."[87]

Well-known parenting magazines published parents' concerns about their sons becoming sissies. "Was our boy a 'sissy'?", queried one mother in *Parents' Magazine* in April 1951. The mother narrates: "I began to lie awake at night mulling over some rather ticklish thoughts. I was troubled by the realization that there was something 'sissy', yes, downright 'girlish' about my young son Donnie. This is a thought that a mother can hardly face."[88] Horrified, the mother "watched the other little boys in the neighbourhood play ball," and saw her son refusing "to join them."[89] This incident was enough for the mother; parental measures had to be taken to ensure the boy became properly masculine and by extension heterosexual. To bring the boy to the normative standards of boyhood, the parents resorted to a few well-known masculinizing methods. "My husband took Donnie to the movies and often chose westerns. While Donnie liked them, he didn't act them out." The frustrated mother further reflected, and concluded that her son's sissy tendencies were not defective biology; instead, the boy's effeminacy, including his "girlish" behaviours, was due to her own too close relationship with her son. "It was not so much the problem of a 'sissy' boy, but it was the problem of a mother who unconsciously insisted on being the centre of a boy's universe." Donnie's effeminate habits might disappear in time, but there was "an over strong pull toward a mother" that caused the small boy to avoid the "normal sex pattern." The author ends the essay with advice for mothers whose boys have revealed non-masculine behaviours: "You will have to let him go. In order to get back a son who can grow to be the kind of son you want, you will have to give him to his father."[90]

Prominent psychologists of the time promoted the view that mothers who were too devoted and overprotective would turn healthy boys into mama's boys.[91] By extension this raised the spectre of homosexuality. A sissy, or mama's boy, was passive, pampered, and coddled excessively by his parents, particularly by his mother. The mama's boy was implicitly marked as abnormal and as inadequately masculine. Psychologist Samuel Laycock, in a 1946 *Maclean's* article, was preoccupied with boys who were dangerously less than masculine. In his view, boyhood was an important stage in a son's development, and mothers could not tamper with it without the spectre of the mama's boy emerging:

The "mama's boy" who has been coddled and tied to his mother's apron strings is likely to suffer in this stage of his development. His mother won't let him play with "rough" boys. She keeps him dressed up in fine clothes and has him as a constant companion. Such boys are apt to get so tied emotionally to their mothers that they never can get free and are never able to fall in love with the opposite sex ... It is easy to see that this sort of devotion, if it lasts into manhood, makes the chances of a really happy marriage practically nil.[92]

Laycock saw mothers as a potential threat to boys as they developed heterosexually, and he blamed mothers for triggering future sexual deviance as their sons grew up. In a *Chatelaine* article in 1956, he reflected the postwar mindscape about sexual deviancy, reinforcing the notion that effeminacy in little boys was an indicator of and precursor to homosexuality: "In some homes boys either do not get on well with their father or are not encouraged to identify with his manly qualities. Sometimes they have an over possessive mother who ties them too tightly to her apron strings. They become 'mama's boys' and develop feminine characteristics. Some authorities think this is why some boys do not develop normally and why they become sex deviates."[93]

Laycock, drawing largely from sex-role theory, warned parents that boys needed masculine fathers in order to acquire the appropriate heterosexual masculinity. He also warned mothers who were too possessive of their boys that they might be turning them into sexual deviants. Indeed, some academics saw the term "mama's boy" as an effective method for keeping boys en route to a positive masculine identity. For instance, sociologist Frederick Elkin told readers of his book *The Child and Society* that the boy who was "kidded about being a Momma's boy"[94] was only being helped back into an appropriate masculine sex role. Elkin further noted that teasing by calling him a mama's boy was as justified as labelling a girl a tomboy; it helped both boy and girl shift back into appropriate gender roles.

Highlighting the social dangers posed by overprotective mothers, some psychiatrists went so far as to claim that mothers' overprotection of their sons directly caused motor vehicle accidents when boys were old enough to drive. Addressing the American Association of Motor Vehicle Administrators, the chief psychiatrist at St. Joseph's hospital in London, Ontario, noted that after examining the past boyhood relationships of men in car accidents, he found that "early histories of these accident prone men had shown that the mother figure was dominant in the home and the father withdrawn, resulting in the child identifying with the mother."[95]

Mothers were instructed to not be emotionally tied to their sons lest the boy's masculinity be damaged. For instance, one divorced mother asked child experts Ilg and Ames for advice about establishing a better relationship with her troublesome eight-year-old son. The mother was upbraided by the experts for using emasculating endearments with her son such as "my lovely son," "my sweetheart son," "my darling boy." Boys, the psychologists noted, "hate this kind of thing." However, the real danger these psychologists saw was that the mother allowed herself "to be too tied up with this boy emotionally." [96] Experts imagined that boys whose fathers were missing or absent for long periods of time suffered from a compensatory flow of affection from the mother toward the boy. This was too much emotion. Such a flow of emotion and expressions of tenderness, experts thought, would turn the boy into a "sissy" and by extension posed a threat to the rigidity of the boundary that separated abnormal from normal.

Postwar gender ideology asserted that the normal boy was naturally aggressive, while the normal girl was demure and passive. According to Deborah Stearns, in patriarchal societies where males are accorded higher status, girls are often restricted in their expressions of emotions such as anger and aggression.[97] Aggression and anger thus come to be seen as a normative component in males and as marking a natural difference between males and females. A key feature of normative boyhood was the belief that a boy was more aggressive and destructive and hence, more of a problem than girls, who were viewed as easy to bring up and unlikely to be a cause for concern. Parents would not have the same kind of problems with girls as they did with boys. Consider the following passage from a short story published in Maclean's on 15 December 1946. In it, a father discusses with his wife the differences between raising boys and girls: "It'll be easier with a girl, anyway, dear. We won't have any of the big problems parents have with boys. Girls are so easy to raise. You just feed them and love them and dress them up for parties."[98] This illuminates how the assumed potential for boys to cause "big problems" was positioned in direct contrast to girls' assumed passivity and acquiescence to authority, parental or otherwise. The sole purpose of daughters was social decoration and amusement.

Postwar psychological studies of sex differences between boys and girls reinforced the idea that normal boys were aggressive, while normal girls were far less emphatic, less bold, and less audacious. To capture this ideological point, one psychologist stated that "in our culture, aggressive outgoing behaviour is as normal in the male child as quiescent nonassertive behavior is in the female."[99] The researcher added with conviction that "extensive research findings have been reported in the literature which consistently shows that boys are more aggressive and generally more 'unmanageable' than girls."[100] The notion that boys were inherently more aggressive than girls was consistent with the wider discourse that saw males in general as not only more aggressive, but also larger, more domineering, and more muscular than females. As one leading expert on masculinity and femininity stated in Maclean's in 1948: "The typical masculine personality is aggressive and domineering. There is little room for sympathy and sentiment. Physically the body is large, strong, and muscular. The voice is deep and booming. Femininity is marked by a passive and submissive nature. Physically the feminine individual is small and weak. The voice is soft and melodious. Such individuals are tender, sympathetic and sentimental."[101] These psychologists viewed aggression and dominance as a natural and even desirable part of the boyhood world, and boys who did not measure up to this standard were thought, among other things, to be sissies.

The "sissy" label was given to boys who were unathletic and who hesitated to engage in rough physical play. Nancy Cleaver, a child advice columnist for the *Stouffville Tribune*, told parents in her column of 15 February 1951 that "no parent wants his child to be a coward. How often a father is annoyed at his son's hesitation to risk physical harm in outdoor activity. He wants his boy to excel in sports and not be a sissy."[102] Postwar adults often viewed sport as the route to indoctrination in male domination and hegemony for Canadian boys and as a key strategy to ward off potential "sissydom." Clearly, "sissy" boys were pathologized, viewed as unstable and unhealthy and—within the politics of postwar masculinity—as the antithesis of a stable, "normal" healthy boy. "Practical" psychologist Janet Power, who promoted herself as a mother of "three of the kind of children you'd like to know,"[103]castigated one mother who had turned her normal boy into a sissy by not letting him become normalized through traditional masculine practices:

> When Stan plays outside he doesn't seem to have any real fun. If his friends are playing ball he always makes sure he's not in the way of the ball. He never really enters into things at all as if he is afraid of getting hurt. I know he won't get hurt because I keep an eye on things and caution him not to go out when ROUGH BOYS are around. Well, mother, it looks as if you're a SUCCESS … in making Stan a sissy! … Never shield a normal boy from the kind of play that's essential to his growth. Boys are … noisy, rough, unmindful of the NICITIES of life. They are bubbling over with energy … waste energy … frightening to us more timid grown-ups! Don't be afraid of Stan's getting hurt … Most lively boys pick up a scratch or two in their play, but few of their accidents are serious. Let Stan go out and TAKE WHAT COMES … Once in awhile turn your back on his activities, so that he doesn't feel that you are MINDING him! Sometimes … a boy has to learn caution the hard way … his own way. You can't rear a healthy boy in a downy nest! His playtime experiences can give him the SELF-CONFIDENCE he will need to FACE HIS LIFE AS IT COMES.[104]

Power's advice needs to be understood in the broader context of the anxiety and fear about the "feminization" of men's masculinity and the heightened anxieties and postwar fears over effeminacy in boys. Boys who displayed abnormal or "deviant" behaviour were considered a threat to the stability of the nuclear family and by extension to the nation state.

It is also important to remember that Power's version of boyhood substantiated the notion that violent play was essential to the healthy development of a normal boy. Drawing on the essentialized idea that boys "are bubbling over with energy," Power rebuked the mother for overprotecting her son, thus making him a sissy. Furthermore, a mother who shielded a boy from engaging in naturally violent play thwarted his innate being. Since boys were naturally noisy, rough, and unmindful, instead of discouraging this behaviour, parents should embrace it, for it provided boys with manly experiences that prepared them for venturing out into the world. Power urged mothers to turn a blind eye to their boys' aggressive play so that they could be socialized into an acceptable version of masculinity.

Mothers were viewed as unable to offer the discipline that a male presence brought to the family. The father was assumed to be the masculine presence that would control the boy's natural animosity toward his mother. It was understood there was little a mother could do to alleviate the tensions between herself and her son, since much of the hostility was a natural part of the relationship between son and mother. In 29 November 1960, the *Toronto Daily Star* published the views of two popular psychologists, Ilg and Ames, who made this point clear: "Even under ideal conditions there is a lot of this kind of disciplinary trouble between mother and almost any son from seven through to 15."[105] Sex-role theorists assumed that boys' malice toward their mothers notably increased when a masculine presence was absent. Ilg and Ames warned mothers that as normal boys got older their natural hostility and resentfulness toward them would increase, "especially when there is no father present to clamp down on them."[106] A weak mother, unable to apply appropriate amounts of discipline to a problem son, was cast against the authoritarian and manly father, who could administer the necessary quantities of discipline when needed.

As in the case of working mothers, there was some defence of women in their relations with their sons. Providing an oppositional discourse, Drinker and Schreier, in a withering critique of the mom-bashing rhetoric so pervasive at that time, argued in a 1954 article in *Journal of Higher Education* that while no one could deny that some mothers frustrated their sons, this did not logically lead to the conclusion that a "dogma" could be made out of the unverifiable theory that all mothers were "potentially dangerous" to their sons. Drinker and Schreier were closer to the truth when they suggested that the notion that mothers are potentially dangerous to their son's masculine development, and that women are a frustrating influence on men and boys, had little to do with "truth" but everything to do with the upholding of "patriarchal values."[107]

Drinker and Schreier provided a contrasting and more critical perspective on moms and sons, albeit a minority one in the postwar period.

CONCLUSION

During the postwar period, as society struggled to return to "normal," various public commentators attempted to reconstruct patriarchal and heterosexist relations. Psychologists and social commentators, among others, defined the best environment in which to raise a "normal boy" as a middle-class home that included a stay-at-home mother and an involved father. This narrow version of boyhood emerged in a province that was frantic with uncertainty, insecurity, instability, and gender anxiety brought about by a convergence of historical developments, which included a decade of economic depression followed by wartime disruptions in marital, familial, and labour relations. The exalted version of boyhood was woven into the patriarchal family structure and its attendant familialist ideology, which was thought central in safeguarding an increasingly corporate and bureaucratic society. Thus the postwar era witnessed a resurgence of traditional gender roles for men and women, one in which notions of stability and security depended on the ideal boy having an "appropriately" masculine father: one who was neither weak nor hypermasculine; one who was wise and who fulfilled the postwar responsibilities of breadwinning manhood; and one who as a result secured an appropriate heterosexual identity for his son. At the same time, mothers were told to not be overprotective of their boys or too distant from them, lest the boy become a sissy and grow into a deviant (i.e., a homosexual). In a time of intense policing and regulation of "sexual deviance," it mattered greatly for a mother to prevent her boys from becoming sissies or mama's boys. At the same time, mothers were warned not to neglect their sons, as this would establish "excessive aggressive pressures" that were imagined to cause wars.

The prevailing discourses of boyhood sought to erase differences along the lines of class, race, and ethnicity and evoked notions of a healthy, normal home—notions that were normalized as the Anglo-Protestant middle-class ideal. It was thought that traditional values and family consciousness would breed sturdy boys who would grow up to conquer urban perils while becoming pillars of the social order. Much of postwar thought imagined that safe, secure, "normal" households structured as nuclear families would allow parents to perform an incalculable national service, that of transmitting traditional values to their boys, who would grow into the "right" kind of men, that is, men who would fulfill the responsibilities of manhood by providing security and stability for Canada's seemingly fragile democracy. Yet some questions lingered: What was meant by the right kind of man? And what did postwar commentators see as the most important values to invest in the ideal boyhood? I turn to these questions, and others, in the next chapter.

One for All:
Teamwork and the Ideal Boyhood

2

The growth of corporate culture in postwar Ontario compelled corporations to draw attention to the problems of administration and management that arose when men worked in groups rather than individually. What corporations required during the postwar period was the right kind of man, one who would slip neatly into the new corporate economy. Some adults remained committed to the notion of rugged individualism as a boyhood value; others more aggressively promoted a version of boyhood based on a deeper, collective male identity. In the age of anonymous bureaucracies, concerned as they were more with fitting in than with standing out, proponents of this version of boyhood played down rugged individualism and played up teamwork, togetherness, cooperation, group fidelity, collective identity, and company loyalty.

In this model of boyhood, important distinctions based on class or race between and among boys were erased as a greater sense of "togetherness" between and among males was sought. This version of boyhood was classless— or at least, organizations such as the Boy Scouts wanted it to be.[1] It was no less competitive than in the past, but in the past, strife between and among boys had been more openly promoted than in the postwar era. In the past, the once autonomous male self who engaged in individual combat had been the ideal. However, running alongside the growth of corporate culture, a new version of boyhood was emerging, one that was influenced by the experiences of the Second World War and shaped by the threat of communism. A boy's character was now to be a mix of modern military and postwar corporate virtues—teamwork, togetherness, selflessness, loyalty, hard work, duty, and discipline. The group, not the individual, was to be emphasized and valued. And among other things, the boy who would become the organization man had develop an aversion to independent entrepreneurship.[2] Such boys would grow up to become assets for any far-sighted corporation.

This chapter begins by examining the postwar value of teamwork and its relation to the ideal boyhood. Teamwork as a core boyhood value ran alongside other postwar values such as conformity, togetherness, self-sacrifice, the disciplining of desire, and recognition of the group. All of these were in turn harnessed to productivity, work efficiency, and the accumulation of profit, which happened to be the postwar goals advanced by industry and corporations alike. Responding to postwar anxieties and insecurities, adult discourses about boyhood focused on building boys who would adopt the value of teamwork as a way to ensure social order and the state's stability. This chapter also explores how some adults promoted sport as having moral worth because it taught boys the value of teamwork, along with other corporate virtues such as team loyalty, civic responsibility, self-sacrifice, and subordination to leadership. It moves on to examine social and cultural commentators' efforts to place within public discourse the centrality of male bonds. Their goal in this was to re-establish a greater sense of male intimacy through public narratives that situated boys as natural playmates of other boys. Finally, by exploring discourses that centred on boyhood and the gang, this chapter examines how the boy gang functioned as a model for corporate or factory life.

TEAMWORK AND THE BOYHOOD IDEAL

The ideal model of boyhood embraced a reworked understanding of teamwork. This new understanding served the interests of major institutions of power such as government, bureaucracies, and industry, and no longer only God and country. In Toronto in October 1942, during an address to a convention of the American Federation of Labor, Prime Minister William Lyon Mackenzie King called for the establishment of labour–management committees "in every industry in our country."[3] His remarks signalled the start of one the "most successful and long lived cooperative experiments in Canadian industrial relations, the Labour-Management Production Committees."[4] A central aim of these committees was to promote "teamwork" between labour and management. The Labour-Management Cooperation Service published a bulletin titled *Teamwork in Industry;* it also developed films and radio projects intended to expand the appeal of teamwork as a concept. According to McInnis, at times these "tactics degenerated to the level where a mawkish cartoon character, known as Tommy Teamwork, was enlisted to remind production workers of the importance of cooperation."[5] The emphasis on "teamwork" is not surprising, given that the immediate postwar years had seen a surge in labour strikes, where "communities across Canada took to picket lines in unprecedented numbers, shutting down almost every major industry at various points between 1945 and 1947."[6]

On 22 September 1949, the *Essex Free Press* informed its readers that since 1946, strikes and lockouts had "idled more manpower and caused loss of more production time than in any year in our history."[7] Given the rising tensions between labour and management, and between companies and unions, it is little wonder that government and business interests often invoked concepts such as teamwork, cooperation, and fair play as a way to encourage increased productivity and to bring organized labour under control.[8]

The hope was that the rhetoric of teamwork would achieve cooperation without coercion or conflict. Speaking in the interests of industry, one public commentator stated that teamwork was to be the single greatest factor in establishing postwar security: "Most of us recognize that we are threatened by postwar dangers that are just as grave as if not more grave than the wartime dangers we have survived and surmounted … Our only hope lies in a new invigorating spirit … and a deep conviction that teamwork … is the answer."[9] It had been teamwork that "broke Germany's back,"[10] and "teamwork" was to be the "key to survival" for Canadians living in an "atomic age."[11] In the midst of the Cold War, it was imagined that teamwork would also play a key role in halting the spread of communism.

Teamwork became an increasingly important postwar value, for it was seen as a way to combat communist efforts, real or imagined, to create disunity and strife in democratic nations. Lewis Milligan, a columnist for the *Essex Free Press,* warned readers that "the mightiest ally of Russia is strife, conflicts, and wars in every capitalist nation."[12] Similarly, on 27 March 1947, an editorial in the *Acton Free Press* alerted readers that "there are godless forces at work with a planned program. These forces exploit and ride to power on moral confusion, weak will and self will, disunity and discontent."[13] Popular commentators and others suggested that the virtue of teamwork would be vital to democracy's victory over communism.

As a regulatory discourse, teamwork came to be viewed as an antidote for a variety of postwar problems that were thought to be threatening social decline and disintegration. An editorial in the *Acton Free Press* on 15 August 1946, titled "The Same Answer," made this point clear:

> Strikes, divorces, political disputes. The headlines, these days have a common denominator. It is the lowest possible denominator—the denominator of selfishness. They all spell social break down—trouble in the world. But they also have a common answer—teamwork.
>
> The strikes and lockouts which are ripping up the fabric of democracy can be settled by violence which injures everybody; by compromise which satisfies nobody; or by teamwork which enriches all.

> Marriage rows can end in a divorce which breaks up the home and leaves the children at loose ends; by a grin-and-bear-it stalemate which is little but an "undeclared divorce"; or by teamwork which gives the whole family something to fight for instead of something to fight about.
>
> International disputes can be ended by an atom bomb which, next time, is likely to end the world along with the war; by craven mutual appeasement which, at best, is only a breathing spell—a postponement of the big eruption; or by teamwork where each nation finds its destiny and contributes to the concern of the whole.
>
> Teamwork makes the maintenance of unity more important than the production of utensils or the jurisdiction of unions. It makes the people you work with more important than the things you work at. It makes holding to the Democratic way more important than each having his own way, and it makes winning our international opponents the real key to ending disputes.
>
> The President of the UNO Security Council may thus have very different problems than the returned soldier who is gripped by the industrial wrangles he finds back home. The latter, in turn, may have different problems than the newlyweds in their first tiff. But to all of their problems there is one and the same answer. They all depend on revolutionary teamwork to achieve a world that works.[14]

At this time, strikes, industrial strife, political disputes, divorce, adultery, and other forms of conflict all were threatening to undermine the state's stability and security. Teamwork was a way to maintain and strengthen the social order by instilling in an anxious population the values of cooperation and togetherness. Thus teamwork was placed alongside the two godheads of postwar industry: productivity and efficiency. If industries could reduce labour unrest, improve quality control, implement accident prevention, and reduce employee absenteeism, they would become more efficient and thus more profitable, but to achieve these things, they needed men who had internalized the value of teamwork.[15]

Within what some experts of the time described as an increasingly "strenuous market,"[16] men as workers and managers were encouraged to work together as teams against other teams: "To compete successfully against larger firms the small company must develop efficiency," declared one Canadian manufacturer, "and to achieve top efficiency, labour and management must be willing to work together toward that objective in an organized fashion."[17] Echoing this sentiment was R.G. Flood, supervisor of Employee Relations at Canadian General Electric Co., who suggested that management and labour must work together as a team in order to be as productive and successful during the postwar as they had been during wartime.[18] But in the postwar era, the ideology of teamwork became little more than a way to regulate and maintain the social, economic, and gender order. The 1940s and 1950s had been marked by an anti-communist campaign that saw the expulsion of communists and communist sympathizers from many Canadian unions, as well as by intensifying public scrutiny of perceived "sexual deviancy" that resulted in a significant campaign against gay men by the Canadian government.[19]

During the postwar period, both in industry and in the growing corporate culture, teamwork, togetherness, and fair play became increasingly significant male values. Shaped by the emergence of new corporate systems and situated within the expanding world of postwar capitalism, these values—along with other values such as controlled aggression—became central in the development of an appropriate boyhood. They were equated with a proper boyhood masculinity and transmitted through sport. In 1946, at the annual Oakville Sports Association hockey night, Tom Daly, "ambassador at large" for Toronto's baseball and hockey clubs, told more than 100 boys that "when you become an athlete you have come into manhood."[20]

SPORT, TEAMWORK, AND THE IDEAL BOYHOOD: BUILDING AN EFFICIENT, PRODUCTIVE ONTARIO

For corporate capitalism to continue to expand, it would have to replace the economic individualism of the past with a new corporate consciousness. This change would lead individuals to sacrifice themselves for the good of the company. At a time when postwar capitalism depended heavily on teamwork and fair play, some adults promoted sport as a good vehicle for teaching boys teamwork as well as other corporate virtues, such as loyalty, sacrifice, promptness, civic responsibility, and subordination to leadership. "Teamwork, rather than individual play" was most important in hockey, declared one NHL coach.[21] In a similar vein, speaking at a boys hockey banquet in Unionville in 1951, guest speaker Father Flannigan from St. Michael's College in Toronto told the large audience that "good sportsmanship, team work and the ability to get along with others" were essential in building a boy's character.[22]

Through organized sport, some members of the Canadian press sought to inject boyhood with a greater degree of group consciousness. *Saturday Night* on 18 January 1949 printed an article by Kimball McIlroy titled "Shall I Let My Son Play Hockey?" In it, McIlroy asked: "What benefit does the average boy derive from participation in such hard team sports as [hockey, rugby, and baseball]?" Answering his own question, he continued:

> Well in the first place he learns to take hard knocks without whimpering. He's going to have to take hard knocks as he grows older, and it's a good thing to get used to them early. In the second place, he will learn

the value of cooperation. He sees that the twelve men on a rugby team can't get anywhere as individuals, and that success comes only through planning and teamwork. He discovers the necessity of submerging some of his own ambitions for the general welfare. Thirdly, he's developing himself physically. Despite all risks of injury, the graduating athlete is almost invariably a much healthier boy than the comparable non-athlete.[23]

Employing reasoning linked to the postwar values of teamwork, togetherness, collectivity, and cooperation, McIlroy portrayed boyhood in a contradictory way. Boyhood was a time when boys needed to learn how to individually "take it," not just for themselves, however, but for the sake of the team. The hard, physical lessons learned on the playground or the hockey rink were good preparation for the game of life. One child advice columnist advised parents that young boys, like nation-states and corporations, should, when faced with bigger, tougher boys, stand firm and take their bumps and lumps. The columnist concluded that in the boy's best interests, he "needs to be taught to take what comes cheerfully without crying, to risk scratches, get a dab of Mercurochrome when he needs it and get back into play."[24] One teacher from St. John's Training School for Catholic boys advocated a straightforward and uncomplicated formula when it came to boys and sport: "If they can take it in sport, they can take it in life."[25] Corporate and industrial success depended on the maximum efforts of all employees. Despite the risk of injury or physical or emotional harm, boys, like men, had to learn to take their lumps while continuing to put forth a maximum effort for the welfare of the group.

Public commentators never tired of emphasizing that team success depended on the maximum productivity of *all* members. No surprise, then, that "teamwork," along with the ability to perform "unselfishly" and "fairly" as well as "aggressively," stood out as accolades when applied to boys and men. In September 1947, in a child advice column in *Parents' Magazine,* the writer made this point clear:

> Our son, aged ten, was not aggressive enough, and as a result, several of the boys in the neighbourhood bullied him almost constantly. He began to lose confidence in himself ... I talked the matter over with the physical director of our YMCA and my son was enrolled with the nine to eleven age group. Instead of being taught boxing as I had expected, he was put on the basketball team and given instruction in swimming. The result of the teamwork is wonderful. My son sees that any unfairness while playing is punished by penalties that the whole team suffers.[26]

Capitalism, like patriarchy, needs rules in order to flourish. Rules, which are set by the politically powerful, regulate social action and must be adhered to if the social and economic order is to be maintained.[27] Hierarchal relationships of superior to subordinate, of employer to worker, of masculinity to femininity, are structured by relations of power embedded in rules. Yet even in democracies, rules do not represent *all* citizens. Instead, rules often serve the elite, such as dominant industrialists and well-connected corporations. If people play fair and follow the already established rules, gender relations remain stable, patriarchal privilege is buttressed, and industrial and corporate profits grow. So it is not hard to see why the quintessential athlete of the postwar era, like the quintessential employee, was team-oriented, played by the rules, and faced the consequences of competition with equanimity and fortitude. One would hear no whining after a close but hard-fought loss and no gloating after a win: "defeat without whimpering and victory without gloating," as one academic put it in a 1955 article in *Journal of Educational Sociology* titled "The Contribution of School Athletics to the Growing Boy."[28] Sports and the ideology of teamwork aided corporations and industry alike by shifting the responsibility for failure onto the shoulders of the individual competitor. Good sportsmanship required that athletes play fair and by the rules and that they blame no one but themselves for a defeat, while modestly sharing credit for victories with fellow players and coaches.

All of this brings to mind the image of Gregory Peck in *The Man in the Gray Flannel Suit* (1956).[29] Like Peck's breadwinning character, Thomas Rath, the model of boyhood outlined in the preceding paragraph promoted the prototypical organization man. Clearly, individualism and autonomous self-reliance were not pronounced in this model of boyhood. A corporation's impersonal bureaucratic structure was designed to prevent the expression of individual or entrepreneurial spirit; at the same time, it promoted teamwork and fair play. A successful nineteenth-century boyhood had emphasized self-reliance and individualism; in the postwar era, a successful boyhood was built around the collective, with boys working together in teams, and with the emphasis on teamwork, cooperation, selflessness, and togetherness. These boyhood values were seen as necessary to "bring harmony to a tired and fear-stricken world."[30] Of course, these same values were also necessary to create a productive and efficient economy in an increasingly bureaucratic Province of Ontario. That was the message conveyed by Franz Martin, advertising and sales promotion manager for Chrysler Corporation of Canada, at the 1958 annual Bosses' Night of the Leamington Junior Chamber of Commerce: "The evolution of the boss-employee relationship was just as spectacular as evolution in science and engineering. It has brought us from the Scrooge–Cratchit way of working together to a modern way of getting things done—through teamwork, cooperation and good personal relationships."[31]

In the Cold War era, many adults in positions of power (who included Franz Martin) viewed the codification of teamwork as an important means for securing an elusive stability in a culture that dreaded disunity, strife, and division. An important task of those in power during the postwar era in Ontario was to cultivate some sense of unity, some sense of teamwork, togetherness, and aggression among boys, especially among newly arrived immigrant boys, who were headed for different slots on the social, economic, and occupational hierarchy. Thus team sports were promoted not only to occupy increasing amounts of youth leisure time but also to support socialization by providing a model and an actual system where boys were slotted into specialized roles of varying prestige and importance and were expected to leave aside individual gains in order to cooperate for the good of the team. At the time, industrial capitalism and corporate culture were entrenching themselves. Boys would encounter the organizational patterns of the adult-managed world of team sports again when they grew into men and entered the world of corporate or industrial work.[32]

The values of togetherness, teamwork, and loyalty promoted by social commentators, and the corporate spirit those commentators worked to impose through activities such as sport, were not designed to prepare boys for life in an egalitarian society. On the contrary, the exalted values of cooperation and fair play and the increasing emphasis on teamwork and togetherness described the relationship of future members of a hierarchal, capitalist, and more and more bureaucratic society. This suggests that a major function of public rhetoric as it related to constructing a prevailing narrative of an appropriate masculinity was to develop in boys an allegiance to the rules governing competition for positions in the social order.

Allegiance to hockey, for example, included acceptance of the uneven social and economic consequences of the rough-and-tumble sport; at the same time, hockey prepared boys "for a man's role in the world," as one team of psychologists from Toronto's Institute of Child Study declared.[33] In this way the world of boys, predicated on competitiveness and controlled violence, became established as the training ground for a successful masculinity. If boys could "take it" during their boyhood days and withstand the roughhousing of their male friends, surely they would be able to "take it" as men, engaged in the roughhousing of the new corporate culture.

This appears to have been the view held by Dr. Spock, who saw violence and aggression as natural to a "normal" boyhood and as a necessity for the development of an appropriate postwar corporate masculinity. But he added that boys' natural propensity for violence became a problem if it was not controlled. Accordingly, organized sport (among other methods) was a useful means to help boys control and discipline their aggression. It was useful because boys would learn to work with other boys in a formal structure that had rules and conventions. These rules and conventions would in turn discipline their assumed naturally aggressive tendencies. Here is Spock:

> As boys get into the 6-to-10-year-old period, their games of make-believe violence are better organized. A crowd that wants to play war divides itself into teams, makes rules of the game. At the high-school and college level, make-believe no longer satisfies. Organized athletics, games, debates, and competitions for school jobs take its place. All these call for aggressiveness. But the fierce feelings are strictly controlled by dozens of rules and conventions.[34]

For Spock, and for other postwar experts, any attempt to extinguish a boy's aggressive instincts was misguided. If he was to compete successfully as an adult in the postwar corporate culture, a boy needed to *refine* his aggressive instincts: "And when a person goes out into the world and takes a job, he still needs his aggressive instincts, but they are further refined and civilized. He works to make his business concern successful." For parents who remained concerned over their young son's aggressive tendencies, Spock went on to reassure them that a young boy's aggression was simply an indicator that he was on a natural path toward becoming a valuable postwar citizen: "In other words, when your child at 2 bangs another over the head, or at 4 plays shooting, or at 9 enjoys blood-and-thunder comic books, he is just passing through the necessary stages in the taming of his aggressive instincts that will make him a worth-while-citizen."[35]

In sports books marketed to parents but intended for boys, the heroes were moral exemplars who downplayed individuality and emphasized teamwork. Ed Winfield's 1953 *Safe on Second Base* was lauded in the popular media as a particularly good book for boys, for it placed "wholesome stress on sportsmanship and team play."[36] Sports columnist Scott Young was singled out as an outstanding author of boys sports books. His 1953 narrative of a Canadian hockey school, *Boy on Defense*,[37] was touted as "a superior novel for Canadian boys" largely because it emphasized physical robustness, teamwork, and fair play.[38] One year before his *Boy on Defense* appeared, reviewers advised readers that Young's 1952 narrative *Scrubs on Skates* had "universal interest to boys,"[39] was one of the "best boy books" to arrive in a long time,[40] and was loaded "with demonstrations of right and wrong behaviour of several kinds."[41] Sports books such as *Scrubs on Skates* were viewed as pedagogical tools for developing attitudes of togetherness, racial equality, teamwork, fair play, discipline, and masculine courage and for fostering conflict resolution skills in such a way that individual desires and honours were subordinated to the common good.

The give and take of sports competition introduced in microcosm many of the social situations of modern postwar living. Social commentators hoped to reach young boys through sports-related books and to channel their enthusiasm into more desirable patterns of social interaction. In 1952, in his *Globe and Mail* review of *Scrubs on Skates,* William Arthur Deacon argued for abandoning an older version of boyhood that valued individual heroism: "Every moving novel requires a moral of some kind and a discipline of some sort. Mr. Young gets his discipline from discarding the boy hero idea in favour of the discipline of team effort; and his moral is erasing race prejudice through equality on the ice. A boy's ancestry does not count when he is trying to get the puck into the net."[42]

J.L. Charlesworth, a book reviewer for *Saturday Night,* echoed these sentiments two weeks later when he celebrated *Scrubs on Skates* for its moral worth to boys. According to Charlesworth, books like *Scrubs on Skates* helped the "rebirth of a proper attitude in the lad, the development of a new appreciation of team play and sportsmanlike understanding."[43] They taught boys rules, teamwork, and how to work with others. They were ideal texts to prepare boys for life in a more organized, corporate capitalist society. Postwar corporate culture demanded both conformity and a cooperative atmosphere that shunned conflict and fostered togetherness. If corporate culture was to flourish in a society so deeply divided by race and social class, it mattered greatly that a boy's race, social class, or ancestry not generate conflict. Texts like *Scrubs on Skates* instilled the necessary character traits for achieving corporate ends. Adults saw them as moral guidebooks, as enjoyable reads, and as manuals for building a corporate character in boys that would ensure economic survival in a modern age.

Many postwar texts encouraged and naturalized hegemonic forms of masculinity; in effect, they were attempts to inject corporate behaviour and success ideologies into the ideal of boyhood. They distinguished between an appropriate boyhood and an inappropriate one based on the relationships between boyhood, team sports, and, for example, reading. In the 1 September 1956 issue of *Saturday Night,* for example, Brian Cahill drew out for readers some of the contours of an acceptable postwar boyhood and its relationship to specific gendered activities: "He is a quiet lad, healthy enough but not very interested in organized sports and team athletics. This puts him in a tough spot in our neighbourhood where it would seem, the sight of a young boy sitting quietly under a tree reading a book sets everyone's teeth on edge."[44]

Team sports were a type of male interaction that perpetuated male privilege and supported hegemonic versions of masculinity; at the same time, they mimicked the attitudes and social relationships needed to sustain postwar relations of production. Not surprisingly, then, cast against the masculine practices that emphasized boys' physicality and engagement in organized team play, the passive act of reading alone was largely viewed as an abnormal, feminine practice.

It was vital that the normal, healthy boy show a strong interest in competitive sports. "Boys desire athletic competition," wrote Kimball McIlroy in *Saturday Night* in January 1949.[45] For McIlroy, the craving for competition and bodily contact grew increasingly strong in boys soon after babyhood. "The average healthy boy begins to evince a disquieting interest in outdoor sports of the kind that call for hard bodily contact." The happy, "healthy" boy naturally desired the "hard," physical dimensions of sport for both the apparent pleasure of it and for the psychological benefits to be had from engaging in it. "The boy," McIlroy added, "has the terrific psychological advantage of having participated, of having done what the others were doing, of having been permitted to be one of the group rather than ... an isolated and probably unhappy outsider."[46] This statement, like many others, emphasized that boyhood required a strong sense of cooperation, institutional loyalty, and willingness to subordinate personal interests to those of the group. Yet at the same time, team athletics offered an arena for unashamedly celebrating male skill and strength, for glorifying comradeship and team spirit without women and the feminine.

Throughout the postwar period, images of boys filled the sports pages of Ontario's newspapers. Carol Dyhouse remarks that college histories are full of tributes to former sporting heroes and essentially function as "hymns to the male body."[47] Adrian Bingham notes that newspaper sports pages have served a similar function for the wider culture.[48] This was exemplified on the sports pages of three prominent postwar newspapers in Ontario. Although appropriate boy conduct was heralded in newspapers' front-page photographs, in fiction, and in advice columns to adults, the lessons were concentrated and most explicit in photographs presented in newspapers' sports sections. The sports section forged formidable links among boyhood, masculinity, and sports by celebrating boys' apparent commitment to postwar values of teamwork, selflessness, courage, and fair play along with athletic proficiency, competitiveness, and skill.[49] An extraordinary number of photographs appeared throughout the postwar period in a variety of domains, showing young boys playing team sports such as hockey, baseball, football, or basketball. Presentations depicted boys dressed in masculine armour (hockey equipment),[50] smiling and sweaty as they posed in hockey nets,[51] change rooms, and elsewhere. On 12 June 1946, the *Globe and Mail* included four photographs from different moments of a boys softball jamboree.[52] The first two, taken at home plate, are of young boys up to bat swinging at the ball while an "excited mob" cheers the action. The boys' bodies and the value of teamwork are the central themes in this composition; their male bodies depict masculine strength and demonstrate competitive, team-oriented sporting prowess within a theatre of manliness. The remaining photographs portray moments after the jamboree. One shows the boy who was the "captain and pitcher" borne on the shoulders of his teammates in masculine celebration of their triumph. The photographs together represent sports as an all-boy domain; the absence of females, except as fans, strengthens this notion.

Visual texts such as this, coupled with the increasing amount of public rhetoric about the value of teamwork, helped focus public attention on playing by the rules as the hallmark of a wholesome boyhood.[53] In the hope of channelling the fiercely competitive feelings of players and coaches into acceptable forms of behaviour, public commentators and others encouraged young boys to internalize the sporting codes that graced the front pages of the popular media. The ideal athlete was conceptualized as one who accepted the rules. In the best of all possible worlds, boys would compete fiercely but unselfishly. Perhaps this is why the 1950 Ontario Royal Commission on Education selected a number of masculine virtues, such as duty, loyalty, courage, endurance, and discipline, as the cornerstones for building a safe and secure postwar society in Ontario, and why it distilled these virtues into the "cardinal" virtue of "unselfishness."[54] Boys' winning ways must not be tainted by a loss of individual self-control. Real athletes would rather lose than take unfair advantage or cheat even if they could get away with it. In the game of life, as found in postwar bureaucracies or industrial labour relations, and as in the game of hockey, it was crucial for men to cooperate with the legitimate authority. Cooperation with authorities in hockey or in the growing corporate culture meant accepting officials' or bosses' decisions without question or dissension. This is precisely why we find public statements such as the one uttered by a Second World War pilot in a 1947 *Globe and Mail* article titled "Teamwork Pays in Air As in Hockey, Says Ace," in which he noted that his "success" in becoming a "top scorer" in shooting down "Jerries" during the war was attributable to "teamwork" and by doing "what he was told."[55] What more could the military, or a corporation, ask from a man?

While sport was used to instill in boys the values of obedience, teamwork, and fair play, it was also used to prop up a flagging masculinity. Sport, Varda Burstyn has remarked, is a "master narrative of masculinity."[56] For Burstyn, sport becomes particularly important, socially and politically, at moments of gender unease and "provides points of identification, masculine regroupment, and symbolic affirmation in a social landscape marked by changing gender, race and class relations."[57] Not surprisingly, then, sport was imagined to be useful in rejuvenating a perceived flagging postwar masculinity and by extension providing a way to ensure postwar stability. Shaped by Cold War anxieties around the "specter of regimented Soviet he-men"[58] and the perceived decline in masculinity in Western nations, some commentators called for increased federal funding and guidance for organized sports in Canada to develop a healthier citizenry, and, more importantly, to build healthier future soldiers and corporate men. The degree, for instance, of Russia's demonstrated "domination" at a 1956 international winter sporting competition in Italy was a gender bell-wether for *Globe and Mail* columnist Jim Vipond. According to him, Canadian manhood was lagging far behind the manhood of the Communist countries—a significant point if war with Russia should break out: "Healthy athletes make healthy soldiers. Should a war break out, and let's hope it never will, Russia will be able to muster somewhere between 80 to 90 percent of its manhood without fear of medical rejection. Here in Canada, if the last war is any criterion, approximately 40 percent of our recruits will be rejected as medically unfit for military service."[59]

Vipond was not the only one to issue a warning about Canada's flagging manhood. In June 1950 an MP in Ottawa noted that during the last war "the physical condition of about forty-five percent of those who tried to enlist was a pretty sorry indictment against us."[60] Fears were growing that the country was developing less than masculine boys and the threat this posed to postwar stability. In this context, sport was thought useful not only in training males in the values and conventions of the factory or corporation, but also in "preparing males for exercising violence in the service of nation."[61]

In the sports pages, which were intended for adults, masculinity emerged as a visually overt theme. In his analysis of how gender was constructed in Britain's popular press during the interwar period, social historian Adrian Bingham remarked that sport pages have typically offered a space where "male skill and strength" can be celebrated unashamedly and where "comradeship and team spirit" can be glorified in the "absence of women."[62] The extensive visual representations of boyhood in sports sections rejuvenated a flagging masculinity and indicated that boyhood was a time to celebrate sporting prowess and to claim male camaraderie in male-only spaces. A November 1948 item is a classic example: it reveals two wholesome, dirty-faced boys fresh from racing and rolling in the soft, cold mud of the soccer field.[63] Constructed to appear like two gladiators, muddy, tired, and worn, the two boys, arms draped around each other, embrace in homosocial, masculine solidarity after they have "battled" for victory at the Toronto intermediate public school soccer finals.[64] Items such as this one promoted teamwork as well as male camaraderie forged through struggle and competition; as Bruce Kidd has noted, they also publicly celebrated the dramatic achievements of top male athletes, thereby validating male claims "to the most important positions in society."[65] After the war, boys were routinely made more newsworthy, and their accomplishments were celebrated through public displays. All of this invested them with higher social value than girls. There were no comparable items for female athletes, and this reinforced and inscribed the gendered nature of sport.

HOCKEY, CONTROLLED AGGRESSION, AND BOYHOOD

In *Along Olympic Road* (1951), radio broadcaster and writer Foster Hewitt described the hockey rink as an "outdoor nursery" for Canadian boys.[66] Adults imagined that boys acquired an appropriate character by playing hockey. On 26 February 1959 the *Acton Free Press* editorialized that "most Canadian parents like to see their boys try a hand at organized hockey" as a way to build their boy's character.[67] Advertisements declared that "pro hockey is every kid's dream" and that "in PeeWee leagues from coast to coast[,] Canadian boys are battling it out with stick and puck."[68] This reflected an assumption that all Canadian boys (but not girls) visualized a lifetime of skates, sticks, pucks, and ice rinks. Sanctioning male violence, adults fantasized about boys' epic victories against worthy adversaries and about male bonding within what Kimmel called "purified pockets of virility," defined as all-male spaces under the tutelage of male coaches.[69] The actual physical setting was constructed as a theatre of masculine power and aggression for boys to be team "rivals," "battling" each other as they learned valuable lessons about how to stand up for themselves in the face of aggression, take their lumps, and compete as a team and for their team.

Hockey was heralded within popular discourse as *the* place (rather than *a* place) where athletic activity could instill moral virtues to make young boys work or battle ready. A 1946 advertisement for Hiram Walker titled "The Canadian Way" depicted a father and a young boy at a professional hockey game, watching two players on the ice battling for the puck. The ad copy read: "It's the fightingest game of the season. Every heart beats madly with the joy of battle. And, we must develop it in our children. We must make it strong within them so that in time to come, when the destiny of our nation is placed in their hands, they will be fair-minded in their decisions, unbiased in their judgments."[70]

In the print media, normative masculinity served as a marketing ploy for advertisers to attract their male target audience. This, too, linked masculinity to positively sanctioned violence and controlled aggression with regard to issues of national security. Hockey was viewed as an appropriate training ground for masculinity and corporate citizenship. Through gender initiation it would instill in boys a postwar character built on the virtues of teamwork, fair play, and controlled aggression. Certainly, hockey was not promoted as a way to *eliminate* the virility supposedly forged in the crucible of masculine competition. Rather, it was suggested that sport would temper individual competitive aspirations and superimpose on them the ethos of the team player.

But there were limits to adults' tolerance of boys' demonstrations of virility. In Preston, Ontario, when a twelve-year-old boy was punched and stabbed by another boy of the same age, the police officer in charge of the incident rationalized the violence: "The two schools are close together. It's only natural that boys will fight, but there shouldn't be any fighting which will cause wounding and possible serious harm. It must be stopped immediately."[71] Here, the speaker was establishing fighting as "normal" boy behaviour, while attempting to steer a middle course in the relationship between boyhood and fighting. Fighting, then, was part of boyhood, and adults should be concerned about it only when the logic of violence and "aggressive masculinity" was extended to its inevitable conclusion—that is, when boyish behaviour became overly violent, out of control, unstable, and immoderate so that it resembled the violence associated with fascism, totalitarianism, or a wildcat strike. In 1946, for example, while never suggesting that violence was not a key feature of North American masculinity, the chief of neuropsychiatry for the British Army publicly condemned the "more patriarchal culture" of Hitler's fascist Germany for creating the social conditions from which an overly violent "cult of aggressive masculinity" was able to grow.[72] The issue, then, in the postwar context was not the fighting itself, but whether boys fought by the rules. Normalcy for boys was equated with violence and aggression, but these must be in moderation, legitimate, controlled, and within the framework of established rules.

In short, public statements about sport supported hegemonic forms of masculinity while also reinforcing the social relationships and attitudes needed to sustain an increasingly corporate economy. The hockey culture promoted through public discourse served as a metaphor for corporate culture, in that it exposed boys to the same institutional values and was organized to replicate the milieu of competition and group cooperation that characterized the corporate experience. Through hockey, adults hoped to create the proper corporate character, where boys would learn the value of teamwork and controlled aggression and perhaps become accustomed to being selected and sorted into different categories: first string, second string, bench warmers, and spectators. Team coaches faced formidable problems when trying to build an efficient team. They were obligated to place boys in specific positions of unequal rank, where they would be expected to carry out assignments of unequal prestige and value. Hockey coaches, like corporate managers, held enormous power over players and used that power to overcome their players' resistance through threats of benching or reduced playing time. The concept of teamwork worked alongside the postwar virtue of togetherness, in a way that discouraged invidious comparisons about the relative worth of contributions made by hard-working but lowly teammates or co-workers and that may have offered one ideological solution to the problem of player (or worker) conflict, resistance, or rebellion.

BUILDING BODIES, BUILDING CORPORATIONS

Smiling, trim, muscular, and healthy boys would become men of similar traits and attributes—something that was important for an increasingly white-collar Ontario. The 1940s and 1950s saw a heightened demand for white-collar workers in Ontario ("white-collar" here is understood as an "occupational category, encompassing managers and professionals as well as mechanical, clerical, and sales people").[73] Ontario's expanding capitalist economy required men who were physically robust and "would start off each morning with a zest for work."[74] Corporations did not want male employees who needed time off work due to illness. "Nervous," anxious weaklings placed a burden on these firms; they consumed corporate resources by seeking advice from in-house nurses; they failed to contribute their utmost to the corporate cause.[75] Given that strong, healthy male foot soldiers were required to wage war in the competitive economy of the new Ontario, the building of strong, healthy boys became a necessity. *Good Health,* a 1955 physical education text authorized by Ontario's Minister of Education, made all of this abundantly clear:

> The employee must also safeguard his firm against engaging employees who will create a heavy drain on its social services. It is the weaklings who become a burden to the company nurse; who increase the rates of group insurance, sick benefit schemes and company pensions. When men are ill they are more prone to accidents. All these considerations prompt employers to scrutinize most carefully the health record of applicants and, once hired, to take measures to maintain the health of their employees.[76]

Corporate profits and male careers depended on boys developing healthy, masculine bodies.

The war had increased awareness that mental and physical health was important for the nation's economic well-being. During and after the war, sickness and absenteeism among industrial and white-collar workers became a cause for concern. Worker absenteeism undercut workforce stability and productivity.[77] As the war came to a close, *Fortune,* an American business magazine, declared worker absenteeism the new "Malady."[78] The article noted that the "new malady" was severely undermining corporate profits. And this "new malady" had spread to Canada, where it would remain a concern within the popular and professional discourse well into the late 1950s. In 1959, the Canadian journal *Teamwork in Industry* published an article titled "Absenteeism Costs Business 500 Million Dollars a Year."[79] Absenteeism was thought to be caused by men who were weak and maladjusted. For the future's sake, to prevent absenteeism among adult male workers, it was important to raise boys with masculine bodies that measured up to normative standards—lean, muscular, and athletic. Such boys would grow into men who could compete with vigour and vitality against other men in an increasingly competitive and capitalist Ontario. It was assumed that an undersized boy whose physical development was "retarded" lacked a "biological slate" on which appropriate vigorous masculinity could be written.[80] Child psychologists Breckenridge and Vincent, in *Child Development* (1949), cited the case of eleven-year-old Johnny S. John, who was thought socially immature for he "lacked the robust health from his early years and his lack of vitality was a handicap in his relationships with his teachers and even more with his classmates."[81] He was "weak and fragile" and "had a reputation of being inactive in games, afraid to take a chance and avoided fighting." In this sense, "Johnny had an added handicap in his physique which varied considerably from his more vigorous masculine classmates."[82] Here, social performance was linked to masculine vitality as expressed by a boy's physical appearance or stature. Johnny, to summarize, did not possess a masculine body that in the future would enable him to establish acceptable relationships in the workforce.

Parenting magazines linked being undersized to attributes typically associated with femininity. From the March 1951 issue of *Parents' Magazine*: "Nine-year-old Johnny was small for his age, a fact which gave his mother and father grave concern because he could not keep pace in play with other children of his own grade in school. This was causing him to become shy and retiring, and was affecting his entire outlook on life."[83] The gender ideology expressed here, which feminized undersized boys, could only make sense to postwar adults if normative boyhood itself was predicated on competitive physical play. Being undersized was equated with being unable to achieve happiness; with being out-muscled literally and figuratively; that is, with being unable to compete now against other boys and later on with other men in the corporate world. To summarize, undersized boys lacked the physique to secure a satisfactory place among other boys and later on in the workforce.

Masculine "normalcy" having been equated with physical aptitude and a muscular, well-built body, it is not surprising that overweight boys, like underweight boys, were a cause for concern.[84] Overweight boys were associated with "softness" and hence femininity and thus, by extension, with homosexuality and the fears it invoked. "Homosexuals frequently do have bodily characteristics of the opposite sex," declared John McCreary in a 1950 issue of *Canadian Journal of Psychology*.[85] Drawing on the work of Terman and Miles on the physical traits of "passive male homosexuals," he went on to highlight how these types of individuals were typically "small, slender, rather delicate," or "the large obese, voluptuous" types.[86]

Overweight boys were often described as oversensitive and timid— terms traditionally associated with femininity.[87] Breckenridge and Vincent described overweight boys as often being "timid and retiring, clumsy and slow," and further noted that they were incapable of holding a secure place among other boys, being "over sensitive and unable to defend themselves against more active comrades."[88] The feminized overweight boy, like the undersized boy, was measured against normative masculine standards and perceived as unable to handle bullying in recognized respectable ways and in accordance with masculinist norms such as standing one's ground, defending oneself, and fighting back against more active, masculine bullies. Implied was that the overweight boy, like the undersized boy, lacked the necessary masculinity to compete successfully against other boys.

Obesity among boys, then, was linked to unmanliness and to the overarching postwar social fear of feminization. Employing a version of mombashing rhetoric underpinned by the general sense of men's emasculation that was so pervasive at the time, Breckenridge and Vincent claimed that the typical overweight boy "lives in an overprotective and over solicitous environment generally with a dominating mother and weak submissive father." While the beleaguered father took his share of the blame, it was the mother who was cast as the primary villain and who took the brunt of the criticism: "The over solicitude and protection of the mother cannot hide her underlying insecurity, possessiveness and often hostility to the child." [89] An overweight boy, then, was imagined to be the product of an overly feminized home inhabited by an emasculated father and a dominant, predatory, possessive mother who did not meet or gratify the masculine needs of her son; as a consequence, the boy overate as a substitute gratification.

Parenting magazines emphasized that boys whose bodies were overweight and who did not fit the normative definition required immediate attention lest their future manhood be jeopardized. A 1945 *Parents' Magazine* article titled "The Doctor Made a Boy of Bill" gave full expression to this ideological point.[90] The author (the boy's mother) tells of the remasculinizing of her twelve-year-old, overweight son Bill. Besides being overweight, Bill demonstrated feminized traits such as being high-strung, nervous, and oversensitive. In the body of the piece, the associative links between Bill and femininity were further strengthened when he was described as possessing a "soft childish face." His less than masculine physicality coupled with his feminized behaviour led Bill's mother to note that he was "a good deal more like a girl than a boy."

Being overweight and possessing feminine "curves" bothered Bill. At school, he was ridiculed by other boys about his feminine shape. He was embarrassed about undressing when around other boys because they teased him about his weight and its "peculiar distribution." Concerned about Bill's masculinity, his parents sought the advice of their family doctor, who cited a glandular problem and suggested that Bill, as he grew older, might "straighten out on his own accord." Despite this assurance, the doctor hinted at the spectre of homosexuality, warning Bill's parents that if he did not acquire an appropriate masculine physique, "he will grow up with his masculinity seriously threatened. His voice may remain high and thin, these feminine curves will persist, and his sexual development is likely not to be normal."[91] To normalize Bill, a healthy diet was recommended, along with some minor medical attention; however, both resulted in Bill only losing a "few pounds." Bill's obesity was not caused by a glandular problem or a dietary one.

Bill eventually reached the standards of normative masculinity, with its emphasis on a masculine physique, simply by letting biology take its "normal" course. In time, he grew taller and his body became leaner, more lithe, and better muscled. Nature ultimately fashioned his body along normative lines, stylizing him as something radically different than previously: "Bill is a different boy. Physically he is hard muscled instead of flabby. The feminine curves are gone. So are the double set of 'spare tires' around his waist. His voice is deepening ... Emotionally he has matured beyond belief. The weepy spells are over and far between. He is gruffer and vastly more confident in the cocky fashion of the normal male animal."[92]

The narrator reassured readers that Bill had achieved the standards of normative masculinity by letting nature take its course. His achievement of masculine normalcy was recognized and socially acknowledged, evidenced by his mother's claim that at this point "Bill became a normal boy."[93] In keeping with efforts to uphold patriarchal definitions of masculinity, it was noted that emotionally as well, Bill had become more masculine. He no longer suffered outbursts of weeping, a marker of traditional femininity; he was now described as maintaining masculine control over his emotions and feelings. Stories such as this strengthened normative standards of boyhood and suggested that masculine normalcy consisted of boys' bodies being lithe, athletic, hard, and muscled—not undersized, flabby, or soft.

The aim to develop a corporate spirit in boys was both a reflection and a consequence of the social and economic changes that were reshaping postwar Ontario. Some public commentators, advertisers, and others attempted to instill in boys physical and psychological character traits such as the team spirit associated with the modern corporate world. Public discussions about the value of organized team sports for boys, for example, were laden with statements indicating that boys, to be successful and well adjusted, required a strong body, along with a strong commitment to teamwork, a good sense of cooperation, institutional and national loyalty, and a willingness to subordinate themselves to the group. This kind of rhetoric was further taken up in the widely popular Boy Scout Movement.

MALE FRIENDSHIP PATTERNS AND THE BUILDING OF THE ORGANIZATION MAN

Influenced by the increasing demand for white-collar labour and the need to create "organization men," social and cultural commentators made efforts to inject the importance of male bonding into the public discourse. Social commentators sought to re-establish a greater sense of male intimacy through public narratives that situated boys as natural playmates of other boys. What better way to foster postwar corporate values of male togetherness, loyalty, commitment, self-sacrifice, and camaraderie than through a persistent emphasis on culturally sanctioned male alliances? That is, through boys playing well with other boys in male-only contexts, so that as men, they would work well with other men in what William Whyte called the "fraternity-like life" of corporate training programs.[94]

Influenced by psychological discourse, social and cultural commentators assumed that boys at any age naturally wanted to play and socialize with other boys and that they should not intermingle with girls. As one doctor put it: "The boy finds a chum who is a boy. The girl finds a chum who is a girl."[95] The world the doctor presented essentialized and dichotomized gender, with the result that both masculinity and femininity were universalized. The deep internal differences between boys and girls allowed a connection to others of the same sex, while disallowing the opposite. In official education reports of the time such as the *Hope Report*, the dominant rendition of boyhood reflected the views of psychological experts, reiterating boys' preference for playing with other boys, which supposedly occurred naturally at a point coinciding with entrance to grade one.[96] Drawing on theories of child development offered up by postwar psychologists, the *Hope Report* stated that the tendency for boys to only play with boys became increasingly "marked during the middle and later years of childhood."[97] For a boy to play with other boys was regarded as a momentous step in his life, as he "continued toward freedom from earlier ties" by moving away from a dependency on parents, mothers in particular, toward masculine independence and camaraderie with other boys.

Depictions of children's friendship patterns in postwar popular discourse created a spatial and textual separation between the sexes; girls' and boys' worlds rarely merged. Obvious examples of these depictions included an abundance of news items highlighting clubs for boys such as the Boy Scouts, the YMCA, and various informal city clubs. Repeatedly, photographs depicted these as essentially all-male domains where boys only played with other boys. However, these boyhood relationships were viewed largely through masculine connectedness, a bond characteristically experienced and mediated through appreciation of sport, action, or outdoor adventure. Articles with titles such as "Voyageurs of the 20th Century, 27 Boys of Muskoka Camp Plan to Paddle Their Way to Exhibition,"[98] and "Boys Enjoy Jaunts to Canadian Wilds,"[99] contributed to this notion. Yet these articles were essentially about how boys managed human relationships successfully in order to accomplish a team goal. Why? Because the rough-and-tumble days of corporation growth were largely assumed to be over. What corporations needed most, Whyte told parents, was "the adaptable administrator, schooled in managerial skills and concerned primarily with human relations and the techniques of making the corporation a smooth working team."[100]

Other headlines offered a more complex albeit highly traditional rendering of boyhood by adding elements of physical peril when boys acted together with other boys during outdoor adventures. A January 1950 photograph depicted seven smiling boys, hands interclasped in celebration of their joint effort to save a friend from drowning; the text read, "Chain of Pals Saves Youth from River."[101] The photograph seemed to convey the message that "above all else, we boys must not work as individuals. If we work together as a team and coop-erate with each other, we and all others might manage to survive, to be safe and secure." After all, they were, as William Whyte said of white-collar men, "all in the same boat."[102] With masculine solidarity and daring acts of duty and self-sacrifice by the boys for the sake of one another, the group, like their organizational counterparts, endured their masculine ordeals. The photo and text confirmed their boyish loyalty and commitment to one another. Here, the chain imagery was revealing in that it called attention to their having forged a vital link, unwavering, inflexible, united in masculine fidelity, sharing and possessing male courage, and their heroic duty marked by a willingness to face physical danger in order to save a pal's life, and by a deep sense of loyalty.

During the postwar era, loyalty mattered, but a man's company loyalty mattered most. Since the end of the Second World War there had been a marked increase in job movement among white-collar men, a trend that trou-bled growing corporations, which valued loyalty. A "hefty majority" of men, Whyte observed, were demonstrating less company loyalty than they had in the past.[103] "Job changers," as Whyte termed them, were becoming more prominent and more problematic for corporations, which had invested time and money into grooming workers. The growing tendency among professional managers and other white-collar workers to change employers was partly attributable to the characteristics of the postwar labour market, which trended toward full employment, fuelled by the widespread growth in white-collar work, which was so readily available, Bothwell tells us, that these workers "had little trouble finding attractive jobs in post-war Canada."[104] "Corporate treason," that is, the lack of company loyalty among the foot soldiers of the growing managerial professional classes, posed significant problems for corporations that aspired to successfully wage economic war.

Company loyalty, like patriarchy, was built upon the solidarity of males in the context of traditional all-male spheres. Social pedagogues perpetuated the idea that desirable company for boys was not girls, but other boys. Dr. Spock advised parents that "the boy without a father particularly needs opportunity and encouragement to play with other boys, every day if possible ... and to be mainly occupied with boyish pursuits."[105] In 1950, Frank Tumpane reinforced the belief that boys had a natural aversion to femininity, their natural playmates, beginning immediately after birth, being other males. "For several years after he is born, for instance, he does his utmost, not only not to understand females, but to avoid them altogether. Desirable company, to him, is synonymous with males his own age."[106] According to Tumpane, boyhood was a homosocial space for boys to be with other boys without the assumed toxic intrusion of females. Tumpane sounded a note of despair, suggesting that boys were under the unfortunate illusion that "this male state will last forever."[107] Notwithstanding his claim that the male state might not last forever, it was also the case that the act of boys playing with other boys, in particular in gangs, could be extended well into manhood.

BOYHOOD AND THE GANG

The boy gang served as a model for corporate or factory life. The corporate life of boys as manifested in the boy gang was thought by adults to foster in them corporate or company values as well as social principles such as loyalty, trust, selflessness, and the welfare of the group; it also tethered boys to the task of being a good group member, that is, one who worked well on a team and who developed allegiances with other males. All of this, of course, fell along gender lines. The postwar logic seemed to be that if you did good for the company or the corporation, then the company or corporation would do good by you. This in turn informed the adult perspective on boy gangs—that is, the notion that boys who learned cooperative relationships among themselves would later, as men, develop cooperative relationships in corporate or factory life. Boys, it was assumed, were not born with the ability to cooperate; they had to learn that skill gradually, in gangs.

Gang life was viewed as a natural stage in boys' development. In *Boyology* (1922), H.W. Gibson claimed that the "the hermit or recluse is always regarded as an abnormal being, for it is a law of nature for bees to go in swarms, cattle in herds, birds in flocks, fishes in schools, and boys in gangs."[108] Although written decades earlier, Gibson's concept of boyhood and the "gang instinct" was highly influential in the postwar era and informed public opinion about the nature of boys and their "hard-wired" tendency to "spontaneously" organize into gangs as part of a "normal" malehood. "Most boys," declared an article in the *Toronto Daily Star*, "naturally play in gangs and the gang instinct is inherent in almost every normal boy with a superabundance of energy."[109]

In postwar Ontario, it was widely assumed that the gang instinct emerged in a boy at about the age of eight.[110] Official education reports put the age at which boys belonged to gangs between eight and twelve: "The period from 8 to 12 or 12-plus years seems to be a separate stage in development. The child seems to be a completed product, desiring the prerogatives of an adult: with others of his own age he organizes clubs and gangs; he shows an intensification of the spirit and other adult influences."[111]

Other child experts agreed. In *Child Development* (1949), Breckenridge and Vincent promoted the idea that from ages four to ten the boy moved forward from solitary and parallel play into genuine gang play.[112] This view was supported by academics. A.R. Crane, for example, in a 1952 issue of *Journal of Genetic Psychology*, asserted that boys between the "ages of nine and thirteen were thought to naturally want to form pre-adolescent single-sex gangs."[113] However, not all experts agreed that the gang instinct was hard-wired to emerge in boys as young as eight; instead, they suggested that it happened around the age of twelve. Charles E. Hendry, a professor of social work at the University of Toronto, reported that the "gang" was a natural and almost "inevitable" outcome of boys' activities between the ages of twelve and sixteen.[114] Despite these differing opinions, there was unanimous agreement, among experts and social commentators, that being in a gang was an inevitability of boyhood.

The gang was the bridge on which boys marched toward a successful, secure manhood. The gang socialized the growing boy, emancipated him from family ties, and prepared him for the greater corporate world. In 1948 a *Globe and Mail* editorial opined that "until boys are about eight years old, family ties have precedence in their lives," but that when they reach adolescence, these ties grow weaker and "outside interests exert a powerful sway." At this age, "boys in a neighbourhood, of similar age and congenial spirit, tend to form a gang, held together with deep loyalties to each other."[115] In the postwar years, loyalty, selflessness, and group welfare were all important values for building a corporate psychology in boys. Breckenridge and Vincent argued that "the gang teaches lessons that force consideration of others." According to them, group loyalties fostered in gangs gradually forced a child to "curb his most self-centered impulses in favour of group welfare." What happened to boys who were selfish, who were not committed to the group's welfare or did not "curb" their impulses? "Discipline is prompt and relentless," Breckenridge and Vincent observed. "Black eyes and bloody noses are all part of the experience for boys" and helped whip boys into line.[116] Like the organization man, the boy had laws to obey and official relationships to be observed, and in many instances he cooperated with other boys in the discharge of those relationships.

Yet adults displayed simultaneous and contradictory attitudes toward boy gangs. On the one hand, they worried deeply about boy gangs and their propensity to cause social disorder. At the same time, adults promoted the idea that gangs were useful tools for building better boys. In large part, this ambivalence had to do ethnicity, class, and age.[117] According to Hagedorn, in the Industrial Age (1925–60), when adults discussed a gang, they typically defined it as an "unsupervised, lower class peer group."[118] Sangster observes that adult fears of boy gangs—in particular, gangs from non-Anglo communities—"took on more intensified form during the Depression, and became especially prominent in the 1940s and 1950s." Adolescent boy gangs, she notes, "were seen as breeding grounds for delinquency because they encouraged truancy, theft, violence, and in your face antagonism to the adult world."[119] Some sociologists of the time defined gangs as "sub-cultures organized by working class boys."[120] Albert Cohen's *Delinquent Boys: The Culture of the Gang* (1955)[121] and Herbert Bloch and Arthur Neiderhoffer's *The Gang* (1958)[122] both focused on the problems of the adolescent underprivileged boy. It was the underprivileged adolescent boy gangs, largely from immigrant newcomer communities, that prompted the most anxiety in adults, which in turn caused a worrisome preoccupation around gangs during the postwar era.[123]

Social and cultural commentators perceived boy gangs whose members were under the age of fourteen, not so much as an immediate threat to society, but as a useful tool for producing good boys. In late 1945, after returning from overseas, George Singleton, community secretary of the Broadview YMCA in Toronto, launched a new method in Ontario for approaching boys that some believed placed Ontario "boy workers" on the "threshold of a new day in boys' work."[124] The experiment was based on accepting the important fact that boys under the age of fourteen form little gangs. The process involved transforming the "gangs into little clubs with worthwhile objectives."[125] Boy work was not new in Ontario, but the method had now changed. Boys were no longer expected to find their way to the YMCA or other organizations; rather, boy workers went into the local communities to work with boys: "The present system of central buildings with their gyms, swimming pools, billiard tables and so on will remain. But, in addition, trained workers will emerge from 'nerve centers' to take fun and recreation and education to districts and communities using facilities of churches and schools where necessary. But usually a neighbourhood parlor or cellar."[126]

For example, when one boy worker heard of a gang of "little-girl-scarers," he went out to meet them: "The gang jumped him from a garage roof, not realizing his commando training was useful to him. When the riot ended they grinned and invited him to gang headquarters. Three meetings later, all attended by a boy-worker, another club was formed."[127] The end result was held successful, according to the boy worker. It was thought that the program paid broad dividends in creating better boys.[128] The boy worker in this case was trying to build better boys before they reached the "retirement age of 14," an age when boys were thought to be moving out of boyhood into adolescence and no longer encouraged to be part of the club.[129]

Julia Grant has argued that at the turn of the twentieth century, peers played a leading role in inculcating masculinity.[130] Thus, instead of substituting adult authority for peer influence, boy workers tried to "harness" the "gang spirit" to develop leadership and masculinity.[131] Over the ensuing decades, this portion of the dominant boyhood discourse, grounded in recapitulation theory,[132] remained largely unchanged. Boy workers in the postwar period saw that the gang spirit could be redirected from antisocial behaviour and manipulated to build better boys.

Hence, instead of breaking up gangs, experts counselled boy workers to "harness" gang spirit and direct it toward the greater good. A 1946 *Toronto Star* headline had one expert issuing this order: "Don't Smash That Boy Gang, Harness It."[133] In that article, boy expert David Nicholson, a former YMCA official in Toronto, claimed that "boys naturally like to get together. That's normal and healthy. The most impressionable thing to a boy is his gang's reaction." Nicholson encouraged boy workers to "get to know the gang and if you can manage it, become at least a friend of that gang."[134] Other adults in authority advocated the same approach. The Chief Constable of the Kitchener–Waterloo police characterized boys in more nefarious terms after nine young lads between the ages of ten and twelve were caught vandalizing.

> Gangsterism is natural to boys and the object should not be to stamp out gangsterism but to turn it to its proper ends ... These gangs of boys who have been causing trouble lately are not Bad Boys. They are just normal, high spirited boys who have no direction. Not one of them is criminal, nor should they be treated as such. What is a hockey team or a football team but a "gang" that is being used for a good purpose.[135]

The link here between boy gangs and sports teams was not coincidental. By suggesting that a gang was like a team, the speaker positioned the gang as just another societal institution that could be exploited to reproduce the social relationships required to maintain the existing social order. Moreover, this approach sought to show that with a worthy objective, as well as reasonable adult male interest and supervision, the social dangers of the gang would be lessened.

Postwar assumptions about the "gang instinct" assumed that it was essentially a neutral force, one that if properly channelled could be manipulated in socially beneficial ways. One July 1948 *Globe* editorial advised that "the gang spirit is natural, but it can and ought to be channeled into constructive and useful purposes."[136] A 1956 Boy Scout fundraising appeal made this ideological assertion in an attempt to induce funds from the general public: "Most boys naturally play in gangs and the gang instinct is inherent in almost every normal boy ... It can be a force in his life for good or evil."[137] The funding appeal informed readers that the gang instinct "can be used to build up those qualities so essential to good citizenship and is an asset both to the community and the boy."[138] In June 1951 a male doctor told the sixth annual conference of United Church women that "the United Church of Canada is using the gang instinct of boys in working with them."[139] He added that the church program, which claimed to be working with about 10,000 boys, emphasized "achievement as a member of a group rather than as an individual."[140] The premise was that boy workers and boy organizations had to capture the gang, not oppose it. By working with and through gangs, they could teach boys important lessons in corporate loyalty, cooperation, and becoming goods (male) citizens..

After the horrors of the Second World War, some commentators posited that the gang spirit in boys must be directed toward constructive channels. The gang spirit, if left unsupervised or corrupted by men with evil intentions, could have appalling consequences for boys and society at large. In July 1948, a *Globe* editorial argued that tyrants like Hitler had manipulated and abused the gang spirit for their own evil purposes: "The gang instinct has frequently been exploited by unscrupulous men for various reasons. Hitler made use of it in his early storm troops, who later grew up to become a virtual army of ruffians."[141] The editorialist feared that if the gang spirit was left unsupervised or in the hands of bad men, gangs of young boys would grow into associations (or perhaps unions) of corrupt men who ruthlessly sought their own advantage by manipulating provincial and municipal governments. This was not the wholesome gang life imagined by postwar boy workers or parents on which to build a safe, secure tomorrow.

In their search for safety and security, parents were encouraged to welcome normal, wholesome gang life as an avenue for sound social development for the boy and his friends. According to child experts like Breckenridge and Vincent, no other group, except the family itself, was of such fundamental importance for boys' social development. As a gang member, the boy would acquire the "we" feeling and would learn cooperation with others as well as a sense of fair play. Boys would develop leadership skills and "make normal social contacts."[142] Parents were to allow boy gangs into their homes and make a headquarters where boys could meet. Parenting magazines suggested that garages, backyards, and basements would do as long as the boys were always under reasonable adult supervision. Parenting magazines often published moral stories that encouraged this method of boy work. In *Parents' Magazine* in February 1950, one mother wrote about her son being away from home so often and how she resolved this issue:

> Our house is small and our son age seven had no room to entertain his playmates. So most of the time he wanted to go visiting instead of having friends in to see him. We decided to build a playhouse in the backyard. Using packing cases and scrap lumber, we built a small house ten feet square, he helped decorate the walls and furnish it by building some rough chairs, a little table and some shelves to hold toys and games. His gang moved in and made it a neighbourhood play center. Now our son is content to stay at home part of the time and play host to his friends.[143]

Directed, supervised, purposeful gang play would mould the right kind of boy, who would acquire the postwar corporate values of good citizenship, fair play, and cooperation; at the same time, he would avoid the undirected, unsupervised gang play found in the streets.

The postwar era required men who could work in teams. That being the goal, boyhood was conceived by adults as a time when boys naturally sought the company and companionship of other boys. Those who did not fit this model were pathologized or deemed socially suspicious and in need of special help—boyhood must not be a solitary time:

> It is the withdrawn child who needs the most attention from parents, teachers, everyone interested in youth ... Unfortunately, aggressive or delinquent behaviour on the part of children too often occupies the limelight ... It is true that such a child may get himself into trouble but, by and large, that trouble is not often as serious as that of the child who is withdrawn. Psychiatrists, psychologists, social workers, all professional people who work in the field of mental health know that many a withdrawn child, allowed to go his mental way unheeded, may get so far from reality, from his fellows and family, that he will be unable to come back again.[144]

Within the strictures of normative boyhood, more latitude was given to boys who demonstrated antisocial "masculine" behaviours such as being overly aggressive, than to boys who were shy or who desired to be alone.

CONCLUSION

Patriarchy and capitalism are reproduced, in part, because those who benefit from them usually have the power to prevent the rules from being changed.[145] An acceptable boyhood valued such things as playing by the rules, teamwork, and fair play—attributes that supported the dominant structures of society. This model of boyhood relied upon conformity, self-sacrifice, the disciplining of desire, and recognition of the group; these in turn were harnessed to productivity, work efficiency, and the accumulation of profit, which were postwar goals for both industry and corporations. Thus, ideas such as teamwork and following rules came to be inculcated in boys, in order to advance the corporate objectives of those who would employ them as adults. In addition, the postwar effort to establish teamwork as a central virtue in the making of an ideal boyhood functioned to elide differences based on race, class, and religion. Postwar commentators sought to stabilize the supposedly fragile postwar democracy by fostering a version of boyhood that worked against the aims of communists and communist sympathizers, who were thought to be targeting and exploiting social differences in order to undermine the Canadian way of life. But there was a problem with all of this: the idea of teamwork became instrumental to the increasingly competitive market rather than oriented toward a wider social and ethical framework, so that its primary function became the perpetuation of the corporate capitalist status quo and the reproduction of class and race hierarchies and the gender order rather than a critical reflection upon them.

As a response to postwar economic and social developments, adult discourses about boyhood focused on building boys who would slide easily into the culture of corporations, the army, or other bureaucratic organizations. The attributes required by an increasingly industrial, corporate society turned out to be remarkably the same as for military preparedness. These discourses, which called to mind the "Organization Man," the generic manager, or the team player, emphasized a unity between the individual and the company; they also fostered obedience, uniformity, and company loyalty and stressed the centrality of the organization versus a fading individual entrepreneurship—the team was to be the hero, not the man.

Although pervasive, this discourse was not altogether uncontested. Coexisting with the Organization Man discourse was an older and less visible discourse that emphasized a version of boyhood that rested on individualism and self-reliance. I discuss this second, less visible discourse in the next chapter.

3

One above All:
The Heroic Ideal in Boyhood

Competing models of masculinity emerged as traditional notions of rugged individual manliness were superseded by a much more corporate mindset. Some adults promoted a version of boyhood that would help boys become men in grey flannel suits, who would slide easily into corporate culture. Yet there was also an element of continuity, with other adults attempting to hold on to an older version of boyhood, one characterized by rugged individualism, by a frontier entrepreneurial masculinity bent on individual conquest. This version of boyhood was concerned more with standing out than with fitting in; it played down teamwork and played up individualism. In this view, the boy was self-sufficient, willing to take risks, able, forceful, ambitious, strong willed, assertive, independent, and heroic. He sought out difficulties, embodied the spirit of early capitalism, and called to mind, not the organization man, but what might be referred to as the heroic entrepreneur.[1]

"Entrepreneurship" is a gendered concept; the entrepreneur has always been assumed to be male.[2] Research on gender and entrepreneurship has shown that entrepreneurial figures have long been closely linked to hypermasculinity: "the entrepreneur as conqueror of unexplored territories, the lonely hero, and the patriarch."[3] According to Connell, the jargon surrounding the entrepreneur is full of "lurid gender terminology: thrusting entrepreneurs, opening up virgin territory, aggressive lending, etc."[4] To the dismay of postwar commentators such as C. Wright Mills, the rugged, self-reliant entrepreneur made up only a fraction of a male population dominated by organization men.[5]

Foundational texts on entrepreneurship include Joseph Schumpeter's *The Theory of Economic Development* (1934) and the same author's *Business Cycles: A Theoretical, Historical, and Statistical Analysis of the Capitalist Process* (1939). For Schumpeter, an entrepreneur was a risk taker, daring, decisive, independent, able, and implicitly male. He was driven "by a will to conquer, motivated by an impulse to fight, to prove oneself superior to others, to succeed for the sake, not of the fruits of success, but of success itself." The entrepreneur, Schumpeter wrote, "seeks out difficulties" and "delights in ventures."[6] Finally, the entrepreneur was, according to Schumpeter, a man of "super-normal qualities of intellect and will."[7] The ideal entrepreneur, who was associated with and framed by notions of hegemonic masculinity, helped define the heroic entrepreneurial boyhood found in postwar discourse.

The less celebrated, less heroic, more domesticated salaried managers of the modern bureaucracies were decidedly not entrepreneurs. They had, as William H. Whyte wrote in his 1956 bestseller *The Organization Man,* an aversion to independence, venture, and entrepreneurship.[8] The large army of postwar organization men could not fill the crucial role played by the entrepreneur in Ontario's expanding corporate, bureaucratic society. Entrepreneurs had once been society's fountainheads, pillars of strength who ensured economic survival by providing innovation, initiative, and leadership.[9] The ordinary businessman or salaried manager was content to fit quietly into the commonplace routine imposed on him by postwar bureaucracies. In a 1959 issue of *Administrative Science Quarterly,* one academic wrote that the businessman "simply followed traditional lines and fell into already established patterns and routines."[10] Only the entrepreneur had the will, the intelligence, and the force of character to break the mould of custom and tradition. Only the entrepreneur had the initiative, imagination, and leadership that would ensure the future of capitalism.[11]

BOYHOOD AND THE HEROIC IDEAL

The entrepreneur was viewed as hero in search of adventure and treasure. The call to adventure took the hero away from his domestic setting; he was courageous in the face of danger, master of both himself and the situation. The postwar years saw a rise in the number of exemplars of young (white) boyhood (but not girlhood). Boys were acclaimed for carrying out individual deeds of courage. The *Evening Telegram* in January 1946 carried the headline "Boy's Quick Action Helps Save Eight"; the accompanying story celebrated the "quick action" of eleven-year-old Jerry LaPlante, who saved the lives of eight young children when their house burned down.[12] On 13 January 1945, the *Globe and Mail* celebrated a fourteen-year-old as a "boy hero" after he rescued two small children from a burning cottage.[13] Boys were lauded for other lifesaving heroics; on the front page of the *Toronto Daily Star* in March 1948, Ted Boniface, a twelve-year-old boy, was praised for saving four children from drowning on different occasions.[14] Texts such as these may well have fed the capitalist machine by proliferating narratives that encouraged and attempted to instill in boys values that promoted a rugged, heroic entrepreneurial boyhood.

The image of the ideal entrepreneur has historically drawn from heroic themes such as self-sacrifice.[15] In the print media, paeans to boy heroism were never more fulsome than during the postwar years. Unlike narratives promoting a collective male identity, these could be read by adults as exemplifying a successful entrepreneurial boyhood. An *Evening Telegram* headline in 1948, "Admiration for a Hero, 11 Years Old," fronted the story of David Western, the youngest winner of the Albert Medal. The Albert Medal, first struck in 1866, was named after Prince Albert and was originally intended to recognize saving a life at sea. In 1867 the award was extended to cover civilian bravery—in particular, saving life on land. Western won the award by courageously saving three skaters after they plunged through thin ice.[16] A 1948 news item from the *Toronto Daily Star* told the story of thirteen-year-old Roger Lacelle, who was awarded the Royal Humane Society Bronze Medal for "making three trips through blazing oil on the St. Lawrence River" in a rowboat to save crew members after a shipping collision.[17] Yet another news story featured Robert Thomas Waters, who in 1954, at age thirteen, in "complete disregard for his own safety," fought his way through "heavy bush and swamp" to rescue the trapped pilot of a downed Lancaster bomber. His courageous action won him the George Medal for gallantry, which made him the only civilian of thirty-one recipients to win the award.[18] According to the ideology of entrepreneurship, individual character led to material success; the heroic boy accumulated public praise and awards, the entrepreneur accumulated financial wealth.

The abundance of exemplars of postwar entrepreneurial boyhood assuaged males' anxieties over their masculinity. Collective or individual masculinity requires constant confirmation from others, public or private, but its "short lived thrill can only be resuscitated if it is embellished and elaborated in countless freeze-framed narratives about heroic males among men."[19] Although the narratives varied, the sexist prioritizing of boys and masculinity over girls and femininity always predominated. Readers were often enrolled as witnesses to instances of white boys' heroic success. Accounts of boys' heroism and their triumphs over adversity met the need for constant reassurance about the state of postwar masculinity.

The abundance of similar versions of postwar boyhood also paraded what were thought to be the crucial virtues for safeguarding a nation, both economically and otherwise. The boy in each narrative, like the ideal entrepreneur, was willing to take risks and was strong enough to face situations that required physical and mental strength. Routinely noted for his "quick actions" in high-risk emergencies, the boy exemplified decisiveness; he was not reflective, passive, or wavering. The boy was glad to endure hardships and take physical risks for the sake of others. Demonstrating steady nerves, intelligence, readiness, physical and moral courage, and masculine confidence, the boy came to symbolize the national hero.

Robert Von der Osten, having analyzed the gender ideology found in four generations of juvenile fiction, remarked that the 1950s masculine hero was often characterized by competence, self-control, and courage coupled with the ability to solve problems efficiently.[20] Canadians read stories of boys being self-lessly heroic, thus making public and explicit that certain attributes, such as courage, competence, physical daring, steady nerves, leadership, and decisive-ness, were required in boys. The stories taught that having such attributes, and using them, was a mark of true boyhood. It is not hard to see that stories about boys offered an articulation of boyhood designed to help ease adult readers' anxieties and fears about the dangers of the postwar world.

The entrepreneur must overcome barriers and obstacles. In venturing, he finds that competition, bankers, suppliers, and customers present serious, venture-threatening obstacles that must be overcome. To acquire the entre-preneurial virtues of courage and individual heroism, boys needed to develop their masculine potential. The print media offered frequent examples of boys who demonstrated moral and physical courage. A 1946 story described how a six-year-old boy "limped on charred feet across a field of snow" to obtain aid for his baby brother caught in a house fire. The story conferred masculine honour on the young boy, praising him for his "gallant effort" despite it being in vain.[21] Boys were never too young to be heroes. Six-year-old Randy Tays, who carried his five-year-old playmate a quarter of a mile after a freight train had crushed the boy's foot, was publicly praised for acting "like a man in a king-sized emergency."[22] These types of stories conferred individual masculine honour and the status of "little manhood" on boys. The actions of the boys were invested in and tethered to traditional notions of masculinity; dauntless in the face of danger and not averse to risk, the boy/man was expected to negotiate and overcome landscapes full of hardships. More subtly, these narratives also rendered and strengthened the notion that boys took more risks and experi-enced less emotional and physical fear in new situations than girls. In other words, the narratives suggested that boys began exploration outward, which led to external performance in the broader world, where the accumulation of power could be had, away from postwar domesticity and the safety of home.

Patriarchy constituted the subtext for understanding the entrepreneur. A feature of this subtext was the alliance between capital and men, which was mutually self-serving because of a shared interest in the control over and subordination of women.[23] Echoing a long patriarchal tradition in which males are the strong saviours of the weak damsel in distress, individual boys were depicted in the popular press doing their self-sacrificing duty by saving passive females. A 1954 *Globe and Mail* item praised a seven-year-old boy, who lost his right foot under a locomotive as he shielded his sisters when all were trapped on a railway bridge.[24] Linking the boy's actions to dominant representations of masculinity found in the mythology of the American West, the father explained the boy's actions this way: "Roy Rogers was his hero ... He [the boy] wanted to grow up and be a cowboy like Roy Rogers and do heroic things. He didn't know he was going to be a hero so early in life."[25] The text reveals that he may have lost a limb, but he had been socially and emotionally compensated for it by having established himself "so early in life" as a masculine hero, as capable of courageous actions. Other narratives strengthened the idea that individual boys were in the business of saving girls: "Boys, 7, Save Little Girl from Spadina Rd. Creek";[26] "Boy, 13, Jumps into Lake Rescues Scarborough Girl, 4."[27] Stories of young masculinity such as these achieved meaning through, among other things, the oppositional relationship to images of femininity that often positioned females as passive and helpless.

Common patriarchal values were also maintained in narratives that lauded boys for saving their mothers. Some representative headlines include "Boy, 11, Saves Mother from Chilly Lake Water,"[28] "11-year-Old Boy Pulls Mother from Flames,"[29] "Boy, 14, Saves Mother,"[30] and "Mother Saved from Flames by Son, Age 11."[31] Or, for example, consider the 7 January 1950 headline in the *Toronto Telegram*, which read, "Boy Leads Way as 3 Escape Blazing Cottage."[32] The accompanying text reported that "with her 10-year-old son Paul leading the way, Mrs. Louis Alexander carried her two-year-old daughter Judy to safety."[33] Such narratives invested boyhood with bravery as a highly valued masculine practice. The narratives suggested that each boy knew what to do in the moment of crisis and was no less a hero than the soldier who rushed into the thick of battle to rescue a fallen comrade, or the entrepreneur who forged ahead into new unexplored territories. Boy heroes maintained relationships within society by saving females in need or by controlling outcomes through strong physical action. This association between boys and physical strength and action perpetuated a model of boyhood that rested on the idea of boys being naturally adventurous, strong, independent, and decisive in emergencies while performing loyal community service.

It is not surprising that at a time when traditional gender roles were being reasserted, the view that boys were natural heroes justified excluding girls from heroic adventure stories. The Dow Award provides an example. Inaugurated in April 1946 and sponsored by the Montreal brewing company, Dow Brewery, with recipients chosen by Canadian news editors, the Dow Award was given to individual Canadians who had performed outstanding acts of heroism.[34] Individuals who received the award were given a $100 Canada Savings Bond, and their accounts of heroism were published in various well-known print outlets such as *Maclean's*, the *Toronto Daily Star*, the *Globe and Mail*, and the

Toronto Telegram. Of the twenty awards analyzed, women or girls received five, men or young boys fifteen. The men and boys featured as "heroes" in the various Dow Awards were typically depicted as muscular and powerfully built; the emphasis here was on the selfless, individual hero triumphing over extremely perilous circumstances and attempting to overcome long odds. For instance, consider the following account of a Dow Award given to a young boy from Ontario in 1951, published in *Maclean's*. Ten-year-old Gerald Blair of Renfrew, Ontario, while carrying out a masculine deed, was "fatally injured by truck after pushing woman off road":[35] "Knocked unconscious by the terrific impact, Gerry was rushed to the hospital but failed to rally. He gave his life so that another might live. The instinctive heroism of this 10 year old boy merits the praises of all Canadians. We are proud to add his name to the list of those who won THE DOW AWARD for outstanding bravery."[36]

As with the entrepreneur, the premium here was on individual male effort. Gender-defined accounts such as these upheld dominant gender ideologies of the time by displaying physically and morally courageous boys who had been compelled by "instinct" to acts of individual heroism and self-sacrifice.

These narratives had patriarchal power at their heart. The self-sacrificing boy was valorized as the leader, the doer, the active protector, the postwar savior, and in this way, to some degree, these values were established as naturally male. One outcome of the belief that boys were the natural leaders was that girls were constructed as largely dependent on masculine leadership, expertise, and ingenuity; another was the perpetuation of the myth of "masculinity as the legitimate site of action and power."[37] This is not surprising, given the general conflation between masculinity and leadership by psychologists during the postwar period. Throughout those years, women were thought responsible for the expressive functions of caring and nurturing, while men were considered responsible for instrumental functions of struggle and leadership.[38] In a 1946 address to the education section of the Chemical Institute of Canada, one psychologist asserted that "it is a basic necessity of feminine psychology that a man do the leading." He stressed, without irony, that he was not an anti-feminist, further remarking "that more mature communities are controlled by the male psychology" and citing as evidence that "the great discoveries in the intellectual frontier, in the arts as well as the sciences, owe their development to the male psychology."[39] The dominant message delivered by narratives of individual male heroism rested on the notion that the two sexes were suited to different activities as a result of inborn variations. Thus, boys were naturally suited for heroic, daring endeavours such as safeguarding democracy and competing in the economy, while girls were intended to be passive observers.

According to the overt politics of masculinity, individual boys were self-sufficient, willing to take risks, forceful, assertive, and independent; they also embodied the spirit of entrepreneurial capitalism and called to mind, not the organization man, but the older heroic entrepreneur. This view coalesced within postwar discourse, which in turn promoted a version of normative boyhood that supported the need to build boys who would become entrepreneurs, guardians of the nation-state, and defenders of patriarchal values. Nowhere was this better expressed in popular discourse than in representations of the boy and his dog.

A BOY AND HIS DOG: BUILDING THE ENTREPRENEURIAL SPIRIT

Any understanding of postwar boyhood as a form of social construction misses the mark entirely if it does not consider the theme of a boy and his dog. It is necessary to refine the analysis of boyhood to see how and why cultural and social forces positioned the dog as a primary accoutrement of normative boyhood. The unique importance of a dog to a boy was stressed throughout the postwar years. A 1955 news item published in the *Toronto Star* asserted that there was no greater association or attachment for a boy than his dog.[40]

The abundance of news items, photographs, prose, and poems featuring a boy and his dog testified to the power of this theme throughout the postwar years. Its constant repetition in the print media and in movies fostered the notion that the relationship between a boy and his dog was both powerful and unique. Popular Hollywood films about that relationship included *The Biscuit Eater*[41] (1940), *A Boy and His Dog* (1946), *The Tender Years* (1948), *Good Bye, My Lady* (1956), and *Old Yeller* (1957). One film critic of the era wrote rather cynically, after viewing it, that "*The Tender Years* is simply another stab at one of the most sentimental of all themes—the story of a boy and his dog."[42] In postwar Ontario, the strong appeal of the boy-and-his-dog theme was evidenced by the television hit series *Lassie*.[43] Similarly, children's books routinely employed the boy–dog theme. Examples include Leland Sillman's *The Daredevil* (1948),[44] Catherine Anthony Clark's *The Golden Pine Cone* (1950),[45] Lois Lanski's *Davy and His Dog* (1956),[46] and Louise Rorke's *Lefty's Adventure* (1950),[47] which was marketed as "an exciting and moving story about a boy and his dog."[48] Similarly, Morley Callaghan's *Luke Baldwin's Vow* (1948)[49] and Farley Mowat's *The Dog Who Wouldn't Be* (1957)[50] prominently featured relationships between boys and their dogs.

In October 1948, one book reviewer declared: "The story of a boy and a dog holds perennial appeal to all readers of almost any age."[51] Book reviewers praised boy–dog tales as sweet, cheerful, and charming. A *Globe and Mail* review of James Street's *Good Bye, My Lady* (1954) told readers that the "Dog-Boy Tale Is Winsome."[52] This reviewer described the story's enchanting atmosphere, making special mention of the warm and loving relationship between the boy and his dog, which was the novel's central theme. Given the postwar preoccupation with boyhood in general, and the power of the boy-and-his-dog theme in particular, it is no surprise that in 1949, Longmans, Green called upon Canadian author Jack Hambleton to write some boys books. To inspire the reluctant writer, the publisher provided him with a simple formula for them: "Get a boy and a dog and a horse together and put them in some of the settings and experiences [Northern Ontario wilderness] you know, and you've a story."[53] Dogs, boys, other animals, include some masculine adventure and risk, and situate it in the rugged Ontario wilderness, and you have a boy book.

But why dogs? One answer is that emotions mean being human, but normative boyhood in general, and an entrepreneurial boyhood in particular, were constructed on premises that rejected public displays of the kinder, gentler emotions. It was widely held that "feminine" displays of emotions were for sissies. Entrepreneurialism typically denied male emotion and emotional attachment to others, and when it came to human relationships, words like loyalty, tenderness, sympathy, sensitivity, and gentleness were located in the "feminine" and stood in direct opposition to the notion of the ideal entrepreneur.[54] The heroic entrepreneur required emotional detachment, a freedom to move unhindered and unfettered by emotions in order to meet the demands of entrepreneurialism. Entrepreneurs were alone in the world, isolated emotionally by their independence. Emotional investments were hindrances. Within this restraint, to whom, then, were boys, and by extension future heroic entrepreneurs, to become emotionally attached? Who could they trust?

Certainly, something or someone was required for them emotionally. Adults believed that boy–dog bonding was a necessary masculine vehicle; a boy could cry with and express his fears and anxieties to his dog. Boys might be despised or ridiculed for showing "feminine" emotions to other boys, their fathers, or even their mothers; dogs were a safe and secure but still "appropriate" relationship within which to do so. A photograph titled "A Boy with His Dog" won first prize in the *Toronto Star's* 1947 amateur snapshot contest.[55] That photograph expressed a striking archetype of the boy and his dog, one that evoked innocent and tender joy between the two, as if they were lovers gloriously and happily smitten with each other. This interdependence, which was a peculiar feature of the boy–dog relationship, would have been obvious to the *Star*'s readers. The photographer had constructed a profound relationship between the boy and his dog, a relationship formed by understanding, tenderness, mutual respect, and camaraderie. The photographer's had turned their interdependence into an image of natural beauty.

Other writers echoed these heightened sentiments and made the relationship between boys and their dogs something mystical or eternal, something that only a few significant relationships could surpass in terms of power, sentiment, and substance. In 1954 the *Toronto Daily Star* published a poem that included these lines: "The christening of a child, An old man's death; A wedding in the church, A marriage feast, A little boy leading a dog along."[56] This passage epitomized the sentimental indulgence that characterized the boy-and-his-dog theme. The boy and his dog were imbued with an exaggerated sense of passion and mystical importance, while being elevated beyond the material, turbulent world and discursively linked to human events that carried potent personal and social significance. The strong postwar bond between boys and dogs made one author state that he "can't imagine a children's heaven without dogs."[57]

In 1947, child advice columnist Angelo Patri agreed that dogs could function as human substitutes, providing boys with pals with whom to share the trials of boyhood:

> This matter of the dog in the family is important, especially so when a boy—it is usually a boy—feels lonely, feels the need for affection, for companionship in the hours when the puzzles of life bewilder him … A dog can be a very close friend to such a boy. He shares his moods of sadness, of gladness, as no human being can. He feels the boy's spirit before the boy does and acts accordingly.[58]

Patri here was echoing typical postwar sentiments about boy–dog relationships reaching mystical levels beyond anything offered by another human being. Postwar poems reinforced the idea that boys and dogs were pals, friends, and close intimates. An excerpt from a 1952 poem exemplified this point, "A boy and his dog, pals, playmates, friends. They sure understand each others' thought: Watching them there, quite lost to the world, a beautiful sight."[59] This and Patri's example highlight how emotion was forged between boys and dogs. The boy's primal spiritual essence was leashed to the dog's; the dog was the only being with access to the boy's deep emotional and spiritual level. For the boy, the dog was a safe haven, a retreat from a turbulent and unwelcoming world in which he could not display emotion without being branded as feminine.

A multitude of postwar depictions of boys and their dogs from a variety of social and cultural domains reinforced the assertion that boys and their dogs were inseparable. A January 1946 news item expressed this typical postwar theme: "A boy stood close to his dog, a big, black-and-white setter. The rope around the dog's neck was wrapped several times around the boy's hand. These two were not going to be separated without a struggle."[60] Postwar accounts painted each boy–dog relationship as unique and as underpinned by a strong sense of security, fidelity, and loyalty even in death. Capturing this point was a 1957 *Toronto Daily Star* headline: "Boy, 13, Going to Spend $140.00 on Funeral for His Pet Dog."[61] The story told of a young boy who refused to bury his dog in the backyard of his home, opting instead for a luxurious funeral. Reportedly, the dog was to be "buried in a silk lined casket in a concrete vault"; the "plot will receive perpetual care."[62] The father questioned the boy's decision and was rebuked: "He [the boy] asked me if I'd bury a pal of mine in the backyard and they certainly have been pals."[63] Or take for example one sentimental November 1952 front-page story that identified a boy, ravaged by disease, who expressed his only and perhaps last request as "an eagerness to have a dog."[64] Thus, embodied by good companionship, unconditional love, purity, and unshakeable fidelity, the friendship between boys and dogs expressed these key attributes.

Shaped by the social impulse to build a boy in the spirit of an older, more rugged ideal masculinity for boys and for adults alike, the essence of a boy's relationship to his dog was based on a deep sense of masculine fidelity and courage. This is evidenced when social commentators repeatedly lauded young boys and their dogs for heroically and selflessly saving each other's lives through displays of daring and physical action. A news item of 7 June 1951 celebrated the heroics of a five-year-old boy's dog and his valiant but vain attempt to save his boy master from a fire. The headline read "Dog Pulls Clothes, but Pal, 5, Burns."[65] The accompanying text noted that "the boy and his dog were ... great pals." Similarly, a 1948 *Toronto Star* headline captured the overarching sentiment of the boy–dog relationship: "Rescue Dog First, Boy of 14 Insists." This item told of a boy in an overturned boat who selflessly refused rescue until his dog Buster was rescued first.[66] This text asserted the virtues of entrepreneurial masculinity, bravery, risk taking, and courage: the boy, without regard for himself, courageously demonstrated fidelity in the face of imminent danger by first saving his "true" pal. Similar testimonials of boys' virtues are apparent in the following 1949 news item: "Boy, 13, Saves Dog from Speed River."[67] This boy of 13 was publicly lauded for "risking his life in the swirling water of the Speed river" to rescue his dog Cookie from drowning.[68] A 1948 *Globe and Mail* story identified the egalitarian relationship between boys and dogs: "True pals in times of peril."[69] This item told how a boy, 14 years old, risked "his own life to save his shaggy, mongrel collie."[70] Another front-page headline, in the *Toronto Evening Telegram* in 1948, mentioned how a 14-year-old boy acted like the Biblical character "Samson" by clubbing a marauding wolf that had been attacking his dog.[71] In each of these examples, the boy accomplished the supremely heroic masculine task of mastering himself while facing danger and meeting the call of duty to a worthy friend. Consciously facing peril was the true test of fidelity and masculine courage.

In the traditional research on entrepreneurship it is customary to perceive and understand it as something extraordinary and as highly different from managing. The difference rests in that entrepreneurship incorporates elements of hegemonic masculinity—independence, taking the initiative, bearing risk— and is particularly suited for certain people, not "mere mortals."[72] Something of this can be seen in stories about boys who garnered national recognition and awards for saving dogs. One boy, featured in the *Globe and Mail* on 21 July 1953, was publicly lauded and raised to national status for risking his own life for the sake of a dog. The headline read: "Saved Dog in Canyon, Gets Award."[73] The 14-year-old B.C. boy "proved that a boy can be a dog's best friend" and received the 1953 National Humane Act Award for rescuing a dog stranded on a rocky ledge after it had been swept down a river.[74] This news story reworked the common phrase "a dog is a boy's best friend." The reworked phrase emphasized how the boy–dog relationship was largely egalitarian, binding boy and dog together through mutual trust, tenderness, and appreciation.

Although a boy's relationship with his dog included emotion, it was centred on masculine action. A possible function of these narratives was to articulate a version of entrepreneurial masculinity that emphasized a reciprocated physical way of relating to others. Although boys were assumed to naturally form gangs, and although same-sex friendships were considered normal, the closest association a boy had was assumed to be with his dog, and that relationship emphasized physical enactments of affection. Boyhood and dogs were intertwined with values of hegemonic masculinity such as individual risk, loyalty, and physical strength; it follows that expressions of love between boy and dog were most often framed by physical action. The entrepreneurial boyhood discourse assumed that biology compelled boys to seek adventure and physical risks, and these required a masculinized, trustworthy companion for times of need.

Farley Mowat's *The Dog Who Wouldn't Be*[75] illuminates the importance that a dog had in a boy's life and how that relationship centred on adventure and physical action. Early in Mowat's novel, an eight-year-old boy discusses a limitation for him as his family moves from Ontario to Saskatchewan:

> If there was one drawback to the new life in Saskatoon, it was that we had no dog. During my lifetime we had owned, or had been owned by, a steady succession of dogs. As a newborn baby I had been guarded by a Border collie named Sapper who was one day doused with boiling water by a vicious neighbour, and who went insane as a result. But

there had always been other dogs during my first eight years, until we moved to the west and became, for the moment dogless. The prairies could be only half real to a boy without a dog.[76]

Why would the prairies be half real to a boy without a dog? Mowat presented the prairies as a Western frontier, where men with guns and boys with dogs could roam wide-open masculine vastness. In Mowat's mind, this was a complete contrast to the feminized "physical and mental confines" of the "staid Anglo-Saxon province of Ontario."[77] This brand of rugged individualism, which stood juxtaposed to the family, posited that on the prairies, boys could begin their exploration outward, like little entrepreneurs, engaging with the world away from the safety of home. All of this being so, a "real" boy invested with a natural sense of physical adventure and exploration, compelled by biology, needed a trusty masculine companion to explore the wide-open Western frontier. The best companion for this, a dog, showed masculine loyalty and faithfulness. Dogs had always been esteemed in Western culture for these traits and as "companions, hunters and guards."[78]

An ideal entrepreneur sets himself apart from others, physically, geographically, socially, and psychologically. Such a person requires "personal self-denial."[79] Interestingly, then, each of the above examples cultivated the image of a solitary boy and his dog—together alone. One can glimpse here an aspect of the heroic entrepreneur version of boyhood, which emphasized traditional features of hegemonic masculinity and self-reliance expressed in solitary manly adventure. Like the entrepreneur, the boy and his dog were sallying forth into the dangerous rugged wilds of nature in solitude, not with adults, rarely with other boys, not with girls or mothers, but decidedly alone. Moreover, the rugged outdoors and dangerous circumstances often framed a boy's relationship with his dog and accentuated the need for physical courage and bravery. This also allowed the boy to determine on whom to rely, since the test for true masculine friendship was the degree to which one could count on another during physical danger and crisis. If dogs were boys' "true pals," then others, such as parents, adults, and other boys and girls, were tainted with falseness, rendered to some degree untrustworthy in their relations with boys.

Not only in the world of sport, then, but also in general public statements about boyhood, bodies mattered. Toughness, physical endurance, and a belief in the power of the body have historically been hallmarks of a successful entrepreneurial masculinity.[80] The efforts of self-denying boys emphasized the physical exertion of boys' bodies, often in the rugged outdoors. If the promise of postwar security and the growth of capitalism rested on individual boys' masculinity, than a boy's body was a crucial site of this. The news items discussed above repeatedly alluded to the courage of a boy forcing his body into action, marshalling the masculine body to great heroic, individual ends. The accounts fostered the image of boys as little masculine adventurers, independent, mentally free, decisive in spite of uncertainty, who either sought out or found themselves in danger, danger situated in or against the elements of nature, lakes, rivers, wild animals, and so on. In contrast to the organization man, and against the backdrop of social and political turbulence and insecurity and the need for economic growth, these stories presented boys as physically engaged in masculine acts of courage and physical daring, as exercising sound judgment in order to bring about safe and secure happy endings. The young males, exposed to loss or physical injury, were filled with an endless masculine spirit that could later be utilized to spark the mobilization of resources that would bring about economic growth. News stories like these helped fuse the boy–dog relationship with entrepreneurial values such as individual risk taking, physical struggle, and outdoor action, all predicated on a world characterized by urgent danger and peril.

Yet this patriarchal posture toward boys' bodies found in many public statements was not unique to this model of boyhood. Public commentators routinely taught that an acceptable model of boyhood of any kind was one where bodily pain was to be endured and that to survive pain and overcome physical hardship was courageous and appropriately masculine. It is not hard to see that the ideology of male heroism and its hollow morality of embodied power worship most likely implanted visions of individual and group male ecstasy and masculine courage in the minds of some men and boys during the postwar era and well beyond. For example, one Ontario academic, whose work was published in the late 1960s, found that among boys, physical courage was most often cited as evidence of a boy's masculinity.[81] Certainly, some men and boys would have learned the dominant cultural message that if they could not take it—that is, internalize patriarchal values as men or boys— then the social, economic, and political rewards of individual male effort or male camaraderie, including social prestige, public recognition, and financial gain, would not be forthcoming.

Ultimately for some, boys were expected to interact with the world in a way that aligned itself with and was informed by a more traditional style of masculinity. Social commentators tried to use their public authority to establish a model of boyhood that took for granted the values of self-reliance, decisiveness, risk taking, and rugged individualism. We might also see social commentators' attempts to naturalize this version of boyhood as an attempt to prop up a supposedly flagging masculinity. That is, as social commentators tried to establish the "authority" of this boyhood, they were also trying to reaffirm the status of masculine identity and authority by repeatedly drawing on past representations of hegemonic masculinity at a time of significant gender unease. Nowhere is this better seen than in the Boy Scout Movement.

SELF-RELIANCE, RUGGED INDIVIDUALISM, AND THE BOY SCOUT MOVEMENT

When former British prime minister Lord Rosebery wished aloud that his nation's manhood was made up entirely of old Scouts, he was not wishing for anything different from Ontario's immediate postwar Premier George Drew (1943–48).[82] In February 1945, when Drew addressed the annual meeting of the Provisional Council of Ontario Boy Scouts, he expressed the hope that a time would come when "every boy or girl in this country belonged to the Boy Scouts or Girl Guides."[83] Linking nationalistic aims of citizenship to the largely Christian, character-building program of the Boy Scouts, Premier Drew stated: "I can think of no better basis for citizenship than a full understanding of the undertaking that every Scout gives: To do my duty, to God and King, to help other people at all times."[84] Drew, like the Boy Scouts, prioritized the three tenets—character, Christianity, and citizenship—for producing well-rounded boys who understood their obligation to God and mankind. Drew was not alone in lauding the Scouts as an instrument for safeguarding democracy in Ontario. Less than a year later, meeting with Ontario boy scouts and scout leaders— 20,000 Boy Scouts and Wolves—in Toronto's Varsity Stadium, Lord Rowallan, Chief Scout of the British Empire, blustered that "much could be prevented in the way of saving the world if more could be persuaded to interest themselves in the Scout movement."[85] By associating them with military masculinity, Lord Rowallan further linked the Scouts to their "brothers who fought bravely and courageously" in Europe during the Second World War.[86]

Other boy leaders expressed similar sentiments about the importance of the Boys Scouts for building good citizens. In 1945 the President of the Boy Scouts Association of Canada emphasized the need to function as a collective when he declared that "Scouts of today will be the responsible citizens of tomorrow" and that "standing together as brothers they can help wonderfully to keep the world's peace."[87] As the Second World War ended and people began worrying more about the dangers confronting an ever-changing world, concerned adults believed that boys' moral state was of vital importance to stave off social disorder and to protect a fragile postwar democracy. In 1946, Major General Dan Spry, Chief Executive Commissioner of the Canadian Boy Scout Movement, posited that "those things for which we have been fighting are not going to be handed to us on a platter. None wanted destruction and dissension and yet the world is full of antagonisms despite the general desire for peace."[88] Peace, he continued, rested on boys' masculinity and "depended on the minds and souls of the mass of the people"; the "job of scouting was to bring up boys who will approach their responsibilities as citizens with the Scout background of tolerance, fellowship and service."[89]

Within the Scouting movement, the job of making better boys was given to men. Specifically, despite claims to inclusiveness suggesting that the Scout movement was blind to issues of class and race, the Boy Scouts aimed at recruiting mostly men from the new white-collar and professional classes. Managers, executives, salesmen, bank officers, professional men, lawyers, and businessmen were solicited to volunteer their time and energy. In 1948, one Boy Scout representative stated that officers of the association "have been stressing the need for leadership in scouting by public, business and professional men."[90] Prominent men filled the administrative ranks of the Scouting movement. Rhys M. Sale, President of Ford of Canada, Sidney Smith, President of the University of Toronto, and Fred Finlay, who surrendered his job as Secretary of the Bank of Nova Scotia to assume the position of Chief Executive Commissioner of the Boy Scout Association, are but a few examples from the early 1950s. These were the men who were found in the upper ranks of the Scouting movement. A *Globe and Mail* editorial recapped all of this most accurately by suggesting that the Scouting Association's Advisory Board "reads like a directory of the city's business and professional men."[91]

The ideal Boy Scout was self-reliant. A Simpson's advertisement published in the *Globe and Mail* in 1945 conflated character building in boys with nation building and commemorated the Scouting movement as "Canada's Future ... in Training." The same ad listed attributes that boys should internalize in order to secure their privileged position in society: "What they are taught, what lessons they learn now will influence the future of our nation. The Boy Scout movement teaches boys to be self-reliant, trustworthy and honourable, healthy in body, spirit and mind." [92] Echoing similar sentiments were others who maintained that Canada's most valuable resource was well-built boys. Addressing the 36th annual meeting of the Ontario council of the Boy Scouts Association in February 1947, Reverend Reginald Howden of Barrie remarked that "true greatness of Canada depends not so much on the abundance of her natural resources as on the strength of character of her citizens."[93] In the view of the editors of the *Newmarket Era and Express*, the Scouts even provided a better opportunity than competitive sports for building an appropriate character in boys: "In our opinion, what boys learn from scouting is more valuable than what they learn from competitive sports because the scout program provides a wider field of activity and learning. Their programs do not stress physical skills alone. Importance is put into the building of character as well."[94]

Yet despite the overall assertion that the Scouting movement built better boys, the adults in charge of the Boy Scouts appeared torn at times between building and preparing boys for the emerging corporate culture and fostering in boys an older style of masculinity. To do both, of course, was contradictory, for one model of boyhood was based on notions of teamwork and collectivity while the other worshipped self-reliance and rugged individualism.[95] Certainly, the Scouting movement itself was largely an all-male hierarchal structure that promoted obedience and the ability to follow orders; this mirrored many postwar bureaucratic organizations.[96] So there is little doubt that the social relationships encouraged in the movement replicated those found in many postwar bureaucracies. Yet despite the ambivalence around boyhood, the rhetoric of the Scouting movement tended to emphasize the values of self-reliance and rugged individualism. One *Globe and Mail* editorial touted citizenship training, for example, as less about building or strengthening community and more about fostering the manly virtue of self-reliance in boys:

> The handicrafts, thrift, patriotism, rules of health, the chivalry, independence and pride of citizenship which Scouting teaches are practiced and cherished by the boys because they are presented in interesting and enjoyable ways. Field operations, conservation, kindness to animals— all these and more make the outdoors a real and vivid world in which each boy has an important part. His camp life teaches him not only self-reliance, but the wonderful heritage which that self-reliance helps to develop and protect.[97]

Efforts by the Scouting movement to retain an older, more physical, more self-reliant style of masculinity were tied to the ideology of Nature. "Scouting gives a boy a sense of honor and loyalty ... it teaches him to be self-reliant," remarked a 1955 editorial in the *Newmarket Era and Express*. The editorial went on to suggest that "through open-air exercises and self-care, a boy gains a sound mind in a healthy body. Cheery comradeship and the enjoyment of nature give him happiness." The idea here that nature "makes a man of a boy"[98] is not surprising, given that the classic venue for masculine epic testing has always been the wilderness.[99] Drawing on long-standing beliefs about the value of the rugged wilderness in making an appropriate boyhood, postwar commentators envisioned a return to Nature as the dominant way to build better, more self-reliant boys.[100] Vincent Massey, the Governor General of Canada, noted in 1948 that the Scouting movement's emphasis on rugged outdoor activities allowed boys to explore the world in wholesome ways. "Boys have a natural love of adventure," he remarked, adding that "one of the essential products of scouting is that ruggedness which belongs to Canadian life."[101] It was assumed that cities were sickly and artificial environments,[102] where walls and sidewalks confined boys' assumed nature, thus preventing them from acquiring necessary masculine skills to build the nation. Many opined, for example, that the rapid urbanization of postwar Ontario led inevitably to effeminacy, poor health, and nervousness, evidenced by the lack of masculine men fit for war service. R.J. Renison, in the *Globe and Mail* in November 1945, wrote that Canadians had been shocked to learn that about 40 percent of their country's young men had been not fit for active service during wartime.[103] He noted that "physical degeneration" among males, previously encountered only among the "effete and overcrowded inhabitants of the slums of great cities in old countries," had emerged in Ontario.[104]

Driven by the essentialist belief that urban life had little to offer the moral education of boys, the Scouts sought to restore boys to their assumed natural element by mimicking the pioneer experience. By acquiring self-reliance, boys and men would be able to demonstrate the skills their forefathers needed to survive. One Boy Scout leader in 1958 put it this way:

> The Boy Scouts and similar organizations have rendered valuable service to urban communities by training young men in woods lore. The youths they train will be men, and their training will make them better men. There is a constant need of such men, possessed of the pioneer skills on the many Canadian frontiers that still challenge strength and determination. It would be unfortunate, and a great loss to the country if only those reared in rugged, isolated environments could answer that challenge.[105]

The above passage invoked a mythologized past, where men learned to how to be men in the rugged outdoors. Out of this construction of the past and its relationship to a mythologized masculinity came the notion held by Scout leaders and others, that the rugged outdoors was the best context to help a boy become a man.

"Help a Boy Become a Man" was the tag line for a 1947 Boy Scout fundraising campaign that sought public financial support to build a permanent campsite for the Toronto District Cubs and Scouts (now the Haliburton Scout Reserve) while highlighting that the Boy Scouts were chiefly a character-building organization.[106] The Toronto District Cubs and Scouts had found the "ideal country for 'men-in-the-making.'"[107] Called "Boys Land," the camp, it was imagined, would transform effeminate city boys into "real" boys. The rhetoric and content of the appeal spoke to postwar masculine fears that only a project that instilled self-reliance, rugged outdoor skills, and traditional values could save future generations of boys from becoming feminized. However, it was the geographic location that was thought to make it ideal for making men out of boys. The staked-out Boys Land property, in the heart of Haliburton County in Central Ontario, comprised 4,000 acres of lakes, forests, trails, and wildlife. The retreat would offer a permanent homosocial place where boys could be boys with one another under the influence of adult males, safely placed in the context of rugged nature.

In the postwar period, many adults perceived a return to nature as the best way to develop and remasculinize boys. "Think of the appeal to boys," one Boy Scout fundraiser implored. This particular entreaty rested on the idea that boys could return to their natural habitat, given that they were best suited for nature, not civilization and the corrupting feminine influences of the city: "If you were a normal, healthy boy, how'd you like to go camping next summer in Haliburton? Or if the wildest animal you'd ever seen was the neighbour's pup or a Jersey cow, how'd you like to track a deer, porcupine, foxes, perhaps, even a bear?"[108]

Through Scouting, boys developed "a keenness of mind, a fitness of body and ideals of loyalty and comradeship which breed good citizens. Because of this—and because if you were a boy you couldn't wait to go camping next summer in Haliburton."[109] In short, it was thought that the outdoor location of Boys Land, coupled with Scouting's physical program, would counter postwar feminization and instill an older, more rugged, more self-reliant version of masculinity in the boys.

The Scouting movement sought to mould boys into a successful masculinity through woodcraft and hearty doses of rugged outdoor adventure that tested and honed self-reliance. Being able to spear a fish, and knowing which outdoor berries were safe to eat, may not have seemed vital to later manhood, yet the link between these skills and masculinizing boys was not far-fetched. To illustrate, in 1954, Scouts from Welland, Ontario, tramped deep into the bush on a "survival test." Over two days, they "speared fish, ate roots and berries, drank birchbark coffee and slept in spruce tents." Demonstrating a racist ideology, some Scout officials noted that learning a few outdoor camping survival tricks was central to developing an appropriate masculinity. "The most important thing wasn't that the boys picked up a few Indian dodges ... but that they displayed self-reliance, a quality of manhood."[110] Other male adults viewed the Boy Scouts as a useful public tool for forging and socializing boys into a "true manhood." In a 1946 testimony, Charles Baugh, the territorial commander of the Salvation Army for Canada, wrote with deep and abiding praise about the Scouting movement's ability to guide boys into successful manhood: "I have followed with interest and growing esteem throughout the years the activities of the Boy Scouts. It probably would have made a great difference to my life had the Scouts been available in my youthful days. Not the least among the blessings of the modern era is the effective and matured instrument for the development of true manhood and citizenship."[111]

The Scouting movement, with its emphasis on outdoor adventure and rugged self-reliance, spoke to fears of a "crisis" in masculinity and degeneracy in men. "Building Boys Is Better Than Mending Men" read a fundraising campaign centring on the fear that men had lost their manliness once the traditional frontier was lost: "We must expect a strong increase of emotional imbalance and social maladjustment if the impossibility to realize frontier ideals becomes evident."[112] As a result of the "crisis" in masculinity, men seemed to be in more psychological danger than women. This it was assumed that character-building organizations for males, such as the Boy Scouts, required more government funding than organizations for girls. In 1950, the question was raised in one provincial legislature of why the government had budgeted $2,500 for the Boys Scouts but only $1,000 for Girl Guides. The justification was that "fewer women than men need guidance."[113] Although limited, the above evidence reveals, to some extent, postwar assumptions about gender roles. Given that the Scouts were allocated more resources than the Guides, it seems reasonable to assume that adults were governed by the belief that boys were more likely to transgress notions of an ideal masculinity than girls were to stray from their accepted gender roles. In short, it was assumed that boys would simply cause more trouble.

Scouting offered boys contradictory messages regarding how to be a man. On the one hand, the Scouts attempted to prepare boys for life in a more organized, interdependent, corporate society. Yet at the same time, they did not at all denounce rugged individualism as an anachronistic vestige of nineteenth-century masculinity. Rather, they demonstrated a tendency to promote this model of masculinity over the corporate boyhood as an antidote to an increasingly feminized society.

CONCLUSION

The pattern of boyhood outlined above was formed in relation to the entire complex structure of gender relations. In terms of other boyhoods, the self-reliant, entrepreneurial boyhood existed in tension with the corporate boyhood and with pathologized boyhoods such as the sissy and of course with women and girls. Although only partial, the historical displacement of the older entrepreneurial boyhood by the modern businessman/bureaucratic boyhood was plainly linked to economic transformations and to the rise of bureaucracies. The dominance of corporations during the postwar period created the need for white-collar men who could fit in, not stand out. Corporations desired men who would follow the rules and help the team win. Yet many adults remained committed to encouraging individualistic impulses and self-reliance in boys.

Public statements about boyhood often drew on an older style of masculinity and ideology to promote a model of boyhood that was closely aligned with historical understandings of the heroic entrepreneur. Furthermore, public commentators had been defining and solidifying gender identity over the postwar period by repeatedly offering up to the public a particular version of boyhood. Many adults would have read about boys living up to a gender identity that had been produced and reproduced for years: boys acting like rugged, self-reliant individuals, decisive, physically daring, and above all often saviours of women. All of this promoted and publicly affirmed a version of a boyhood gender identity. Moreover, in these public campaigns, masculinity was further associated with action, doing, and power as aspects of a normal boyhood.

Public commentators mobilized the popular concern over the fate of postwar masculinity to their own patriarchal benefit by upholding traditional male narratives infused with older versions of hegemonic masculinity. This should not be overlooked, because for some men, the "death" of the individual male "warrior" or "hero" was the most pressing issue of the Cold War era.[114] As noted, the sexist elevation of boys and masculinity over girls and femininity predominated even though the narratives varied. As the everyday narratives so clearly revealed, readers were often enrolled as witnesses to manufactured instances of boys' heroic success. Accounts of boys' heroism and of their triumphs over adversity met the need for constant confirmation of a vibrant postwar masculinity.

As Ontarians strove to regulate boyhood, a key issue was "the bad boy." In the next chapter, I examine the boyhood-ideal-in-reverse.

Dissonant Ideas:
Other Boyhoods

4

As Ontarians strove to regulate boyhood, a key issue was the bad boy. For many adults, this version of boyhood stood in direct contrast to the normal boy. The bad boy was imagined as probably from a working-poor neighbourhood and as incapable of integrating himself with the "normal" world, and thus as a potential delinquent. Commentators taught the reading public that bad boys came from urban, not rural environments.[1] The bad boy preferred disorder, committed physical acts of social transgression, hated morality, and denied society's laws. He was capable of misdemeanours and petty crimes. The bad boy was dangerous to a society concerned about security. "From earliest childhood," postwar experts warned adults, the problem boy did not "think and act in the ways of the community." His nature, they cautioned, found "all submissiveness ... odious and he refuses to respect any rule."[2] This understanding of the bad boy motivated middle-class experts, including psychologists, to encourage individual men and groups of men (and some women) to develop methods, volunteer time, and donate money to create masculinity-building organizations and boys clubs that would rejuvenate a "healthy" masculinity and, by extension, suppress bad boy behaviour.[3]

This chapter focuses on the public statements that constructed the postwar bad boy, or juvenile delinquent. Although these labels are used interchangeably, the term juvenile delinquent is primarily a legal one that defines a particular kind of person in Ontario courts of law. Carrigan, in his history of juvenile delinquency in Canada, states that in Ontario a juvenile delinquent was someone under the age of sixteen who committed criminal acts such as theft or vandalism.[4] Canada's 1908 Juvenile Delinquency Act defined a juvenile delinquent as "any boy or girl apparently or actually under the age of sixteen years."[5] The *Hope Report* offered an official definition of delinquent but refrained from limiting it to an age or to specific acts of criminality. Rather, the commission classified a delinquent as a child or youth in possession of an antisocial attitude.

According to the *Hope Report,* a delinquent was marked by "stealing, stubborn-ness, waywardness, truancy, trespassing, fighting, sex offenses, etc."[6]

Sangster has remarked that in postwar English Canada, the image of the juvenile delinquent was male-defined.[7] Although researchers, theorists, and popular discourse often employed it as a gender-neutral term, much of the postwar preoccupation with juvenile delinquency was focused on boys' social and moral transgressions and their impact on society.[8] For adults concerned with Ontario's stability and security, the main problem was the misguided, poor or working-class, often immigrant boy.[9] Boys clubs were central to addressing the issue of problem boys. Boy workers believed that through boys clubs, they could fill the gap left by the enforced absence of fathers, occupy boys' time constructively, and prevent boys from causing trouble and assuming lives of future deviancy. By investing time, money, and manpower in the regulation of boyhood, Ontario boy workers attempted to build future, law-abiding citizens who would be honest, play fair, and safeguard the future. Of course, a belief that they could instill a masculine character into boys began with the assumption that boys were not innately bad.

"NO SUCH THING AS A BAD BOY"[10]

It was a dominant postwar belief that there was "no such thing as a bad boy":

> Despite the fact that Cpl. Charles Holman of the Royal Canadian Mounted Police has felt the tang of salt spray on his lips while har-pooning whales from a canoe in Hudson's Bay; lived dangerously in the underworld of black market and narcotics; done his share of lonely patrols on the blizzard swept plains of the west and the icy waters of the north and acted as a guard and escort for the recent tour of Queen Elizabeth and the Duke of Edinburgh—he still gets his greatest thrill in proving to society there is no such thing as a bad boy.[11]

Many postwar child experts viewed boyhood as a pliable time in a boy's life—that is, a time when his moral character was forming and his personality contained the seeds of both good and bad. Canadian child psychologist and educator W.E. Blatz registered his thoughts on this subject in *Maclean's* on 1 March 1946: "Every child has within him or her the seeds of good and the seeds of bad; that any child can be made a useful member of society under constant parental guidance and discipline. But that if childish faults and mistakes go uncorrected they may make problem adults—perhaps even jailbirds."[12]

Although opinions varied, most people thought that boys were not born bad or with a biological predisposition to delinquency. Reflecting the decline of previously dominant hereditarian or eugenic thinking, it was thought that boys, good or bad, were shaped by their social and environmental circumstances. In 1954, a man from Belle River, Ontario, explained to readers of the *Globe and Mail* that "children are not born bad. They are not born with any behaviour patterns. They acquire—learn—their patterns and ethics and moral codes. Society teaches them that."[13] Sidney Katz, in a *Maclean's* article in January 1951, summed up the prevailing social knowledge about delinquency: "No child is born criminal; no child is 'naturally' bad: no child has an inherited criminal streak." Here, Katz was reflecting typical postwar beliefs: "No child is born a delinquent. But children do learn. From the world that surrounds them, first in their homes, later in schools, churches, communities. If a child is brought up in an environment where his physical and emotional needs are not met properly then he will behave differently from the child raised in an environment where they are."[14]

Postwar popular psychological advice suggested that antisocial behaviour in children was a learned behaviour, a by-product of their world, in particular an outcome of their home life. For example, a 1954 Ontario report produced by a select committee appointed by the Ontario legislature to study and report on the broader problems of delinquent individuals made special note that a root cause of delinquent behaviour was "an unhappy home atmosphere."[15] This understanding of boyhood development placed boys in a special period in their lives, where if they were raised in a "happy" home, in which their emotional and psychological needs were adequately provided for by two well adjusted hetero-sexual parents, a well adjusted, normal boy and future citizen would emerge.

As already mentioned, the belief that there was no hereditarian explana-tion for delinquent behaviour was something of a change from past beliefs. When discussing Toronto's working-class "boy problem" between 1860 and 1930, Bryan Hogeveen, for example, points out that in the late 1910s medical doctors and psychiatrists emerged on the juvenile justice scene to offer contro-versial theories about juvenile deviance. According to Hogeveen, these experts, who drew on the white Anglo eugenics movement, explained delinquency as an outcome of inferior breeding and defective genes. This class-related theo-retical explanation led to solutions such as "permanent incarceration, steriliza-tion, and, for recent immigrants deportation."[16] It wasn't until the mid-1920s that a change in perspective reshaped understandings of juvenile delinquency. Influenced by the work of W.E. Blatz's environmental psychological approach to social problems, notes Hogeveen, "juvenile offenders were (re)constituted as deterministic subjects who were the product of social, psychological, and economic forces situated in their social milieu."[17] Blatz's approach continued to shape attitudes and beliefs about the causes of juvenile delinquency throughout the postwar years. One outcome of his approach was to lay down the idea that there really was no such thing as a bad boy.

So, were bad boys simply normal boys inside? Some experts believed that bad boys were "average boys with average interests and family backgrounds."[18] Certainly, for many the bad boy had an "essential good" core, which suggested that boy workers could "take these impulses as expressed in these patterns of conduct and direct them so that they will bring happiness and success to the boy."[19] One *Globe and Mail* reporter interviewed sixteen boys from a "bad district" and found "truth in the claim that every boy has some good in him."[20] Some commentators, such as well-known Harvard criminologist Sheldon Glueck, did not believe that boys were naturally good inside or born morally neutral. "All humans are born criminals—that is, socially not adjusted," he asserted.[21] The theoretical core of this psychological model enabled Glueck to flaunt hyperbole and rhetoric in his claim that very young boys, if given the chance, would commit heinous crimes, even murder. "A six-month old baby," Glueck contended, "if physically capable, would steal without conscience, kill when peeved and destroy with vicious abandon."[22] These impulses were considered part of a "normal" boyhood; without proper guidance from experts to keep them in check, disaster would inevitably follow for both boys and society.

Popular postwar understandings of boyhood development accepted the idea that many of the qualities that distinguished bad boys were simply "part of the normal development of almost every boy."[23] In "Will Your Youngster Turn to Crime?", *Maclean's* writer June Callwood cited Glueck, who argued that boys' antisocial behaviour was part of any normal, well-adjusted boyhood: "It was imagined that most normal boys have a period of aggression and resistance to authority, or try to sneak into the movies, or pilfer candy bars from store counters, or hate school and pay little attention to their teacher. At some period of their childhood most boys destroy property or seem to enjoy hurting animals and other children."[24]

A widely held belief was that the bad boy possessed the same desirable character traits as the normal boy. "Look at what kind of a person the delinquent is," declared Glueck. "He's not all bad, by any means. He's fearless, adventurous, aggressive, energetic, strong—just the sort of citizen we want. We shouldn't lose him."[25] Unlike a "mama's pet," who was thought to have "been robbed of all his guts by his mother," rendering him unfit as a future citizen, the bad boy was imagined to possess the character traits that had the potential to make him a good citizen, one who could face the dangers of an increasingly turbulent world.[26] In the bad boy, Glueck and others saw enormous potential, for he was the most resourceful and "self-reliant of boys."[27] In other words, the bad boy, according to experts, had all the right character traits to be a productive citizen. The problem, according to these same experts, was that he possessed these traits in excess. "The tough boy is the potential leader," claimed one expert in 1947. "He has a strong will and strong character. And his only difficulty is that they are not controlled."[28] It was not his aggressive ways or his capacity for violence that most troubled postwar experts; it was the boy's inability to control these things.

The normal, well-adjusted boy was self-disciplined and self-controlled; the maladjusted bad boy was thought to lack discipline and impulse control. Boys were assumed to be naturally aggressive and potentially violent; thus, an "appropriate" boyhood masculinity was defined by a boy's ability to exercise self-control and to master his impulses. The normal boy was adventuresome and somewhat aggressive and impulsive; the bad boy was excessively so. The normal boy disliked anything effeminate; the bad boy demonstrated an extreme hostility to anything feminine. The normal boy disliked school but liked to read comics; the bad boy hated school, was truant, did less well academically despite equal intelligence, and was addicted to comics. The belief that bad boys had the right character traits but in excess lent value to the idea that if these traits—in particular the extreme inclination to danger, excitement, or risk—were not properly channelled, then boys would inevitably get into conflicts with the law or other authorities.

The experts agreed that the bad boy needed to acquire self-discipline in order to override his impulses, resist temptations, and do what society needed to be done. According to Sheldon and Eleanor Glueck, necessary social mechanisms, methods, and strategies were needed to "curb" without extinguishing these primal urges. Parents and other adults in the environment could help control and condition boys to live appropriately in society, so the argument ran. This view was made clear by one doctor in a 12 February 1947 article in the *Globe and Mail:* "Under the pressure of his environment and his parents' discipline and example, the child learns to curb these urges in the first ten years of his life. But if these pressures are drastically distorted from normal, the child cannot learn properly to live in society."[29]

The concept of self-control would have been appealing to postwar adults in positions of relative power. If boys, especially working-class boys, would do what they were expected to do on their own, there would be no need for external controls. The hope, then, was that bad boys would develop and internalize the sort of self-control and willpower required to prevent themselves from doing what postwar experts and other middle-class adults viewed as socially *undesirable.* From a white, Anglo, middle-class perspective (the one often articulated by experts and other social commentators), the marshalling of the bad boy's willpower—in particular the working-class bad boy's willpower—toward socially desirable ends was central to ensuring the stability and safety of the existing social order.

It was widely assumed that the crimes of manhood began in boyhood. Dominant understandings of gender reflected the idea that adult misfits in society were the result of neglect or abandonment in boyhood; human "dere-licts" were products of a misguided childhood. So opined two psychologists in *Journal of Educational Psychology* in 1956: "The youth who at the age of sixteen is in court for stealing a car frequently is the youth who at the age of ten stole things, lied, and engaged in other misbehavior at home, school, and in the community."[30] Four years earlier, the Gluecks, in *Delinquents in the Making* (1952), had noted that "the majority of adult criminals began their anti-social careers as child delinquents."[31] Five years later, in 1959, a *Star* editorial commented that "today's delinquents start persistently to misbehave at the age of seven."[32]

For some, an "abnormal" boyhood had far more loathsome implications than this: it was linked with sex perversion in adulthood. A 1948 study of sex perverts, including pedophiles, conducted by the Canadian Penal Association, drew a close connection between a shabby boyhood and future degeneracy: "most sex perverts in Canadian penitentiaries are 30 years of age, but they began their abnormal habits in boyhood—between 9 and 14."[33] The sociolog-ical reasoning that constructed adult criminality and perversion in events that happened to boys, opened up theoretical and practical space for boy workers. In the midst of the Cold War, the project of safeguarding society from dangers that threatened to undermine the security and safety of society was simply a matter of building better boys.

The antisocial behaviours of boys were always explainable. What, then, were some of the more popular explanations employed by commentators to under-stand the "boy problem"? As noted earlier, postwar boy experts concurred that the boy problem was not the manifestation of anything innate; rather, it was caused by a variety of social conditions. Slum conditions, broken homes, poor parenting, working mothers, absentee or inadequate fathers, lack of masculine guidance, ineffective schools, toy guns, increased unsupervised leisure time, lack of recreational facilities, and movies and comic books were indicated at various times by different commentators as the root causes of the bad boy.[34] A 1947 item in the *Essex Free Press* put the blame for boys' delinquency on a number of factors including "delinquent parents," "over-indulgence of chil-dren by parents," and the rise of "'progressive' methods of education," which, according to the author, did little to prepare boys for "the rigors of a do-or-die economy."[35] Kenneth Rogers, General Secretary of the Big Brothers Movement, who designed a pamphlet titled *Boys Are Worth It*,[36] which was described by one contemporary as that "admirable little book," also identified a number of contributing factors that led to boy delinquency.[37] Rogers blamed fatherless homes and mother-led families, but he also made it clear that delinquency had "roots in social conditions; poverty, ignorance, parental neglect of children, bad neighbourhoods."[38] Focusing largely on poorer working-class and immigrant districts, boy workers attempted to change the root causes found in the home that would surely contribute to future boy delinquency. As Gleason notes, postwar psychologists were no longer solely interested in addressing delinquent behaviour; their primary objective was to "disseminate a new ideal regarding family life and thus bring parents under their professional [scope]."[39]

Underprivileged neighbourhoods, slum conditions, and "unspeakable homes" were scrutinized and repeatedly noted as primary causes of boy delinquency.[40] In January 1946, speaking of Toronto's boy problem, one local rabbi declared that "slum areas, bad housing, congested quarters and lack of recreational facilities for normal and invigorating play characterized too many parts of Toronto."[41] These conditions, he said, had contributed to the boy problem. The conventional postwar wisdom was, as one boy worker put it, that "if you want better boys in your neighbourhood, you begin by making a better neighbourhood for the boys."[42] Accordingly, social reformers set out to mitigate what they saw as the "appalling influence of sin and vice" in working-poor areas; in their view, such an environment caused "the breakdown of the family" and became the "breeding places for delinquency and crime."[43] In this respect, boy workers of the postwar period, like those of the late nineteenth century, focused mainly on regulating boys from poorer working-class and immigrant districts, whose societal position was marginal. In both eras, reformers attempted to uphold and solidify class hierarchies.[44]

Yet it wasn't only working-poor homes that were imagined as producing delinquent boys. Some commentators, albeit a minority, also viewed wealthy homes as sites for producing future delinquents. An editorial in the *Kingsville Reporter* on 12 August 1948 warned readers that "juvenile delinquency is not confined to the poor. Unbelievable offences are committed by rich boys, and probably three times as many occur that ever reach the courts." The editorial went on to suggest that the cause of any boy going bad had little to do with class location and more to do with a lack of "mutual respect" in the home. Some commentators suggested that mutual respect in a home was undermined by permissive parents who spoiled their children: "The spoiled boy has been robbed of all guts. Life has been sloppy and too easy for him. He has learned cute ways of getting his own way from his mother, who thinks of him as a paragon. If the spoiled boy becomes a delinquent he is sly and sneaky."[45] In the midst of Cold War anxieties over effeminacy and by extension homosexuality, it was imagined that a boy with too much masculine aggression, or "guts," posed as much of a risk to the social order as the boy who had too little.

The lack of masculine guidance was also widely believed to create bad boys. This theme was exploited by welfare organizations such as Toronto's Big Brothers. Operating in Toronto since 1913, this movement boasted that it had helped "thousands of boys" between the ages of eight and sixteen "grow to manhood and good citizenship."[46] The help was often in the form of ensuring that working-class boys received proper masculine guidance. A 1945 promotional advertisement for Big Brothers featured a twelve-year-old boy who had grown up on the "wrong side of the tracks." Revealing postwar anxieties about working-class boyhoods, the text asserted: "Boys like Danny don't get into trouble entirely through their own fault. The psychologists call it poor environment and maladjustment. There is no reason why a deserving kid should fall by the wayside because things aren't right at home ... in nearly every case there is a domestic or environmental maladjustment in the background."[47]

But what comprised environmental maladjustment? Ignoring economic and social conditions, authorities identified the real issue as the lack of male guidance. An excerpt from the same 1945 news item made this clear: "In fully 75 percent of the cases the father of the family is either dead or absent ... and as Dr. Kenneth Rogers general secretary, and Noah Pitcher, his assistant, will tell you, the Little Brother has got himself into trouble in the first place because there was a complete absence of adult male guidance in the house."[48]

A boy who lacked suitable male guidance to internalize masculine qualities such as self-reliance and self-control easily became a "delinquent, a hoodlum or a ne'er-do-well."[49] "Doting" and working mothers, it was imagined, robbed boys of their "independence" and were thought unable to fill the gap left by the father's absence.[50] It was this "psychological as well as a physical" gap that Big Brothers sought to fill.[51]

To provide the kind of guidance boys needed, professional men were required; women were simply incapable of understanding boys. So, at least, ran the argument. According to the Big Brothers movement, only middle-class men could decipher and decode "Little Brothers":

> Big Brothers has stood behind many a boy like Danny and by being a pal instead of a truant officer to him, given him a break he deserves and put his feet along the right path ... It is not, for that matter a welfare agency, but a group of friendly business and professional men of this city who know how to understand that most complex of all mechanisms, the growing spirited boy.[52]

As a result of their structural location and the power, privilege, and status that came along with it, middle-class men were viewed as acceptable role models of masculinity for working-poor boys. To some degree, this class- and gender-based approach would have alleviated middle-class fears about boys who threatened the status quo.

Boy workers were expected to model an appropriate masculinity for troubled boys; they were also encouraged to befriend them. It was thought that by developing a relationship with a boy that resembled friendship, the boy worker would better understand his charge's mind. This relationship was informed by postwar psychological discourse. Unlike boy workers in the past, postwar boy workers drew on psychological findings and applied them to pre-delinquent boys. Toronto's Big Brother Movement, for example, encouraged those who worked with "maladjusted boys" to use psychological and psychiatric resources in order to better understand a boy's "mind." It was the *mind* of the pre-delinquent that interested boy workers, since postwar psychology viewed all conduct as the expression of the individual's mental life. A boy worker who developed a relationship with the boy and thereby understood his mind could prevent the boy from becoming a delinquent: "The relationship with the child is most important, as children need to feel you are trying to understand them, to realize the difficulties which caused the problem." Boy workers who failed to understand the mind of the boy in order to help him could cost both the boy and society a great deal: "If such children don't get the help they need at the time they need it then they are likely to end up in Guelph or Kingston."[53]

The nuclear, well-adjusted, "normal" family was seen in the postwar era as the basis for building a secure society and normal boys. Conversely, broken homes and ineffective parents resulted in bad boys. In the *Church Times* of 14 January 1955, Ontario readers would have encountered an article titled "Boys in Trouble: Fruits of Unspeakable Homes." This article reported on research purportedly demonstrating that out of nearly 900 boys in trouble in England, only "twenty-two have had good normal homes."[54] Speaking to the Lakeshore-Etobicoke Neighbourhood Workers District Association in 1956, W.F. Rutledge, a probation officer from the Metropolitan Toronto Juvenile and Family Court, conveyed a similar message about "unspeakable homes" as a cause of delinquency: "One out of three children who appear in Toronto's Juvenile and Family Court as delinquents comes from a broken home."[55] He paraded proof that "homes where there is constant bickering, drunkenness, selfishness and misunderstanding, all contribute to a child's emotional insecurity." Expressing similar sentiments offered up by other child advice experts, he then concluded that it was typically the boy's failure to connect with middle-class institutions such as schools, churches, and the Scouts that contributed to the boy's delinquency: "it is seldom that a child who has a firm connection with his church, school, boys club, or Scouts appears in Juvenile Court."[56] In this sense, the underprivileged boy was routinely targeted as potentially dangerous and as associated with possible criminality.

Parental neglect or indifference was thought to lead to delinquent boys. In 1946, the secretary of the Kitchener recreational council stated baldly: "We can trace every cause of juvenile delinquency right back to parent neglect."[57] Child experts and others routinely scolded parents for ignoring their parental responsibilities. "A delinquent generation of parents is producing a generation of delinquent children," complained one writer in the *Stouffville Tribune* on 17 March 1949. A *Globe and Mail* news item in 1946 drew a direct link between delinquency and parents who were neglectful of their children and who acted indifferent toward them: "There has been a steady growth in recent years in the number of parents who can't be bothered with their children, it is found by educationists in Toronto who report progressively greater evidence in the schools of juvenile delinquency. They attribute the child delinquent problem to adult irresponsibility."[58]

Various editorials in local newspapers warned parents about the dangers of indifference. It was sometimes mothers, more than fathers, who were cited as the parent who caused the most harm to boys through indifference. An article in the *Stouffville Tribune* on 24 November 1960, titled "Who's to Blame?", told readers that "four out of five delinquent boys say their mothers were indifferent to them. Three out of five boys say their fathers were indifferent to them."[59] Yet it wasn't just parental neglect or indifference that was thought to create the conditions for boy delinquency; parents who adopted permissive parenting practices also came under scrutiny.

During the postwar period, "permissive parents" who made few demands on their children (or none) were seen as raising potential delinquents.[60] The loss of a more masculine, authoritarian approach to parenting, one that sought a child's obedience through rigid rules and strict discipline, and the rise of a supposedly feminized (i.e., permissive) approach to parenting, was thought to correlate with boy delinquency. A 1959 editorial in the *Acton Free Press* titled "Raising Delinquents!" took aim at permissive parenting practices by listing twelve rules for parents to follow if they wanted to raise a boy delinquent:

1. Begin with infancy to give the child everything he wants. In this way he will grow up believing the world owes him a living.
2. When he picks up "bad" words or "dirty" words, laugh at him. That will make him think he is cute. He will run off and pick up some other words that will blow the top of your head.
3. Never give him any spiritual training until he is 21 and then let him decide himself. By the same logic never teach him the English language. Maybe when he is old enough he may want to speak Bantu.
4. Praise him in his presence to all the neighbours: show him how much smarter he is than the neighbour's children.

5. Avoid the use of the word "wrong." It may develop in the child a "guilt complex." This may prepare him to believe that when he is punished later for stealing cars or assaulting women, society is "against him" and that he is being "persecuted."

6. Pick up everything after him; his shoes, his books, his clothes. Do everything for him, so that he will be experienced in throwing burdens on others.

7. Let him read everything he wants. Have no concern whatever for what goes into his mind. Provide him with paper cups for his lips, but let his brain drink out of any dirty container for words and ideas.

8. Quarrel frequently in the presence of your children. In this way they will be prepared for broken homes later on.

9. Give him all the spending money he wants; never let him earn his own.

10. Satisfy every craving of the child for food, drinks, and everything that has to do with the sense of taste and touch, gratifying every sensual desire.

11. Take his part against policemen, teachers and neighbours. They are all "prejudiced" against your child.

12. When he gets into real trouble, always defend yourself and say: "I never could do anything with him."[61]

Despite the tongue-in-cheek tone of the editorial, it does gesture toward the idea that "permissive parenting" practices were thought to create feminized, spoiled, delinquent boys who lacked, among other things, the necessary amount of masculine discipline and self-control.

In the late 1940s and 1950s, Ontarians worried about the Cold War and the fragility of world peace. If boys bore the responsibility for ensuring a more peaceful postwar world, it followed that every boy was worth saving. Reflecting the prevailing sentiment in popular postwar discourse was Louise Baker's novel *Snips and Snails* (1953), which tells the story of a female educator in an all-boys school. Here the narrator remarks on the commitment of one of the main characters to the welfare of boys: "So he [Joe Hargrave] is gone. He died saving a boy named Smith. I am glad some way that the boy's name was Smith—Henry Smith ... In a way, this boy is symbolic of all boys, and even in dying, our friend, Joe Hargrave, made the final commitment to his personal philosophy which was that every boy is worthwhile—worth saving."[62]

While adults generally agreed that boys were worth saving, views were mixed on how best to accomplish this task. Some authorities, such as one Brantford judge, "strongly urged the use of corporeal punishment on Bad-Boys."[63] His rationale was straightforward: "Strapping hurts their dignity, it humiliates them."[64] Another Ontario judge suggested that "the sparing of the rod is what is making today's boy" a juvenile delinquent.[65] Some citizens backed the judges' straightforward method of dealing with problem boys. One resident of Toronto believed that the strap, not education or recreation, would save boys: "The way of the transgressor is hard. Bad-Boys should be shown that. One strapping is better than a jail sentence which soon becomes five or ten. Get out the strap and save the boys before they become murderers or hardened, unemployed crooks."[66]

Yet, influenced by the rise of psychologists and mental hygienists, the postwar era saw experts advocating *less* physical punishment.[67] This reflected a steady shift away from fear of punishment as a deterrent to crime and delinquency, toward a greater emphasis on intervention, prevention, rehabilitation, training, and "correction," especially for the very young.[68] More and more postwar experts viewed planned and supervised recreation and education as the best way to build better boys.

Influenced by postwar psychological understandings of childhood development, concerned individuals, churches, and civic organizations encouraged planned recreational and educational means to offset growing problems among urban boys.[69] In 1946, Toronto mayor Robert Saunders responded to concerns about idle boys, promising that "if any district in the city feels like it would like to have a community centre established I can promise that we will inaugurate an immediate study of the possibilities."[70] Church officials echoed similar views. In March 1946, one Roman Catholic official defended "clubs for boys" and announced the "establishment of recreational centers in every Roman Catholic parish where such facilities do not now exist."[71] One mother of a thirteen-year-old problem boy tapped into the same gendered logic: "More recreational centers and competitive sports and hobbies would keep youngsters out of mischief."[72] She went so far as to suggest that new government policy centred on physical activity should be developed in order to prevent boys from going wrong: "Why can't we have a national physical fitness program in Ontario? ... Grants then could be used for organizing games, sports, and competitive hobbies—all wholesome activities that keep a boy so full of enthusiasm and emulative spirit that he just can't get into mischief, let alone get into bad company and go wrong."[73]

The people just quoted supported the postwar assumption that hobbies and competitive recreation were essential to the development of all boys. They were also constructing boyhood as the origin of the character on which an appropriate manhood was to be built. With the right kind of masculine guidance and the right kind of competitive, organized gateways to forge their character, most boys would develop appropriately masculine traits.

Delinquent boyhoods were seen as restricted, as lacking the supervision and opportunities generally afforded boys from stable homes. One worker stated that delinquent acts were simply recreational or normal play activities gone bad: "delinquency is play behaviour ... it satisfies his need for recreational activity."[74] Such a boy "inevitably uses the materials and methods available to him in his efforts to have a good time. And so many specific acts, legally delinquent, become part and parcel of a boy's play life."[75] For Kenneth Rogers, if boys had worthy objectives with reasonable adult interest, or what one postwar critic called "snoop-ervision," then the dangers to the boy and society were lessened; if the boys had neither, then the dangers were increased.[76] This sentiment was reflected in a poem, titled "BOYS," published by the *Evening Telegram* in 1946:

> Boys are doctors in the making, Priests and parsons, too;
>
> One of them will soon be taking Work now given you;
>
> Left to run the streets unheeded, Scorned by you and me,
>
> And denied assistance needed, Boys may hoodlums be;
>
> Boys in gangs are fond of banding,
>
> Rough and loud at play, what they need is understanding, lest they go astray.
>
> Boys are manhood in the shaping Wise or foolish, we,
>
> From this truth there's no escaping. Sow their destiny.[77]

BOY CLUBS: BUILDING CHARACTER CHAMPIONS

After the Great War, social clubs under religious or community leadership had been deemed more crucial for girls than for boys. After the Second World War, public attention was directed more toward boys than girls.[78] Concerned about the idleness and lack of parental supervision associated with poor working-class boyhoods, public-spirited businessmen and others responded to what they saw as a threat to gender by establishing social clubs to strengthen the character of young boys and to make sure they would grow into strong, responsible men. Between the growing fear of social feminization and the belief that restless boys would undermine the social order by turning to crime, boy's club enthusiasts proposed to keep boys actively involved in the "right" kinds of activities that would build decent masculine habits; this would keep them out of trouble and at the same time create useful citizens. One boy worker remarked that boys clubs were "a pleasant, easy and remarkably effective way of getting young boys together and keeping their energies directed into right kinds of activities."[79] Reminiscing about his own boys club past, a one-time member turned pharmacist noted "the club got the kids off the streets … A lot of us might have ended up in dead-end streets had it not been for the club and its activities."[80]

Boy workers established clubs with the dual goals of preventing pre-delinquent boys from sliding into juvenile delinquency and making "better citizens in the future, and to make their community and city a better place to live."[81] Unlike the Boy Scouts, boys clubs targeted boys from underprivileged, working-class neighbourhoods such as the Ealing district in London, Ontario, and the Dovercourt Park area in Toronto. Boys from areas like these were perceived to be the ones "whose environment or personal attitudes might make them easy prey for an unhappy future."[82] A club for boys was proposed for the Dovercourt Park area in the postwar years, with a budget of $350,000—the first of its size in Toronto. It would be designed explicitly to thwart boy delinquency.[83] Toronto businessmen chose the Dovercourt Park area because, with regard to working-class boys, it was considered to have the greatest need in the metropolitan area.[84] Other clubs attempted to provide wholesome masculine guidance to working-class boys. The Trinity K Club of Toronto targeted boys "of an unhealthy environment" who "had little on which to expend their energies and focus their attention." The club's mandate was simple: get "the kids off the street."[85] Similarly, the Metropolitan Church in Toronto was engaged in a "good deal of careful and quiet work" for "many of the young boys [who] were formerly on the streets."[86]

The Cold War challenged notions that the future was safe and secure. If boys were guided, controlled, and provided with the proper masculine moral training during their formative, character-building years, there would be little fear that they (and, by extension, society) would go wrong afterwards. "Our main purpose is character building," said Robert Shaw, associate regional director for the central area of Boys Clubs of Canada. The clubs' philosophy was based on the "premise that each person has the potential of a good and useful life, with the rewards of satisfaction and happiness."[87] Stated alternatively, if society's future depended on stable, "healthy" men, then society needed to build stable "healthy" boys. Toronto businessman W. Harold Rea, president of Canadian Oil Companies and supporter of clubs for boys, perhaps put the matter best: "Building better boys is better than mending men."[88]

Boys clubs emphasized social responsibility and good citizenship. "To make better citizens in the future, and to make their community and city a better place to live," was how one club summarized its aims.[89] Some clubs in London, Ontario, boasted that "many a London boy has learned to be a better citizen."[90] The clubs' aim of building good citizens carried weight throughout the postwar years. In 1958, the executive director of the Boys Clubs of Canada determined that such programs were essential for building "better citizens."[91]

But which definition of citizenship was being used, and which methods were applied to inculcate this concept?

Good citizenship meant physically fit, dutiful, honest, selfless, obedient citizens, built through sports and hobbies. Two London boys clubs, created primarily "with an eye toward good citizenship," provided boys with opportunities for "hobby and sports education."[92] Echoing the familiar postwar sentiment, the sponsors of this group felt that "clubs are the best possible training in citizenship."[93] In 1954 the National Film Board produced a documentary, *Police Club for Boys*, about Montreal police captain Ovila Pelletier's work with working-class boys.[94] A few years earlier, an April 1949 issue of *Saturday Night* had featured Pelletier, who when questioned on how to turn working-class boys into good citizens, mentioned athletics as the answer. By providing boys who had few if any leisure options with opportunities to learn, play, and watch competitive team sports, he gave them a "pleasing and acceptable alternative to delinquent behaviours."[95] Pelletier explained: "so long as the slums are crowded ... there will be boys getting into trouble. But the club program opens up wide avenues of hope."[96] Pelletier got close to 5,000 boys aged ten to eighteen off the streets by organizing thirty-three hockey clubs and an assortment of other sports teams.[97] But when journalist Miriam Chapin raised questions around gender equality with Captain Pelletier—"What about the girls?"—he employed a patriarchal discourse that was both dismissive and condescending: "Well, you know ... if we get the boys out of the alleys, those girls, they will go home and knit, and that will make me very happy."[98]

The view that good citizenship was built through sports was partly a response to growing concerns about passivity among boys. Vernon F. McAdam, executive director of the Boys Clubs of Canada, captured this sentiment in 1958: "Non-participation and spectator sports are the curse in modern day living and we fully recognize the need for active participation by our young people in all types of programs that will make them better citizens."[99] To counter what psychoanalyst Marynia Farnham, writer Ferdinand Lundberg, and others saw as the postwar "mass production" of "passive weaklings,"[100] the Columbus Boys Club in Toronto, like many other clubs, provided a gymnasium and male counselors as well as a summer camp to enable countless boys "to take the first wavering steps leading from the innocence of boyhood to the destiny of manhood."[101] Organizers of the 1960 campaign to raise $350,000 for the St. Albans Boys Club, a new facility for boys, promoted the fact that the facilities would "include a swimming pool, a gymnasium with portable stage and boxing ring, a recreation room, a library," where boys from crowded homes could congregate.[102] Police Chief Earl Jack of Dundas, Ontario, an organizer of a police-affiliated boys club, stated matter-of-factly: "We subscribe strongly to the old maxim, Keep boys busy and you keep them out of trouble."[103] And keeping boys busy and off the streets was a year-long commitment. The police chief and other concerned citizens of Dundas worked hard to keep boys occupied all year round with various sports: "lacrosse, baseball, softball or swimming in the summer," then "hockey sticks and a place to play in the winter." And "for those boys who did not like hockey there was basketball."[104] The enthusiasm for boys clubs as particular sites for regulating boyhood in a way that made a boy's physicality central to an "ideal" boyhood did not necessarily vanish as the postwar period ended. In 1960, for example, a boys club was formed in Newmarket, Ontario. Guided and led by a local pro wrestler, the club's purpose was to foster interest in physical training among boys, which according to one social commentator, was "a much-needed Canadian interest."[105] Boy training throughout the postwar period centred largely on the physical. In this sense, a prominent feature of the postwar politics of masculinity led boys clubs to create homosocial spaces where boys, separated from women and girls and under male guidance, could engage in masculinity-building activities, which often promoted the development of physical strength, competition and, to some measure, violence.

The difference between bad boys and good citizens was considered small enough to be bridged by physical activity. One news item, "Boy Proud of Distinction: 'Worst in Neighborhood,'" featured boy workers "reclaiming lives of some Toronto children who were potential gangsters and convicts."[106] The story focused on one working-class twelve-year-old "Bad-Boy." In keeping with the gender ideology of the time, he was described as having a "fine physique, with a quick eye and quickly responsive muscles"; but like most bad boys, he was also imagined as having "excessive bravado" and as taking "great pride in his notoriety." The boy in the story seemed to already possess the masculine attributes that could be exploited by boy workers to build "upstanding" citizens who could be entrusted with the promise and hope of the future. The problem was that he had them in excess. Clearly, this boy needed to develop self-control and masculine respect. The solution for reclaiming the boy was straightforward—basketball. Boy workers quickly arranged with the local YMCA recreation officials to enrol him in a basketball program; soon the bad boy became known as the best basketball player in the community. The message for turning a bad boy good was simple: take one bad boy, apply a healthy dose of athletics, and you had, according to many postwar commentators, the "makings of a real citizen."[107]

Through contrived masculinity fables such as this one, charity organizations encouraged the notion that good citizenship for boys was best developed through physical activities like boxing. One story about the masculinizing process, under the headline "Boys Made Good Citizens," told of a working-class thirteen-year-old named Eddie, who was redirected from a shabby boyhood to his destiny of successful manhood. "This is not the old traditional form of rags to riches or sinner to saint," the author wrote. "It's far more conservative than that, dealing simply with most ordinary, yet awesome, process whereby a boy becomes a man."[108] Eddie was thought to be headed in the wrong direction: "He was never what you'd call angelic. He quite often got into the middle of the rough-and–tumble activities that are the heritage of all boys." Having established the essentialist discourse on boyhood, the text made the logical leap: boxing was the solution to Eddie's problems. After being placed in a boys club that provided young males with sports programs, crafts, and vocational training, all under close adult male guidance, Eddie as a result of his "sportsmanship and sporting prowess" in the boxing ring "[was] no longer considered a problem, but a pride." Like the quintessential bad boy, Eddie was thought to have excessive boyish energy and uncontrollable impulsive masculine aggression. By learning to box, he mastered his emotions and developed self-control. To some measure, Eddie had been normalized. In the end, he had learned that to be the right kind of man, he did not have to extinguish such traits, but to control them and direct them to a useful purpose. "He's O.K. now. He'll soon be a man," reassured the text.[109]

Clubs for boys were built on supervised, physical action. In 1945, parents and the presidents of two home and school boys clubs visited the Chesley Avenue Public School in London, Ontario, for a public display of boys' work. There, they saw four boys engaging in "fisticuffs" and "slamming punch for punch."[110] This pugnacious display of masculine vigour and masculinity reportedly stole the show. Two new boys groups were founded in London in 1946 with the stated purposes of getting boys moving and providing them with every opportunity for sports.[111] Even for very young boys, attention to a more physical curriculum was emphasized. A 1954 photograph on the front page of the *Globe and Mail* was full of smiling five-year-old boys participating in the first annual physical demonstration held in the John Innes Community Centre in Toronto.[112] The triumphal masculine tone, central to constructing a traditional yet also collective corporate and military masculinity, was evoked by the "army" of boys naked from the waist up, with arms raised in the air and muscles flexed. The accompanying text labelled the young boys an "Athletic Army of 5-year-olds."[113] Given the significant emphasis on athleticism, it is no wonder that job advertisements for boy workers deemed it "essential" that the successful candidate have a background in "physical education."[114] Most boy workers would have suggested that action was essential to the development of normal boys and, indeed, that it was enough to keep boys out of trouble and mischief and thereby create responsible citizens.

One postwar academic study noted that "approximately one in nine persons in Canada is a postwar immigrant."[115] Not surprisingly, then, boys clubs also promoted themselves as vehicles to "build better Canadians" among immigrant boys through proper training and supervision. In January 1950 a fourteen-year-old boy from an immigrant family won the YMCA's Gold Merit Award, which was, according to one news item, "tantamount" to making him "Toronto's Boy of the Year."[116] John Halcrow, executive secretary of the branch, regarded this boy as symbolic of all that was good in parental training and as an outstanding example of what could be accomplished by "people from other lands who become properly assimilated as Canadians."[117] The downtown Kiwanis Club provided many of Toronto's working-class and immigrant parents with "20,000,000 worry-free minutes"; it also offered experienced instructors for boys to "[sop] up citizenship" while playing basketball or other sports. Governed by the motto, "We Build"—later expanded to "We Build Better Canadians"—the Kiwanis Club promoted the notion that immigrants should not view learning the language as a "bar to physical and mental improvement."[118] Efforts by organizations such as the YMCA to make "better Canadians" of newcomers were not simply benevolent gestures toward a population perceived to be in need of assistance. In a time marked by insecurities and anxieties, institutions strove to regulate and normalize the identities of newcomers in ways that would align them with white, middle-class, Anglo-Protestant ideals.

Boys clubs sought to occupy poor working-class boys' idle time. One 1946 newspaper reported how summer craft classes had taken children off Toronto's streets and "instead of being labeled neighbourhood mischief makers the youngsters are learning to do something constructive."[119] In the immediate postwar period, others echoed these same sentiments: "For several years Toronto's 50 Vacation Church Schools ... have provided a pleasant and educational environment for children. The program was designed mainly to keep the youngsters off the streets during a portion of the summer holidays and has been enthusiastically welcomed especially by parents who live in the crowded downtown areas."[120]

Other male officials believed firmly that supervised recreation was the answer to the problem of juvenile delinquency. "Juvenile Delinquency? No, sir, not in Whitby,"[121] claimed an Ontario police chief, who proudly and publicly noted that the boys in his town were "too busy finding their fun the right way in supervised sport with the Whitby Minor Athletic Association" to partake in delinquent behaviour.[122] The police chief quantified this success with statistics: "This town of some 4,600 population [has] 268 boys between the ages of 7 and 18 years of age who are playing hockey on the 18 teams in the association league. In the summer it's softball, and every boy plays whether he's a star performer or just a lad who wants to have a bit of fun."[123]

These clubs occupied and regulated boys' idle time with the goal of correcting delinquency and moulding them into productive, responsible democratic citizens. One club claimed that "thousands of Toronto youth" might have turned to depravity and crime had they not chosen to spend their leisure time within the organization.[124] In July 1946, the leader of the Toronto Metropolitan boys band publicly and proudly mentioned that none of the more than 100 boys he had trained had appeared in juvenile court.[125] An Ontario probation officer, who saw boys clubs as a way to "nip" boy delinquency in the bud, expressed a similar mindset regarding the value of boys clubs: "Juvenile court records show that no youngster with a membership in a boys club has ever been in trouble."[126]

At the turn of the previous century, boy workers had generally held low expectations for boys, hoping that at best they would develop into modestly productive citizens, if virtues such as obedience were instilled in them through mundane activities such as carpentry and craftwork.[127] In terms of boy workers' expectations of working-class boys, little had changed by the postwar period. In this sense, boys club organizers and boy workers in postwar Ontario generally set their aims and objectives for boys at a fairly low level, promoting the use of unimaginative methods to get boys off the street. To engage young boys, the Mimico Boys Hobbycrafts Club, like many boys clubs, promoted activities categorized as hobby crafts, with men volunteering to work with boys: "110 boys each week with 13 Mimico men acting as volunteer instructors wood work, leatherwork, airplane construction, sheet metal work and plaster moulding."[128] Similarly, Toronto's Columbus Boys Club publicly boasted having 125 to 150 boys a night at the club after school or in the evening to learn a bit about "printing, photography, plastic moulding or other handicrafts."[129] A boys club in Brampton, Ontario, established a hobby shop where boys could "spend their leisure hours making lamps, letter boxes and other handy articles."[130] All of this indicates that many who were engaged in boy work saw idleness as the parent vice; but they also hoped to train boys—in particular working-class boys—in some form of hands-on labour in order to build "better men." "The where to go and what to do winter nights for 300 Mimico boys during the last three years, the Mimico Boys Hobbycrafts Club has concluded another successful season of making models and moulding men."[131]

Ontario boys clubs offered activities such as carpentry, plaster moulding, and leather working—skills that did little to fill the growing demand for white-collar workers in an increasingly bureaucratic Ontario but that were good preparation for the labouring classes. Excluded from boys clubs were activities that might develop white-collar skills. This points to the derogatory assumptions and low expectations that boy workers held regarding the abilities and future occupations of Ontario's working-class boys. Besides maintaining class hierarchies, boys clubs attempted to regenerate men's responsibility to take their "natural" positions as leaders of boys. Boys, as noted previously, were a man's business.

MALE GUIDANCE

Adults lamented the destruction of Canada's finest "young manhood" during the Second World War.[132] As one writer in 1945 put it: "For many bitter years the flower of our country's manhood marched valiantly into the ever demanding jaws of the war machine. Thousands of these gallant youths were devoured and lost."[133] It was thought that with the loss of men came the loss of manhood; in turn, this morphed into concern about the welfare of boys. Without appropriate examples of masculinity, how would boys learn to be men? Without fathers or proper masculine guidance, who would ensure that boys acquired a proper masculinity? The absentee father, be he dead or still posted overseas, became a concern within popular discourse. In 1944 the Toronto police and the Kiwanis Club jointly organized a club for 15 boys whose fathers were overseas. "They didn't have any playground and were headed for trouble until the police and the Kiwanis joined hands to give the boys a break." In this instance, boy workers outfitted the police garage at the Dundas Street West station; it was reported that boys from 7 to 15 "flocked to join." In keeping with normative understandings of gender activities, boys were supervised and instructed in "baseball, swimming, crafts, hockey; sports of every kind got going."[134]

Social commentators adopted the prevailing postwar belief that a male presence in a boy's life could serve as a corrective to delinquency. A 1948 *Globe and Mail* article explored a week in the lives of Toronto's Beanery Boys, a local gang. The reporter offered readers this recommendation with regard to the development and redemption of boys: "But as bad as they are, I believe some of these kids can be salvaged and attracted to decent forms of recreation … If a club could be set up, under the direction of a man whom they respect, it might provide at least a partial solution."[135] The postwar idea that all boys required a masculine presence in their lives was reiterated in countless ways. A photograph in the *Toronto Daily Star* on 12 February 1951 depicted a large group of fathers standing on the side of a snowy hill with arms raised high in a celebratory pose; at their feet sat their "jubilant" sons. The 40 fathers and sons were part of the annual Toronto West End Fathers and Sons Club weekend, billed as a father's "return to childhood in the wilds."[136] Reflecting typical psychological assumptions about the importance of fathers in boys' lives, the club's primary purpose was to "cultivate fathers' interest in their sons."[137] Undergirding father-and-son clubs, such as this one, was the assumption that men and boys needed to retreat to the "wilds," away from feminizing influences, in order to create spiritually and physically based homosocial rituals that would collectively rejuvenate and re-establish masculine bonds.[138] This bond was best established through physical, adventurous action in the wilds. Skiing, hiking, and tobogganing were all on the curriculum.[139]

Postwar attempts to rejuvenate patriarchy fostered the belief that women, and men in professions perceived as feminized, were not the right people to mould a boy's character. Instead, athletic men were seen as the ideal models of masculinity which boys were encouraged to emulate.

> When a man becomes a leader in sports he has a great following among the boys. They follow his daily doings with eager interest. They imitate his game, his clothes, his speech. He is their hero and there is nothing but good in him to their idea ... Their lives become standards for the generation who follow every movement they make and imitate it in their lives ... Mothers, teachers, clergymen have no such attraction.[140]

Strengthening the assumption that adult male athletes best enabled boys were postwar media depictions replete with references to relationships between adult sportsmen and boys. A photograph in the *Globe and Mail* on 26 April 1946 shows George Straith, a star forward on the Victoria basketball team, presenting awards to four young boys who participated in the Kiwanis YMCA three-day sports meet.[141] A May 1948 photo from the same paper shows Bud Poile, of the Toronto Maple Leafs and Chicago Black Hawks, visiting the Scarborough Lions Club to present athletic awards to three young boys.[142] Citations like these reveal the explicit use of the boys club venue as a gender-appropriate setting for transmitting masculinity from older to younger men, primarily through personal example.

An abundance of textual and visual depictions of clean-cut, well-groomed, mostly middle-class white men volunteering and supervising boys of all ages furthered the notion that building better boys was men's business. In 1946, one group of London service clubs, operating under the slogan "Friend-of-the-boy," boasted a membership of "80 business and professional men in this city."[143] Most boys clubs relied heavily on community-minded professional men to supervise boys. The Mimico Hobbycrafts Club for boys boasted thirteen prominent Mimico men as volunteer instructors.[144] Social commentators deemed poor working-class boys to be in need of constant, wholesome, masculine supervision. "Every minute that the boys spent in the clubrooms under the careful surveillance of Bob Strain meant that they were gaining valuable knowledge and were free from bad influences of the street," one news item related.[145] Underprivileged boys from fatherless families were likely in need of "careful surveillance" and appropriate male guidance. In 1945, Nelson McEwen, national boys work secretary of the Canadian YMCA, told members at a father-and-son banquet that boys "needed the help of the experience of older men." He further urged "fathers to unite with their sons" in carrying out boys work programs.[146] The idea that working-class boys required the guidance of middle-class professional men was rendered visible in a 1948 photograph in the *Evening Telegram* that featured a Newsboys Welfare Association executive encircled by young boys listening in rapt attention. The accompanying text described how the executive volunteered his time to hold a weekly basketball clinic with the young boys. The aim, the clinic noted, was to "keep[] the kids off the streets by getting them onto a basketball court."[147] Other public-spirited men ensured that boys clubs were adequately funded to provide recreation for a "real boy's boy": "Now that June is busting out all over and boys will soon be doing the same, a group of Toronto men have joined forces to campaign for a club where the exciting energies of boyhood can be harnessed in a hundred wonderful ways. It will be a club for the real boy's boy, with swimming pool, gymnasium, library and workshop."[148]

In 1947 in London, Ontario, businessman Harry Brennan, proprietor of the London House, was publicly recognized for making the biggest donation to the London Police Boys Club.[149] The same year in the same city, businessmen and professionals were lauded for raising $13,500 to convert the Oxford Street Armoury into a permanent headquarters for boys work activities.[150] In July 1946, Toronto's Ward Two Business Men's Association held its annual carnival; part of the proceeds went to community boys work programs.[151] The *London Free Press* on 17 January 1946 ran a front-page headline about future plans for a "Boys Village," which was to be constructed on a seven-acre plot in East London. The project's estimated cost, $75,000, would be funded by an endowment of $360,000 left to the Salvation Army by wealthy Londoner, Albert McGarvey, for the specific purpose of constructing a boys home. Boys clubs often relied on large donations from well-heeled men; some boys clubs, however, were supported by male, working-class organizations.[152] The Labour Council of London, a body entirely comprised of male delegates from the Canadian Labour Congress, financed and supported local boys clubs. Its stated aim was to support and "assist in the leisure-time education of sons of working classes."[153] Funding came from other sources as well, such as newspapers, which gave generously to boys work programs. Hoping that others would emulate its financial support of the community, the *Globe and Mail* donated funds in 1956 to build a swimming pool at one Toronto Boys Club.[154] The paper made much of its own generosity by repeatedly publishing accounts of the donation. It received accolades from boy workers, who noted that "there is nothing more important than boys' work." [155] The donation for the pool was also meant to inculcate and demonstrate the postwar emphasis on selflessness, collectivity, and male togetherness, all of these, however, contained within a patriarchal world view: "A gift to boys of a swimming pool for their club is an example of enlightened democracy … This large contribution is a Father's Day gift in reverse. But it is right and proper that fathers should give to sons and men should give to boys. For if the time should ever come that adult men stopped giving then boys too, in their turn, would grow up to think only of themselves."[156]

Boys clubs also received donations from unusual sources. In Ottawa, a twenty-four-year-old man on trial for murder testified that having a shabby boyhood caused his crime.[157] The revelation prompted one juror to donate his jury fees to the Ottawa Boys Club, which, he said, "does much to keep young boys off the street."[158] Such items strengthened the notion that building the right kind of boys was a matter for all men.

In the immediate postwar years, some boys clubs received support from national and local police forces. In 1946 the RCMP cooperated with local police forces in Canada to help support local Kiwanis boys clubs—a practice that at the time was viewed as a "radical departure" from traditional RCMP activities.[159] The RCMP believed that during boyhood, boys were under "perpetual evolution and subject to many influences which mark progress along the road of life."[160] Accordingly, the RCMP sought to influence young boys early in their boyhood years to prevent them from becoming future delinquents. The idea was that the respect and admiration the boys learned to hold for "their friends in the police uniform" promised a new understanding on the part of Toronto's future citizens. The RCMP also hoped that young boys would idolize the officers while internalizing the "ideal" masculinity. The RCMP "with its force of clean-cut young constables" told the boys stories of thrilling adventures they encountered in the course of their work.[161] Other methods were used to inculcate boys into a Mountie masculinity, such as singsongs and sporting contests, as well as viewing "good exciting films" such as *Making a Mountie*.[162] Of course, behind the glamorous image of the Canadian Mountie stood a narrow ideal of traditional masculine character rooted in "Anglo-Saxon superiority" and "'proper' deportment."[163] Certainly the image of a physically fit, refined, muscular, strong, pure, aggressive, and youthful Anglo-Saxon Mountie masculinity would have served as a productive vehicle for those adults hoping to put forward ideals to which young boys, in particular boys from working-poor, immigrant communities, could look up to in order to build an "appropriate" masculinity.

CONCLUSION

By the close of the 1950s, organizations to prevent delinquency and offer boys male guidance were still thought necessary. With the news that Russia had successfully launched Sputnik, coupled with the emergence of mass technologies such as television, some adults perceived a greater need for boys clubs than in the past. The world was becoming too complicated and perhaps too dangerous for boys to be without some form of steady masculine guidance. In 1958, Canadian Nobel Peace Prize recipient and future Prime Minister of Canada Lester B. Pearson noted when he was young there had been less need for Big Brother organizations to provide companionship to fatherless boys: "Life was much simpler and not complicated by the sputniks, television and high powered motors with that extra ounce of strength."[164] In light of increasing anxieties emanating from the Cold War, Pearson's anti-modernist comment reflected both a yearning for a simpler, pre-modern past and the notion that more fatherless boys were in need of masculine guidance. Others saw the main purpose of boys clubs as training and building manly boys. In November 1968, one distraught mother wrote to the *Globe and Mail's* advice columnist that her son had too much female companionship, that he "dresses dolls" and "plays house with girls." The columnist drew on the heavily retailed gender ideology of the postwar period: "Get your boy into a boys club … where he will be among male companions and where he will learn how to be manly."[165]

By the 1960s, a shift was occurring in society's attitude toward boys clubs. The notion that boys required more male guidance appeared to be in decline. If large clubs were to be built, they should be promoted for boys *and* girls. This was, perhaps, symbolic of a loosening of traditional gender roles and a diminishing of the postwar preoccupation with boys. In 1964, for example, when a new recreation club in Scarborough Township was built (cost: $400,000), it was promoted for both girls and boys.[166] Another notable development was the decline of small, informal, community-based clubs for boys of the sort that had littered the landscape during the 1940s and 1950s. There is little evidence that the public taste for organizing and running these clubs survived the 1960s. Formal boys club programs still generated moderate enthusiasm. In 1965, the national president of Boys Clubs of Canada stated, perhaps somewhat disingenuously, that the movement "has never been healthier"; he also noted that there had been a slight increase in the number of boys clubs across Canada.[167] Notwithstanding his claims, the evidence suggests otherwise. The Toronto Metropolitan Optimists Boys Club had received $4,000 in government funding annually since 1930; but it received only $2,000 in May 1967, and in 1968 it received none.[168] This lack of financial support may reflect a weakening enthusiasm for Boys Clubs as the 1960s progressed. Why the change in support for boys clubs? Although a deep explanation of the change lies outside the scope of this work, it is worth noting that the decline in support for boys clubs can be read as a by-product of changing social and economic circumstances in Ontario as well as a sharp change in gender relations. As fears and anxieties lessened as the postwar years progressed, male anxieties around the status of boys also diminished.

But anxieties and concerns about boys and boyhood did not end after the postwar era. As I will discuss in the next chapter, heightened male anxieties and intensified concerns about the status of boys, boyhood, and masculinity have reappeared again today.

Changes and Continuities: Historic and Contemporary Boyhood Ideals

5

Looking over the postwar years, it is not hard to see this period as something of a familiar story: concerns about boyhood ran alongside a broader "crisis" in masculinity. Once again, concerns about the status of boyhood have emerged front and centre in the gendered landscape of public discourse. Once again, the idea of boyhood is being used by social commentators, journalists, psychologists, and child experts to shore up patriarchy, thus revealing deep insecurities, ambivalences, and fears about the shifting gender roles in our own current context. Once again, public defenders of patriarchy have cast boys as the new second sex, as disadvantaged in what they imagine to be an increasingly hostile and feminized society. Margaret Wente, a *Globe and Mail* columnist, lauding the emergence of the hugely popular "boy book," *The Dangerous Book for Boys*, noted that this text "has come at an ideal cultural moment," when boys are being disadvantaged by an overly "protective" and "feminized" society.[1] The Iggulden brothers, co-authors of *The Dangerous Book for Boys*, seem to have written the book as a manly riposte to the perceived feminized world in general, and feminists in particular: "The feminist onslaught of the past 30 years," Conn Iggulden notes, "was good for women but bad for us."[2]

Much like during the postwar period, when traditional patriarchal values were threatened by historical developments such as shifts in the labour market, today there exists a hostile tone toward feminism, again due to historical developments such as globalization, economic deregulation, deindustrialization, the proliferation of queer identities, changing immigration patterns, women's emergence as primary breadwinners in Canadian families, and the partial eclipse of the traditional definition of marriage.[3] In the current cultural milieu, the remarkable outpouring of concern over the fate and fitness of Canadian masculinity has once again caused a loose coalition of social commentators, including journalists, educators, academics, media pundits, psychologists, novelists, magazine editors, church groups, and even online readers, to become preoccupied with the idea of boyhood.

This final chapter of *Ontario Boys* explores the current public preoccupation with the idea of boyhood by examining the rhetoric encountered in popular discourses surrounding and emerging from today's "crisis" in masculinity. It then looks at how these particular discourses have run alongside contemporary discussions of boyhood. It also briefly engages with current debates over boys' education. It concludes by arguing that in their quest "to return to normal," a growing number of social commentators, writers, and others have once again projected their gendered fears of the future onto discussions of boyhood development. And, similar to their postwar counterparts, today's social commentators are once again producing patriarchal, heteronormative definitions of masculinity and routinely offering up their version of an ideal boyhood to the Ontario public.

TODAY'S 'CRISIS' IN MASCULINITY: A FAMILIAR RING?

The idea that masculinity is in "crisis" has been expressed, fortified, and legitimated in a number of recent books. Hanna Rosin's much reviewed and talked about *The End of Men and the Rise of Women* (2012), Liza Mundy's *The Richer Sex: How the New Majority of Female Breadwinners Is Transforming Sex, Love, and Family* (2012); and to a lesser extent Kay Hymowitz's *Manning Up: How the Rise of Women Has Turned Men into Boys* (2011) have all argued that women and girls today are now dominant socially and economically.[4] Rosin, Mundy, and Hymowitz are not alone in suggesting that men and boys are disadvantaged in light of what Hymowitz describes as the "radical reversal of the sexual hierarchy,"[5] which has created, in her words, a "New Girl Order."[6] The current gender trouble surrounding men and masculinity has also prompted some academics to produce texts that claim that the new world order is a matriarchy. Prominent books in this genre include Harvey Mansfield's *Manliness* (2006); Roy Baumeister's *Is There Anything Good about Men? How Cultures Flourish by Exploiting Men* (2010); and David Benatar's *The Second Sexism: The Discrimination Against Men and Boys* (2012).[7] There do exist differences between the viewpoints expressed in these books, but they all agree that males are now disadvantaged. Ignoring the structural and systemic privileges that men as a group hold in the current gender order, this backlash politics of masculinity presents the simplistic idea that men and boys are currently victims of an increasingly "feminized" world.

As I have argued elsewhere, the news media have contributed to current anxieties over gender and gender relations.[8] Here are a few examples of news items that have helped fuel current cultural concerns over men and masculinity: "Are Men Being Robbed of Their Masculinity";[9] "What's the

Matter with Men?";[10] "Is the Alpha Male in Danger of Extinction?";[11] "Men Are Redundant";[12] "Men of Extinction: Forget the Whales: It's Time to Save the Males";[13] "Y Chromosome Could Be an Endangered Species";[14] "World's Males Are Under Siege";[15] "Humanity at Risk: Are the Males Going First?";[16] "Death of the Traditional Man";[17] "Manly Men Take a Beating";[18] "Lament for the Days of Manly Men";[19] "Real Men Reeling";[20] "Macho Man to Become Evolutionary Footnote."[21] The July–August 2010 issue of *The Atlantic* had as its cover story "The End of Men: How Women Are Taking Control—of Everything."[22] As I have pointed out elsewhere, drawing on a now familiar patriarchal discourse, the author of the article implicitly suggests that women in general and feminists in particular are to blame for men's malaise.[23] In short, much as happened in the postwar period, significant social, political, and economic changes have once again incited anxieties over the meaning of an "appropriate" Canadian masculinity.

The prevailing discourse shaping the current debate over the meaning of Canadian masculinity suggests that, in the face of the perceived feminization of society, men have lost sight of their assumed "male core." Columnist Christie Blatchford, for example, wrote in the *National Post* in December 2011 that Toronto's men had become feminized, creating a city full of "sissies": "I am wearying of the male as delicate creature. I am wearying of men who are so frequently in touch with their feminine side they … have lost sight of the masculine."[24] The "decline of the male" discourse has been shaped by the conservative men's movement, for which the "crisis in masculinity" is a fundamental component. That discourse, which has made considerable efforts to restore traditional understandings of gender, holds that Canadian men have been emasculated.

For some, the supposed emasculation of Canadian men "has led to the decaying of our cultural muscularity, leaving modern Canadian men limp, whiny, and nostalgic":[25] "When did men become such a bunch of whiners? … It's all part of the wimpification and metrosexualization of the modern man. I never thought I'd hear myself saying this, but I'm starting to pine for the silent, stoic men of yesteryear."[26] This seems to be what an 9 October 2009 editorial in the *Kingston Whig-Standard*, titled "Our Descent into Wimpiness," was pointing at when it complained that Canada had become a land of wimps: "Our once manly and vigorous country—made up of hewers of wood and drawers of water having dominion o'er the land sea to sea, the true north strong and free, home of the coureurs de bois and Sergeant Preston of the Yukon—has descended into a hand-wringing, chattering class of complainers, whiners and wimps."[27]

Likewise, on 11 January 2012 the *Hamilton Spectator* published an article provocatively titled "What's Wrong with Men Today?" Situated in the "crisis in masculinity" discourse, the article starts by unfavourably comparing today's "feminized men" with more seemingly masculine men from the past. In the past, the article suggests, men were real men because they were allowed to be in the company of other real men, engaging in traditional masculine pursuits: "Men of previous generations lived among themselves. They were raised in the shadows of fathers and grandfathers. They went to war. They worked shoulder to shoulder in relative isolation. They spent evenings with each other in seedy bars or men's clubs smoking cigars, drinking the hard stuff, swearing, fighting, watching and listening."[28]

What is fascinating here is what is absent. In the view presented above there is no recognition of the cyclical nature of crises in masculinity, no awareness that concerns over the feminization of men stretch back over a century and emerge as a response to changing social, political, and economic circumstances. Nor is there any recognition that the older version of masculinity as presented and mythologized likely never existed in the way they imagine. Yet in the body of the article, the answer to the initial question—what's wrong with men today?— is supplied. The answer, according to the article, is women: "Over the past few generations, men have been in the company of women. They feel comfortable there. But they're not learning how to be men there ... It takes men to bring up men." The result of being in the company of women, the article concludes, is that today's "men have become very feminized."[29] If masculinity is in "decline" or in "crisis," it is women's fault, so the argument goes. The solution to the problem, at least according to many conservative commentators, is, in part, to establish more male only contexts, where men can once again be men with other men.

Fuelling much of the "male crisis" discourse has been the conservative men's movement,[30] which arose in the late 1980s and had risen to some prominence by the early 1990s. Inspired by the work of mythopoet Robert Bly and his essentialist assumptions about masculinity, the conservative men's movement perceives the values currently privileged in our society and institutions as opposite to the values that are intrinsic in being male. According to this view, men and boys are dysfunctional, unsuccessful, and unhappy because they have lost touch with and have been denied their "essential maleness." Central to this argument is the call for males to rediscover and reclaim their "lost masculinity." The conservative men's movement promotes the belief that in order for men to restore their lost masculinity, they (and boys) need to retreat to male-only spaces where they can reassert their deep, essential masculinity. This line of thought blames women in general and feminists in particular for men's and boys' malaise. It argues that women have little to offer boys in terms of securing an appropriate masculine identity, simply because women cannot know the "deep masculine" and thus cannot develop properly a boy's sense of identity. The conservative men's movement, with its underlying hostility toward feminism and its reassertion of essentialized, unchanging, and mythologized masculine values, holds that it is women who have caused the emasculation of today's males.

All of this reflects the views of a number of male commentators today. In a 2006 *Maclean's* article, conservative writer Marc Steyn suggested that the widespread erosion of manliness in Canadian men had contributed to the 1989 Montreal Massacre during which fourteen women at École Polytechnique were murdered by a single male. "Ignoring how misogyny is central to dominant forms of hegemonic heteronormative masculinity and how this in turn influences violence against women and girls by men and boys, Steyn blamed feminists for supposedly 'weakening' Canadian masculinity."[31] This development, according to Steyn, had prevented the males present at the school's massacre from stopping the killer:

> Yet the defining image of contemporary Canadian maleness is not M Lepine/Gharbi but the professors and the men in that classroom, who, ordered to leave by the lone gunman, meekly did so, and abandoned their female classmates to their fate—an act of abdication that would have been unthinkable in almost any other culture throughout human history. The "men" stood outside in the corridor and, even as they heard the first shots, they did nothing. And, when it was over and Gharbi walked out of the room and past them, they still did nothing. Whatever its other defects, Canadian manhood does not suffer from an excess of testosterone.[32]

In a similar vein, in the *National Post* on 10 December 2011, a male letter writer from Orangeville, Ontario, blamed the fourteen murders at École Polytechnique on today's supposedly feminized males. He argued that real men "would have tried to stop" the mass murderer, Marc Lepine:

> Let's get real: One man alone did this heinous crime in Montreal ... What is not talked about is an important cultural change since the 1960s: The feminization of young men. That is why no male student was man enough to attempt to stop this murderous rampage on that horrible day in Montreal ... Any one of the young men on hand that day at École Polytechnique should have attempted to stop Marc Lepine's murderous rampage. But no male in the engineering class did, as in more modern times, this demanding and gender-biased motif has fallen into desuetude, usurped by a touchy-feely, unmanly, unchivalrous politically correct mush. That is the real shame of this massacre—and of our times.[33]

Unfortunately, this correspondent from Orangeville comes no closer than Steyn to offering a more critical view of gender relations, for he too fails to consider how dominant, patriarchal models of violent (white) masculinity contributed to the horrific events of 6 December 1989. Only when we consider the norms of heteronormative hegemonic masculinity and how they legitimate, fortify, and naturalize male violence against women, girls, and other men and boys do we begin to see the real problem in contemporary gender relations.

But there is more to understanding the supposed "crisis in masculinity" than simply linking it to the rise of the conservative men's movement. The current perceived "crisis in masculinity" also needs to be understood in relation to the changing economic, social, and cultural conditions of a post-industrial neoliberal world order. That order has allowed a small group of corporate-class white men to secure tremendous power and privilege; it has also led to an assault on women as a group.[34] To situate the current politics of masculinity, then, we must briefly theorize the current political context and examine the economic and social project of neoliberalism.

Neoliberalism as a political philosophy has been adopted by a number of governments and international institutions around the world, including in Canada.[35] According to Noam Chomsky, neoliberalism is a system of principles that is both new and based on classical liberal ideas that have been credited to Adam Smith.[36] The basic rules of neoliberalism, Chomsky tells us, are these: liberalize trade through free trade agreements; deregulate various sectors, including the financial sector; let markets set prices; and emphasize privatization.[37] Key to all of this is the idea that governments should simply get out of the way and allow what Michael Apple calls the "eloquent fiction" of the free market to rule.[38] For workers, neoliberal globalization has resulted in significant "efforts to eliminate labour organizations, increase corporate profitability, generate deep cuts to social programs, induce massive layoffs, and create perpetual demands for wage and benefit cuts, and work to eliminate decent jobs in favour of low paying precarious employment."[39] Moreover, according to sociologist Alan Sears, persistent neoliberal "attacks on union bargaining rights and the increased brutality of the law enforcement apparatus" have had especially nefarious consequences for marginalized groups, including non-whites, newcomers to Canada, and "the poor and women."[40] According to Connell, neoliberalism has led to an "assault on the welfare state with an intensification of the gendered division of labour and a redistribution of income from women to men, while imposing more unpaid work on women in the form of caring for children, the elderly and the infirmed."[41] In short, despite shifts in women's participation in the workforce and some gains in education, deep structural inequities persist along gender, race, and class lines.

In Canada, "women bear a disproportionate burden of the problems caused by neoliberal globalization."[42] This is partly due to the ways in which neoliberal ideology has explicitly rejected and erased the political and social significance of gender. Having erased gender (and race as well), it now treats men and women as "equivalent market agents."[43] This strategy works against the aims of gender justice, for it actively ignores the structural inequalities that produce differential outcomes based on gender, race, sexuality, and various other social justice factors. Meg Luxton calls the denial of gender as a social structure one of the "most insidious features of neoliberalism," in that it fails to consider the impact of "society" on the way individuals make choices.[44] In 2010 the Canadian Feminist Alliance for International Action (CFAIA) and the Canadian Labour Congress (CLC) detailed how neoliberal ideology has worked to erase gender at the expense of women and children through recent government policies. Their report noted that the term "gender equality" had been eliminated from the mandate of Canada's primary institution responsible for gender equality in Canada: Status of Women. The same report pointed out that this change had been made in tandem with other significant changes, including these:

> The closing of twelve of the sixteen Status of Women offices, on the principles that women's and men's issues do not need to be separated; The reallocation of funding from organizations that support advocacy for women's human rights to organizations that provide front-line services only; The elimination of funding to the court challenges program, a program created to provide assistance to court cases related to equality rights guaranteed under Canada's constitution; The elimination in 2006 of the funding agreements that had been negotiated with provinces and territories to provide five billion dollars for childcare and early learning programs; The decrease in levels of financial and human resources specifically committed to gender-equality projects in the Canadian International Development Agency and the Department of Foreign Affairs.[45]

In their summary of the current state of gender relations, the CFAIA and the CLC argue that there has been "a systemic erosion of the human rights of women and girls in Canada."[46]

Despite the emergence of second-wave feminism in the mid-1960s and of third-wave feminism in the early 1990s, women today by all accounts remain at a disadvantage compared to men, socially, politically, and economically. Socially, women and girls are routinely reflected in the mass media as objects of sexual desire. A 2007 report published by the American Psychological Association Task Force explored the current hypersexualization of girls and found that in the mass media, which include "television, music videos, music lyrics, movies, magazines, sports media, video games, the Internet and advertising," women and young girls are routinely objectified and hypersexualized.[47] Although there have been some recent changes politically in Canada—for example, Canada at this writing has six female premiers (Alison Redford in Alberta, Christy Clark in British Columbia, Eva Aariak in Nunavut, Kathy Dunderdale in Newfoundland and Labrador, Kathleen Wynne in Ontario, Pauline Marois in Quebec)—it is largely males who oversee the banks, governments, the military, manufacturing, universities, and corporate management.[48] Sherry Cooper, former chief economist for the Bank of Montreal, recently described the corporate financial sector in Canada as a "sea of grey suits and white men."[49]

Economically, Canadian women generally earn less than men. In 2003 the average annual before-tax income of women aged sixteen and over from all sources—including employment earnings, government transfer payments, investment income, and other income—was $24,400. That was just 62 percent of the figure for men, who the same year earned an average of $39,300.[50] Moreover, according to a 2010 Statistics Canada report, differences between women's and men's earnings are found in both professional and non-professional occupational groupings: "Women in medicine and health related occupations earned about 57% as much as men in those occupations; women in business and finance occupations earned about 59% as much as their male counterparts. In non-professional occupations such as sales and service, women earned about 57% of men working in these occupations."[51]

Women are also far more likely to be poor and "precariously employed in part-time, limited term, contractual and non-standard work," the result being ongoing inequities in waged labour and women's inability to accumulate a necessary level of pension savings that will ensure a comfortable old age.[52] Research has also found that more than 50 percent of Canadian women who are single parents live in poverty.[53] Recent research generated by the Canadian Feminist Alliance for International Action indicates that women—especially women of colour, Aboriginal women, immigrant women, and women with disabilities—experience "shockingly high rates of poverty." This draws our attention to the intersection of race, gender, disability, and social class.[54] In sum, despite some gains in some areas—such as education, where women account for 47 percent of Canadian school principals[55]—women as a group in Canada remain socially, politically, and economically disadvantaged. Thus, concerns over the supposed "decline" of Canadian masculinity must be viewed in light of the highly gendered social, political, and economic context of our time: men and boys—especially white, middle-class males—have retained their advantage over women and girls—especially non-white, racialized, working-poor women and girls—when it comes to reaping social, political, and economic benefits.

Yet in this increasingly ideologically conservative time, a loose coalition of social commentators and others are making significant efforts to re-establish the traditional gender order. Today's male crisis alarmists are adamant that the war on men and masculinity has matastasized into a war on boys and boyhood. Discrimination against girls has ended, these people argue. The real problem now, they say, is discrimination against boys and boyhood. It is to these concerns that I will now turn.

IDEAL BOYHOOD IN "CRISIS"

Emerging from the current "crisis in masculinity" has been public concern over the fate and fitness of boys and boyhood. Contemporary discussions about this have taken on the tenor of a moral panic, with social commentators, psychologists, some child experts, and others routinely evoking the idea of "boyhood under siege."[56] For these commentators, a "natural, healthy boyhood is under attack" by the supposed feminization of society.[57] Men and boys remain privileged relative to women and girls, yet this moral panic constructs boys as the "new disadvantaged," as oppressed by women in general and by feminists in particular.[58] This view has been perpetuated in many popular media outlets across the Western democracies since the early 1990s, most of which have consistently fed the public an overabundance of news stories positioning boys as the "new second sex." A 2003 cover story in *Transition* complained about the "Declining Status of Boys in Canada," arguing that boys are no longer valued or publicly supported in Canada compared to girls.[59] With no public support or public acknowledgement of boys' issues, today's boy crisis advocates complain that boys have quickly become Canada's "forgotten" children.

The idea that boys have become the forgotten children of Canada was taken up in a November 2010 report published by the conservative Institute of Marriage and Family Canada. The authors of this report, titled "The Status of Men: Boys Are Lagging," framed the matter in alarmist terms, contending that "men and boys are the forgotten casualty in gender warfare."[60] Reflecting the male crisis perspective and its conservative tendencies, they claimed to know exactly where the blame lay: "in the face of a feminist outlook." The masculinist arguments put forward in reports such as this one produce and reproduce the cultural illusion that boys and men are the "new disadvantaged." Yet this simplistic view fails to consider, among other things, the complex differences between and among males that are structured on varying lines of social class, race, sexuality, and disability.

Many of today's boy crisis advocates argue that men's supposed overall decline in today's society is a result of their "feminization" and that this has its roots in boyhood. A online reader of the *Globe and Mail*, informed by a mixture of misogynist and homophobic discourses, recently argued that "the feminization of boys will just end by producing men, who behave like the worst sort of girls."[61] Ignoring the fact that men's general and dominant social power has remained largely unchanged over time, a *Maclean's* cover story on 25 October 2010 exploited this idea by suggesting that the current emasculation of Canadian men started in boyhood.[62] This article, titled "Are We Raising Our Boys to Be Underachieving Men?", focused mainly on how the feminization of society—in particular the school system—was producing unmotivated boys who were going to grow up to become unmotivated, underachieving, anxious, and uncertain men.[63] A related discussion, based on the *Maclean's* cover story, was held on the daily Christian television show *100 Huntley Street*. There it was suggested that Canadian boys were facing institutional discrimination, evidenced in the way teachers—female teachers in particular—often failed to let boys be boys by allowing them to "hang out, play and bash things." Drawing on an increasingly conservative mainstream culture in Canada, this show's commentators went on to blame women for the overall "evisceration" of Canadian males.[64]

The alleged attack on a "healthy normal boyhood" has led some commentators to suggest that the collective failure to address the emotional, psychological, and physical needs of boys will be catastrophic for some unlucky nations. In a 2006 opinion piece in the *Washington Post*, Leonard Sax, a popular author of various boy crisis articles and books, argued that the motor (i.e., boys) that had historically powered the world was in danger of being worn out: "In Ayn Rand's humorless apocalyptic novel *Atlas Shrugged*, the central characters ask: What would happen if someone turned off the motor that drives the world? We may be living in such a time, a time when the motor that drives the world is running down or stuck in neutral—but only for boys."[65]

Similarly, William Brozo, an American professor, and Richard Whitmire, author of the recent book *Why Boys Fail*, argued in a 2010 opinion piece that one of the most pressing problems nations face today is the "boy problem." For Brozo and Whitmire, the country that "solves" the "boy problem" will be the country that emerges the winner in the global economic sweepstakes: "the global economic race we read so much about—the marathon to produce the most educated workforce, and therefore the most prosperous nation—really comes down to a simple calculation: Whichever nation solves these 'boy troubles' wins the race."[66] Commentators like Brozo and Whitmire actively ignore the global plight of women and girls, who continue to be economically, socially, and politically disadvantaged. They also fail to consider how the current reorganization of global corporate capital has shored up male privilege.[67] And male privilege remains deeply entrenched in Canada. According to Statistics Canada, between 1982 and 2010 "men continued to dominate" the very top tier of Canada's income earners. In 2010, men made up 79 percent of the top

1 percent of income tax filers in Canada.[68] Despite evidence that males remain privileged, male crisis proponents routinely present the idea that boys are in trouble and that they have been left emotionally and physically vulnerable.

Contemporary boy crisis proponents construct boyhood as a precarious time and see boys as confused, frustrated, vulnerable, and fragile. "Our civilization does not understand and fully acknowledge the *fragility* of its male children," complains Michael Gurian in *A Fine Young Man* (1999).[69] From this perspective, boys are the "weaker sex" socially, physically, and emotionally.[70] Rao, in *The Way of Boys* (2009), cautions parents, teachers, and other caregivers to be gentle with boys, for boys "break down a bit after toddlerhood." He then tells readers that "in the years taking them through early grade school, they [boys] will become more emotional, less able to cope for weeks at a time."[71] Rao advises adults to lower their expectations of boys, for high demands will cause boys too much stress.[72] There seems to be a consensus among boy crisis proponents that boys' second-class status in society has contributed to low self-esteem among them. If there is a crisis in self-esteem, they argue, it is not among young girls. For many boy crisis advocates, the solution to bolstering boys' self-esteem lies in letting boys be boys. Today's experts advise parents, caregivers, teachers, and others to stop robbing boys of their "normal developmental struggles" and let them be their active, aggressive, and rambunctious selves.[73]

Today's boy crisis commentators—who include Michael Gurian, Christina Hoff Sommers, William Pollack, Richard Whitmire, Leonard Sax, and more recently Peg Tyre, Meg Meeker, Anthony Rao, and David Benatar—have routinely articulated this view to the reading public, despite research that continues to show that boys tend to have higher self-esteem than girls.[74] Boys' greater overall self-esteem is reflected in research indicating that boys overwhelmingly consider it better to be a boy than a girl, whereas girls do not overwhelmingly consider it better to be a girl than a boy.[75] Yet despite this evidence, by invoking sympathy and drawing the public's attention toward the problem of boys and boyhood and away from issues of girls and girlhood, boy crisis proponents have effectively entrenched male privilege.

In her *Globe and Mail* column of 17 November 2002, Margaret Wente advised her readers to reject the large body of social science research that has demonstrated overwhelmingly that masculinity is a social and historical construct.[76] Instead of drawing from research-based understandings of gender, she went on to promote the outdated view that today's boys are miserable because their assumed intrinsic "boyness" has been devalued.[77] This also appears to be the view of one *Globe and Mail* online reader who, in response to a 14 February 2013 article exploring the current fate and fitness of boyhood, put the matter this way: "There is a nasty attitude that boys are supposed to be little dolls with no flatulence in public, [no] climbing trees, playing hockey on the street, make noise, throw snowballs, etc. And even their once favourite Boy Scouts of Canada has been changed to allow girls ... It is difficult to be a boy these days."[78]

Regarding a solution to the perceived "difficulty" with being a boy today, commentators like the ones mentioned above argue that today's adults need to "celebrate boys' boyness" by placing value on their assumed natural tendencies such as being active, aggressive, and in some cases violent. The notion that a "normal" boyhood's assumed natural behaviours such as aggression have been somehow devalued or pathologized fails to recognize that aggression and the capacity for violent acts have been closely linked to performances and representations of hegemonic versions of masculinity. Not to mention that underpinning such advice is the fear that boys who are not aggressive or violent are somehow really not "normal" boys. Homophobia rears its head here. The fear of ridicule by other boys may pressure a boy into acting aggressively or violently in order to "prove" his masculinity. Then and now, boys who fail to act aggressively or violently seem not "fully masculine" in front of other males, who view them as "wimps" or "sissies."[79] Finally, considering the everyday violence against women and girls, to suggest that boys are naturally aggressive and violent can be dangerous, for it reinforces the association between masculinity and aggression. As adults, we can and should do better for boys *and* girls.

Yet boy crisis advocates argue that one reason for the supposed "masculinity deficit" in boys is a lack of male role models. Toronto writer Elliot Katz wrote in 2010 that Canadian boys have been left bewildered, frustrated, and lost because "they have grown up without strong [male] role models."[80] Similarly, Ontario writer Michael Reist complained in *Raising Boys in a New Kind of World* (2011) that the absence of male role models in boys' lives has harmed their masculine development. For Reist, the problem is that many boys exist in "feminine environments," including "single-mother home[s]."[81] In these feminized contexts, Reist argues, boys have been left without an appropriate male role model who can supply them with the "essential masculinity" that is required for boys' "psychic development." More than a decade earlier, similar views were expressed in Canada's Parliament. In a 2000 parliamentary debate, the member for Nanaimo-Cowichan drew on a homophobic and misogynist discourse as he blamed feminism, divorce, and single-parent families for creating an identity crisis among boys: "A gradual blurring of the sexes occurred that gave young men growing up in many female dominated, single parent homes an identity crisis. This led to a rise in militant homosexuality, a coming out of the closet of gay men and women who also demanded equality."[82]

To be sure, the current discourses about boyhood at work in the rhetoric found in contemporary popular culture, the mass media, and other sites have fashioned a powerful discourse, one that speaks in language that expresses scorn for feminists and that condemns women for undermining boys' masculinity.[83] In a 2003 article titled "Wimps and Barbarians" and published in *Claremont Review of Books,* American academic Terrence O. Moore spoke from this position. Underpinned by homophobic, misogynist, and anti-feminist sentiments, Moore argued that,

> Radical feminism ... has in some ways undermined the relations between the sexes. Radical feminists have not directly changed the character of traditional men. There are still a number of gentlemen who will open doors for ladies at the risk of being told off by the occasional woman out to prove her equality and independence. What feminism has done, in conjunction with political correctness, is deprive overly non-offensive, modern parents of the language traditionally used to bring up boys: "Be a man." "Stick up for your sister." "Quit throwing the ball like a sissy." "Quit crying like a girl." Instead, we have a lot of lukewarm, and androgynous talk about "being a good person" and "showing respect for people." A naturally rambunctious and irascible boy, though, is not too interested in being a good person. For if he achieves that status, what will distinguish him from his prim and proper sister?[84]

Comments like these ignore how boys' struggles may be largely due to socialized and embodied notions of an ideal version of boyhood and not the result of the absence of male role models. For commentators like Moore, the problem with boys "is the man-hating culture perpetuated by the feminists." So it was put by a *National Post* online reader in response to a October 2010 news story promoting boys-only schools as a method for addressing the educational needs of boys.[85]

Yet the call for more male role models for boys as a way to counter the supposed feminization of society has been injected into the field of education.[86] Here, the failure to adopt a more complex view of boyhood and girlhood has led to calls for more male teachers as a means to address the emotional, psychological, and educational needs of boys.[87] From this perspective, hiring more male teachers would "remasculinize" schools, thus making them more "boy-friendly" and countering the perceived damaging effects on boys caused by female teachers and mother-led households. In *The Walrus* in March 2007, two Canadian academics argued this point: "Boys growing up without a male role model at home and hard pressed to find one among their teachers are at considerable risk. Especially in the elementary years, where female teachers represent a large majority, there is always danger that young male students faced year after year with female teachers will begin to resent them as authority figures and switch off learning altogether."[88]

Others have agreed. In an online response to a 19 February 2013 article in the *Globe and Mail,* which reported on the Toronto District School Board's affirmative action plan for hiring more male teachers, one reader had this to say: "Reality is many young boys don't have a role model these days. Broken homes, single moms, and (often) female teachers that don't understand how boys are different from girls ... They expect boys to be still and behave as girls do. Perhaps more male teachers would help offset that."[89]

Others have expressed, as another online reader did, the opinion that the lack of male teachers in Canadian classrooms stems from the lack of males enrolled in university faculties of education. Here, the backlash politics that inform much of the current debate over the call for more male teachers becomes clear: the writer blames "feminists" and "multiculturalists" for making males feel "unwelcome" in university classrooms.[90] Similarly, in an article titled "The Boys at the Back," published in the *New York Times* on 2 February 2013, Christina Hoff Sommers, an academic and well-known boy crisis proponent, argued that recruiting more male teachers should be a key strategy in helping address the educational needs of boys.[91] Of course, the current moral panic about the need for more male role models to address the problems boys are experiencing today—problems that are attributed to the supposed feminization of society—parallels to an extent the campaigns that were mobilized in the 1950s and 1960s to recruit male mentors for boys, including male teachers as proper role models in schools.[92] As I have argued elsewhere, "although there are social, political, and ideological differences, in both contexts the concern over the lack of male role models for boys needs to be understood as inextricably linked to the fear of feminization of boys and its supposed emasculating consequences."[93]

The assumption that boys need male role models and respond best to them remains an important ideological feature from the boy crisis perspective. Remember, though, that a key factor in current efforts to provide boys with male role models is the failure to address issues of gendered power hierarchies. Boys, then and now, are situated as a disempowered group. Girls by implication are privileged, and institutions such as schools are constructed as better suited to meet the needs of girls. Yet as Martino and Rezai-Rashtai note, the "intensified focus on boys as the 'new disadvantaged' ... belies the persistence of male and white privilege, which continues to afflict the participation of girls/women and minority groups in the public sphere."[94] In short, the current moral panic over boys' education, as a result of which significant amounts of limited resources have been allocated to address the problems it supposedly faces, has to some degree created a "structural backlash" against girls.[95]

This is not to suggest that some females have not benefited from feminism—some surely have. But as others have pointed out, the beneficiaries of feminism have largely been middle-class white women, who have made some gains in education, moving slowly into areas long dominated by men, such as math, science, and business.[96] In other words, when it comes to academic achievement, social class and race appear to matter more than gender.[97] Thus, in any given year, an individual Canadian from a family with a higher income is generally more likely to go to university regardless of gender than an individual from a family with a lower income.[98] Middle-class boys are more likely to attend university than working-class girls. Moreover, add to the mix issues of race and ethnicity as they intersect with social class and geographical area and the problem of gender and academic achievement in school becomes far more complex. In Canada, "girls who come from remote Indigenous communities are certainly not outperforming boys in middle-class urban areas."[99] The charge levelled by conservative commentators such as Glenn Reynolds that schools "are a hostile environment for boys" fails to acknowledge that not all boys are failing and that not all girls are succeeding.[100] Unfortunately, boy crisis proponents' anxiety over the loss of white male middle-class privilege has prevented any meaningful dialogue that might take into account how complex and interrelated factors such as social class, sexuality, ethnicity, disability, geographical region, and race intersect to influence which boys and which girls succeed academically and socially in and out of school.

The problem, then, is that today's boy crisis proponents present "boys" as a monolithic and undifferentiated group. This has led to misguided gender-specific intervention strategies such as hiring more male teachers, establishing single-sex settings, and developing "boy-friendly" curricula as a way to address the educational needs of boys. It has also resulted in a failure to consider how social class, ethnicity, race, and sexuality intersect in schools. In his work on urban schools, Michael Katz found that social class was the greatest predictor of who succeeded at school.[101] A recent Toronto District School Board study found that students who speak Spanish, Portuguese, or Somali are at higher risk than any other group of failing the grade ten literacy test. In his analysis of that study, Wayne Martino found that students from the Caribbean, Central and South America, and eastern Africa had significantly higher dropout rates than the rest of the population. This draws our attention to how ethnicities, along with other factors such as social class, powerfully shape student achievement in complex ways.[102]

Moreover, in the context of the "crisis in masculinity" debate, the ongoing discrimination against women in certain subject disciplines is rarely mentioned. According to a 2010 report by the Canadian Natural Sciences and Engineering Research Council, women remain underrepresented in natural sciences, mathematics, and engineering programs.[103] In 2001 and 2002, for example, women made up only 30 percent of all university students in mathematics and physical sciences and just 24 percent of those in engineering and applied sciences.[104] This gender gap has had implications for labour force participation, where women remain a "minority among professionals employed in the natural sciences, engineering, and mathematics."[105] For example, of the 70,000 licensed professional engineers in Ontario in 2009, only about 7 percent were women.[106] Or consider the recent finding from a 2012 report, *Strengthening Canada's Research Capacity: The Gender Dimension*, which found that female researchers in Canada remain significantly underrepresented in academe.[107] Yet male crisis proponents barely mention that, disinclined to enrol in traditionally "girl-unfriendly" classes such as engineering, girls still overwhelmingly enter the "soft" fields of languages, education, humanities, creative arts, and social sciences.[108] Within their fields, women can and do succeed, but their chosen fields often leave them economically dependent on their male counterparts, which continues gender inequities between men and women. Given this level of conceptual naïveté around understandings of gender relations in general, and masculinity in particular in the context of education, it is perhaps not surprising to find that some universities have been considering affirmative action policies for males.

Fuelled by the "crisis in masculinity" mentality, some Canadian universities have considered ways to recruit more males into university classrooms. In 1999 the University of Toronto's Faculty of Education engineered its admissions program to favour male candidates. David Booth, co-coordinator of the elementary pre-service program at the university, remarked that "for now, one factor taken into account when choosing students for the elementary stream is gender ... and, given two equal candidates for a position, the male gets it."[109] Likewise, in the early 2000s McGill University considered whether it should make special efforts to draw more males onto its campus.[110] The University Senate commissioned the Admissions Committee to generate recommendations that could be adopted in order to bring more males to the campus. While an official affirmative action plan for males has yet to be established at McGill, other universities, such as McMaster University, have established new admission practices in order to draw more males into school. Fearing that "an overemphasis of high marks was driving away male medical students," McMaster's medical school changed its admissions process in the late 2000s by de-emphasizing grades and placing greater emphasis on personality tests.[111] Paul Cappon, president and CEO of the Canadian Council on Learning and former vice-president of Laurentian University, has noted that affirmative action for males is becoming increasingly common at law and medical schools at a variety of Canadian universities.[112]

In addition, some Ontario school boards have adopted affirmative action hiring policies for males. Fuelled by concerns over boys' underachievement, school boards across Ontario and elsewhere have sought to hire more male teachers as a means to address boys' educational needs.[113] An internal memo recently sent to principals and teachers of the Toronto District School Board (TDSB) stated that males, along with racial minorities, should be given preference in hiring. Dated 5 February 2013, the TDSB memo, published in the *Globe and Mail*, read: "The first round of TDSB interviews will be granted to teachers candidates that meet one or more of the following criteria in addition to being an outstanding teacher: Male, Racial Minority, French (FSL qualifications), Music (instrumental), Aboriginal."[114] This TDSB action follows similar initiatives such as the Ontario College of Teachers 2004 male teacher initiative, which called for more males in elementary school classrooms to address the educational needs of boys.[115] Hiring more male teachers is guided by the belief that more men in teaching can counter the perceived notion that the workforce is "dominated" by women. In 2000 the Ontario Public School Board Association president, Liz Sandals, worried that little boys are lost in "a sea of women."[116]

The affirmative action plans for males that some Ontario school boards are currently developing are consistent with the conservative "crisis in masculinity" discourse, which sees society as overly feminized. There is, of course, no empirical evidence that simply having a male teacher in the classroom will increase boys' achievement. When it comes to raising student achievement, research has consistently shown that more often than not, what matters is not the gender of the teacher but the teacher's pedagogical approach.[117] Consider also that males, as reflected in the TDSB memo, have been officially identified as a disadvantaged group alongside other groups that have historically and systematically experienced oppression and discrimination. In other words, obscured in the TDSB memo is the fact that racialized minorities, Indigenous populations, and women have appealed at times to affirmative action in their efforts to escape a history of racist and gender oppression and exclusion, in and out of institutions such as schools; by contrast, efforts to implement affirmative action policies for (white) males are born of a desire to *retain* the social, political, and economic advantages for men that have been created by that same history.

Online readers of the 18 February 2013 *Globe and Mail* article that ran the TDSB memo responded to it by trading in a backlash politics, claiming disenfranchisement based on being a male in the education system. According to one online commentator, "the whole education system has been so feminized that boys feel completely out of place as they move through the system ... Boys have been generally made to feel unwelcome."[118] Another reader commented that "our entire education system discriminates against males—from the restrictive playground rules to the domination of language in every subject including math and science. The curriculum and hiring practises are driving males away from the system."[119] Still other readers engaged in a backlash politics that made race and racism explicit. Ignoring the structural privileges that come with being white and male in contemporary society, one of them complained that "to be the white male in Canada is akin to being the Negro of the American 1950's."[120] Still another, using the online name "TheFoxReport," wrote that it is now "socially unacceptable to be white and male." In keeping with the "white male disadvantage discourse," this writer suggested there was a history of discrimination against white males in relation to public institutions: "When it comes to issues like public service hiring, entry into professional schools etc., anybody with a pulse knows that white males have been openly discriminated against for years … For decades now, it has been a 'good thing' to discriminate against males—young white males in particular. Accordingly, we have medical schools, dentistry, the public school system heavily dominated by women."[121]

These simplistic and uneducated reactions to the current concern over "male disadvantage" reflect the broader conservative "crisis in masculinity" discourse, which does little to offer the public a nuanced and productive account of gender constructions, gender relations, and social inequalities.

Productive theories of gender such as those developed by sociologist Raewyn Connell and philosopher Judith Butler can help us understand gender issues, for they highlight how boys' problems are in part the result of their gendered performances of an idealized boyhood. Productive, research-based understandings of gender indicate that an "idealized" boyhood flattens and narrows boys' lives as it remains narrowly predicated on heterosexuality and homophobia and is defined against femininity. In such a boyhood, toughness remains simplistically linked to self-worth, and physical stature alongside sporting prowess is still equated with moral stature. Boyhood, that is, is still wrongly thought of as an outcome of biology or a manifestation of inner essences. Productive accounts of gender demonstrate that gender, which operates within socially given structures of power, is best thought of as a relation, not a psychological property of an individual or an outcome of biology. As Connell has argued, to accept either of these two positions is "foolhardy as they obliterate questions about social structure and the historical dynamic of gender relations."[122]

Despite the well-established understanding in the research literature that gender is a social construction, today's loose coalition of boy crisis advocates continue to write popular books, appear in the media, and publish in mainstream magazines and newspapers, endlessly promoting misleading proscriptions in the popular culture and attempting to misdirect child development discussions toward outdated notions of an essentialized masculinity. Some of the more noteworthy texts in this vein are Gurian's *A Fine Young Man* (1999),[123] Pollack's *Real Boys* (1998),[124] and Hoff Sommers's *The War Against Boys* (2000),[125] and more recently Zimbardo and Duncan's *The Demise of Guys* (2012; e-book),[126] Sax's *Boys Adrift* (2007),[127] Tyre's *The Trouble with Boys* (2008),[128] and Rao's *The Way of Boys* (2009).[129] All of these works implicitly and explicitly blame women in general and feminists in particular for promoting the achievement of girls at the expense of boys. Ideas about an essentialized boyhood are at the heart of boy crisis texts such as these, all of which reflect a deeper albeit unspoken anxiety relating to the need to assert or reclaim masculinity for boys, who are viewed as "at risk" of being feminized by what is imagined by today's loose coalition of social commentators to be an increasingly feminized society. A variety of popular mainstream writers are employing the now familiar strategy of reinforcing and legitimating gender differences that are linked to binary categorizations of the sexed body. Thus, Meeker in *Boys Should Be Boys* and Rao in *The Way of Boys* depict, in a nostalgic and retrograde way, an ideal boyhood: white, middle-class, rambunctious, active, aggressive, attuned to nature, and athletic. This is seldom, if ever, the boyhood in which the vast majority of boys actually live.

Today's boy crisis proponents, like those of the past, tend to assume that there is a fixed, true boyhood, when in fact, societal constructs of boyhood vary over time and compete with one another according to culture, age, and myriad social factors. All males, though, while differently located according to social class, race, disability, ethnicity, sexual orientation, and other factors, share one thing, and that is gender privilege.[130] Because they were born male, men and boys have been granted access to power, position, and resources on a preferential basis. Today's boy crisis advocates, like those in the past, often take these unearned rights for granted. A sense of privilege and entitlement, in fact, comes simply from having been born a boy, then and now.

CONCLUSION

The belief that boyhood is in "crisis" is a commonplace one in contemporary Canadian society, along with the flip side of this discourse—a contempt for women in general and for feminists in particular. That belief has been reiterated time and again in the press and has gained authority from a steady stream of already mentioned news articles, books, essays, and educational policy documents. At particular historical junctures marked by significant social and economic change, narrow, well-defined, and explicit gender ideals are promoted and gain prominence in popular discourse. As a response to threats posed to the existing gender order, whether in the postwar period or today, these gender ideals are constructed, generated, and normalized by many leading social and cultural commentators, often with the effect of retrenching traditional under-standings of heteronormative masculinity.

As we have seen, such is the case now in post-industrial Canada, where a particular version of boyhood is emerging as dominant. This version of boyhood has been generated and sustained as part of a public backlash against the threat of gender uncertainty—an uncertainty that has been brought on by significant social and economic change, including economic restructuring, downsizing, and the loss of well-paid industrialized jobs. This social and polit-ical turbulence, this mixture of uncertainty and danger, fear and change, has produced a search for clarity, stability, and security that has been put alongside gender ideals of boyhood. Once again, the current debates about the status of boyhood within popular discourse have generated and fostered a narrow version of masculinity that typically derogates the feminine and devalues alter-native, more egalitarian models of boyhood.

Conclusion:
Making Ontario Boys, 1945–1960

6

In the immediate postwar years in Ontario there existed a deep preoccupation with boyhood, in reaction to the uncertainty, insecurity, instability, and gender anxiety brought on by Depression era and wartime disruptions in marital, family, and labour relations, rapid postwar economic changes, the emergence of the Cold War, and the looming threat of nuclear annihilation. Shaped by these historical circumstances, motivated by a deep yearning for normality, security, and stability, and resisting shifts in gender relations, public commentators and defenders of hegemonic masculinity positioned boyhood and masculinity alongside their restless search for security, stability, and normalcy. In their quest for "normalcy," a loose coalition of social commentators, journalists, psychologists, child experts, social workers, and others projected their gendered fears of the future onto discussions of boyhood development. By doing so, they attempted to publicly assuage an intense sense of insecurity, instability, and gender trouble by normalizing white, Anglo-Protestant, middle-class, patriarchal, heteronormative definitions of masculinity and routinely offering their version of an appropriately "masculine" boyhood to the public.

The Great Depression dramatically increased male job loss and challenged men's entitlement to waged labour, thereby undermining men's power and status as breadwinners and inciting anxieties over heteronormative masculinity. Male unease and anxiety over the "emasculation" of men caused by the Great Depression was being expressed even three decades later: "The great depression gave women an excuse to introduce their husbands to dirty dishes and diapers. They became 'partners,'" complained two anti-feminist writers in 1969.[1] On top of this came the shift within the labour market during the Second World War that increased women's independence and that led to a breakdown of gendered workplace categories thought previously to be fixed and rigid. Out of this social and political turbulence, this mixture of uncertainty and danger, fear and change, emerged a search for normality, clarity, stability, and security that was put alongside gender ideals of masculinity, femininity, and boyhood and girlhood—and all of this was grounded in constructions of the postwar ideal family.

One leading social manifestation of the search for stability and security, then, was a rush to "return" to traditional understandings of gender, which in part meant the reinstitutionalizing of the patriarchal family and its familialist ideology. Cultural commentators and others stressed that a return to normal was to be equated with establishing a white, middle-class, Anglo-Protestant, heterosexual, nuclear family (and by extension manhood) as the bedrock upon which to safeguard and fulfill the promise of a better postwar Ontario. By the 1960s and 1970s, social conditions that included economic shifts, feminism, and gay and lesbian liberation had undermined the "family decade" and brought to an end the ideological hegemony of the 1950s middle-class nuclear family.[2] But by then, many social commentators in the immediate postwar period had taught their readers that an ideal boyhood was the product of a good, stable nuclear family, led by an involved father and located in a respectable neighbourhood. It was imagined that in these spaces, children—immigrant and working-poor boys in particular—would have more opportunities to develop good habits and traits such as honesty, helpfulness, and a spirit of fair play and teamwork—qualities that were thought to be the very marrow of postwar economic security and stability.

As boys came increasingly to be seen as the future of a stable and secure Ontario, the popular and professional postwar discourse placed increasing emphasis on moral and physical training and character education to ensure that boys would grow up with the desired traits. Social and cultural commentators seemed only too willing to offer up stories for adults and boys alike that reclaimed attributes closely associated with a reworked traditional masculine ideal. Boys and men should value teamwork, selflessness, and fair play. They must be rational, physically and emotionally self-controlled and disciplined, upright and moral, loyal, and obedient. These stories promoted male togetherness and teamwork in all-male contexts, which left little space for mothers or girls or for "feminine" emotions such as compassion and empathy. Advertisements for toys and games promoted an acceptable postwar masculinity for boyhood. Through toy guns and cowboy and sports equipment, adults promoted a narrow version of boyhood that reasserted patriarchal values by re-establishing the breadwinner ideology. Boys as future doctors, engineers, and businessmen filled postwar periodicals. The "crisis" mentality regarding gender during the postwar era provoked adults to attempt to restore a dominant masculinity, and this contributed to popular constructions of boyhood that isolated boys not only from the smothering tendencies of mothers but also from *all* feminine influences.

Influenced by the prominent psychological discourse of the time, postwar commentators privileged a narrow version of boyhood as the cultural standard; they also regulated, disciplined, and marginalized others by rendering public judgments about what was appropriately "masculine." By doing so, they established a public framework where traditional gender roles were vigorously promoted and invoked; they suggested suggested, for example, that real boys, unlike sissies or mamma's boys, avoided anything closely associated with the feminine. Real boys developed "normally" as heterosexuals; they were competitive and aggressive; they preferred sports over other activities such as reading; they played with other boys, not girls, and they joined gangs. Playing with girls was viewed as a sign of latent homosexuality. Mostly, though, in light of the lessons learned from the Second World War and from fears that communism was spreading, an appropriate boyhood during the postwar period depended on the will to act in heroic, selfless ways and on the capacity to physically resist aggression. Social and cultural commentators taught that when boys faced a hostile and menacing enemy (another boy or group of boys, for instance) without the use of force, it was appropriate to question their masculinity. The standard thereby established was applied in such a way as to set apart real boyhoods from inferior boyhoods, an appropriate boyhood from a feminized one. When boys submitted or disengaged from confrontations, adults easily viewed this as a clear sign of "abnormal" or "maladjusted" masculinity; this in turn raised the spectre of effeminacy and, by extension, homosexuality. Postwar public pedagogy taught that boys who could be trampled on or intimidated without resistance ceased to be real boys and became something closer to victimized girls. More often than not, public pedagogues accepted and indeed celebrated the boy "nature" for what they believed it to be—namely volatile, impulsive, and physically aggressive in the face of danger, or of insult or wrongdoing. Thus, adults continuously underscored the cost to boys and to society of masculine inaction. To be passive and victimized was to be feminized, which portended not only the loss of all the authority that an appropriate masculinity conferred but also, quite simply, the end of the democratic world as adults knew it.

To be sure, "normal" boys also showed moderation and self-control when it came to aggression and violence. After the war, in the context of the Cold War and the spread of capitalism, adults recognized the need to naturalize masculinity's links to violence and aggression. Boys' "naturally" aggressive tendencies could then be co-opted by the state to ensure the production of rough-and-ready masculine men who would be willing to go to war, be that war economic or political. Yet at the same time, social and cultural commentators set limits on masculine aggression, promoting the idea that self-control and self-discipline were essential features of an appropriate boyhood. To fight fairly, to stand up for yourself, was a mark of an appropriate masculinity, in the same way that to fight unfairly, or to extend aggression beyond reason, was thought brutish, thuggish, and the mark of a bestial and undesirable masculinity. Hitler and his barbarous hordes had demonstrated to Canadians what could happen when "hypermasculinity" accompanied by its "natural" propensity toward violence was unleashed and went absurdly beyond reason.

This was precisely why the threat of a cruel, bestial, barbarous, undisciplined, and violent masculinity as embodied in the construct of the "bad boy" was of particular public concern. In the postwar years, the bad boy was associated closely with a poor, working-class boyhood. He was thought to contain the seeds of "hypermasculinity" and as such to pose a direct threat to the safety and stability of the social order. A bad boy, so it was thought, had masculinity in abundance; he embodied a version of masculinity that was essentially good but in need of much masculine training, of male mentoring to show him how to control and discipline his masculinity. Psychologists, mental health experts, and other concerned adults had no intention of extinguishing the bad boy's good masculine core, which they viewed as an essential part of being a "good" citizen. To assuage their fears of out-of-control poor working-class bad boys, they instead advocated methods of prevention such as boys clubs, which would direct boys onto the right path. Adults imagined that by inculcating the "right kind of masculinity" in them, they could prevent poor working-class and immigrant boys from sliding into delinquency. At the same time, they would be building these boys into future masculine breadwinners, good citizens, and obedient men who would adopt the prescribed masculine role, pay their taxes, and maintain the existing social order.

The gender contours of an appropriate boyhood were revealed through the psychological orthodoxy of the day, which was adamant in attributing psychopathology in general and sexual perversion in particular to boyhoods that embodied the "feminine." Like manhood, boyhood was predicated on heterosexuality and homophobia. Parents were warned again and again by popular psychologists and other child care gurus to be on guard for signs indicating a failing or deficient masculinity in their sons. Adults were cautioned to be on the lookout for boys who did not engage in the natural rough-and-tumble play, who preferred to play alone, who played with girls, or who enjoyed dolls instead of guns. These were to be taken as omens, signs of impending doom, linked as they were to future homosexuality. This "lack" of masculinity was embodied in the "sissy" and imagined as jeopardizing not only boys' future as proper heterosexual, breadwinning men but also the future stability and security of society. The sissy, who was closely associated with effeminacy and by extension homosexuality, functioned as a familiar discursive device within popular discourse to delineate the tenuous and unstable boundaries of appropriate masculinity for boys. A loose coalition of social commentators, journalists, psychologists, child experts, and social workers invoked the spectre of the sissy as a way to regulate and publicly police the boundaries of boyhood. In doing so, they demonstrated that boyhood was not "self-evident" and that it could not be taken for granted. The mere invocation of the term "sissy" opened up possibilities for gender restructuring, thus revealing the contingent nature of boyhood itself. Certainly, no one was tempted to label as effeminate a boyhood that was described as active and vigorous, aggressive and tough, that expressed a love of sports and the great outdoors. Activity and aggression were markers of a successful boyhood masculinity. For many social and cultural commentators, the opposition between activity and passivity (a traditional sign of effeminacy) was essential in distinguishing an acceptable from an unacceptable boyhood.

There were a few bright and daring individuals who understood gender in the postwar era better than most. Sophie Drinker and Josephine Schreier wrote insightfully in *Journal of Higher Education* about how *patriarchal values* negatively shaped and determined experiences for some women in their quest for intellectual and spiritual growth; at the same time, they pointed out to those who would listen that patriarchal values were informing the psychological discourse that took for "truth" the popular allegation that women in general, and mothers in particular, posed a threat to their son's masculinity.[3] Not until Betty Friedan published *The Feminine Mystique* in 1963 did a full revitalization of women's struggles for equality take shape, and bring modern patriarchal values under closer scrutiny.

The ideology that shaped the idea of boyhood during the postwar era in Ontario was one of the principle tools for reinscribing male privilege onto the basic social and public language of postwar life. At a time when fear, anxiety, doubt, and uncertainty shaped public discourse, public commentators coded boyhood, not girlhood, as inherently heroic and key to the survival of the nation. It is surely no coincidence that ubiquitous gendered images of heroic, wholesome boys engaged in selfless, morally courageous acts of derring-do flooded the textual and visual gendered landscape at a time when women were challenging traditional male power on many different fronts, including in the public sphere. Providing a superabundance of images showing boys situated in traditional master masculine narratives seems to me to have been a means of symbolically taking power away from women and girls in the broader social and political sphere. In a world teetering on the brink, it was boys who were expected to provide safety, security, and leadership. Girls were largely located in discourses of domesticity, and social and cultural commentators taught that it was their responsibility to prepare themselves as future wives, mothers, and homemakers. Boys, by contrast, had outlined for them by adults a more active, public role. Boys were to be the selfless, honest, and decisive future businessmen, administrators, workers, and leaders—and, of course, patriarchs of their own families. And if nature had fitted boys to be future heads of their own families, it only made sense that they take control of and primacy in caring for the broader "social family." Through this ideological representation of boyhood and girlhood, gender differences were naturalized, providing boyhood, not girlhood, with greater possible locations for the exercise of social, political, and economic power and privilege. In this sense, the model of boyhood that was promoted to Ontarians, on the social, political, and economic levels, ran alongside efforts to restore and secure patriarchal power and privilege that had been diminished. In this social, cultural, and political milieu, the idea of boyhood became an ever more crucial site for shoring up patriarchy.

Given the crucial work done by second- and third-wave feminism, it would be hopeful to suggest that since the postwar period the idea of boyhood as constructed by adults for other adults and boys has broadened and moved beyond traditional definitions of masculinity to include a wider range of understandings of boyhood, toward models that are more diverse, egalitarian, and equitable. Yet listening to the current debates about the status of boyhood within popular and professional discourse, you would never know that decades of critical feminist work have created room for alternatives to traditional masculinity, and challenged a masculinity that is predicated on heterosexuality and homophobia and that is defined against femininity; a masculinity in which toughness and physical aggression are simplistically viewed by some adults as "a normal part of boyhood" and physical stature alongside sporting prowess is still equated with moral stature; a masculinity that is still incorrectly thought of as an outcome of biology or a manifestation of inner essences.[4] This book has demonstrated the consequences of the failure to connect such concerns about the state of boyhood to the broader social and historical phenomenon regarding the anxiety around the state of masculinity in times of an anti-feminist backlash, and how this in turn generates and fosters a narrow version of boyhood that typically derogates the feminine and devalues alternative, more egalitarian models of boyhood.

The immediate postwar years have long since passed, but as was shown in Chapter 5, Ontario in the early part of the twenty-first century is still anxious about boys and boyhood, still uneasy about mother-led households, still nervous about absentee fathers and what this means for boys' masculinity.[5] As Chapter 5 outlined, shaped by insecurity, instability, and fears over boys' perceived emasculation, many social and cultural commentators today, like those of the postwar era, continue to project their gendered fears of the future onto discussions of boyhood development. The growing sense of fear over the state of boyhood today among today's social commentators has led them once again to uphold normative, white, patriarchal, heteronormative definitions of masculinity and routinely offer their version of an appropriately "masculine" boyhood to the public.

Why dwell on what has passed into history, in particular the period of postwar Ontario? Ruth Watts has suggested that knowing history is significant because the past sends long tendrils into the present.[6] Uncovering the dominant discourses about boyhood and masculinity found in the postwar popular press and professional periodicals helps us understand how the production and reproduction of ideas about gender take place within a society. Postwar ideas about an acceptable boyhood would have likely shaped and influenced, to some degree or another, the beliefs, attitudes and opinions about boyhood of the girls and boys who grew up during that that era. Those boys and girls are now today's leaders and writers, not to mention grandparents and parents, who in turn are now shaping and influencing another generation of children. Certainly, furthering our understanding of the ways that popular and professional discourse helped shape masculinities in the past as well as in our own time is crucial to understanding who we are now as Canadians. Exploring how boyhood was constructed through history also demonstrates that boyhood, like masculinity, is not ahistorical, asocial, or acultural. Rather, the idea of boyhood is contingent, influenced by historical developments, made in culture and as such subject to change. History is important not only as a record of the past but also as a guide to the present.[7] If we are to engage in thoughtful and meaningful debates about masculinity in general, and boys in particular, we need to know where we have come from in order to better understand where we are heading.

Notes

Notes to Introduction

1 Ruth Roach Pierson, *"They're Still Women After All": The Second World War and Canadian Womanhood* (Toronto: McClelland and Stewart, 1986); Christopher Dummitt, *The Manly Modern: Masculinity in Postwar Canada* (Vancouver: UBC Press, 2007); Cynthia Comacchio, *The Dominion of Youth: Adolescence and the Making of Modern Canada, 1920-1950* (Waterloo: Wilfrid Laurier University Press, 2006); Magda Fahrni and Robert Rutherdale, eds., *Creating Postwar Canada, 1945-1975* (Vancouver: UBC Press, 2008); Tarah Brookfield, *Cold War Comforts: Canadian Women, Child Safety, and Global Insecurity* (Waterloo: Wilfrid Laurier University Press, 2013).

2 On the search for security and stability during the postwar period, see Franca Iacovetta, "Making New Canadians," in Franca Iacovetta and Mariana Valverde, eds., *Gender Conflicts: New Essays in Women's History* (Toronto: University of Toronto Press, 1992); Reginald Whitaker and Gary Marcuse, *Cold War Canada: The Making of a National Insecurity State* (Toronto: University of Toronto Press, 1994); Veronica Strong-Boag, "Canada's Wage Earning Wives and the Construction of the Middle Class, 1945-1960," *Journal of Canadian Studies* 29, no. 3 (1994): 5-25.

3 "Heading Towards Normal," *Georgetown Herald*, 31 October 1945; "The World Is So Full of Boys," *Leamington Post and News*, 28 August 1947.

4 Speaking in front of several hundred women at the formation of a Canadian branch of the Women's International Democratic Federation in 1947 at Toronto's King Edward Hotel, Dr. Gene Weltfish, an American anthropologist, suggested that women's role as citizens was primarily to be caregivers and educators of children and nurturers of men. See "Peace Objective as Women Form Federation Branch," *Globe and Mail*, 29 January 1947.

5 Lorinda B. Cohoon, "Boyhood," in Paula S. Fass, ed., *Encyclopedia of Children and Childhood in History and Society*, vol. 1 (New York: Macmillan Reference USA, 2004), 107; Catherine Burke, "Theories of Childhood," in Fass, ed. *Encyclopedia of Children and Childhood in History and Society*, vol. 3 (New York: Macmillan Reference USA, 2004), 818.

6 Leon J. Saul, *Emotional Maturity: The Development and Dynamics of Personality* (Philadelphia: Lippincott, 1947), 26.

7 Marian E. Breckenridge and E. Lee Vincent, *Child Development: Physical and Psychological Growth Through the School Years* (Philadelphia: W.B. Saunders, 1949), 535.

8 Ontario, *Report of the Royal Commission on Education in Ontario* (Toronto: Baptist Johnston, King's Printer, 1950), 70.

9 Benjamin Spock, *Baby and Child Care* (Montreal: Pocket Books of Canada, 1946, 1965), 415.

10 Cynthia Comacchio, for example, has shown how socially constructed and historically specific meanings come to shape and define understandings of age-related concepts such as "youth," "adolescence," and "teenager." See Comacchio, *The Dominion of Youth*, 2–3.

11 "Claim Indian Boy, 3 Killed by Uncle, 10," *Toronto Daily Star*, 30 August 1946; "Murder Charge Dismissed Against Frail Indian Boy, 13," *Toronto Daily Star*, 14 May 1948; "Sick Indian Boy Sped to Toronto," *Globe and Mail*, 29 July 1949. For more on this, see Jane Helleiner, "'The Right Kind of Children': Childhood, Gender and 'Race' in Canadian Postwar Political Discourse," *Anthropologica* (2001): 143–52.

12 Canada, Truth and Reconciliation Commission of Canada, *Interim Report*, 2012. See also Shelley Goforth, "Aboriginal Healing Methods for Residential School Abuse and Intergenerational Effects: A Review of the Literature," *Native Social Work Journal* 6 (2007): 11–32. See also J.R. Miller, *Shingwauk's Vision: A History of Native Residential Schools* (Toronto: University of Toronto Press, 1996).

13 Truth and Reconciliation Commission, *Interim Report*, 25–26.

14 For a discussion of residential schools and their impact on boys and boyhood, see Kim Anderson, Robert Alexander, and John Swift, "Indigenous Masculinities: Carrying the Bones of the Ancestors," in Christopher J. Greig and Wayne J. Martino, eds., *Canadian Men and Masculinities: Historical and Contemporary Perspectives* (Toronto: Canadian Scholars' Press, 2012), 217–53. See also Ian Mosby, "Administering Colonial Science: Nutrition Research and Human Biomedical Experimentation in Aboriginal Communities and Residential Schools, 1942–1952," *Historie Sociale / Social History* 46, no. 91 (May 2013): 145–72.

15 Timothy J. Stanley, *Contesting White Supremacy: School Segregation, Anti-Racism, and the Making of Chinese Canadians* (Vancouver: UBC Press, 2011); Franca Iacovetta, *Gatekeepers: Reshaping Immigrant Lives in Cold War Canada* (Toronto: Between the Lines, 2006).

16 Comacchio, *The Dominion of Youth*; see also Comacchio, *The Infinite Bonds of Family: Domesticity in Canada, 1850–1940* (Toronto: University of Toronto Press, 1999); Comacchio, *Nations Are Built of Babies: Saving Ontario's Mothers and Children, 1900–1940* (Montreal and Kingston: McGill–Queen's University Press, 1993); Rebecca Priegert Coulter and Helen Harper, *History Is Hers: Women Educators in Twentieth Century Ontario* (Calgary: Detselig, 2005); Christopher Dummitt, "Finding a Place for Father: Selling the Barbeque in Postwar Canada," *Journal of the Canadian Historical Association* 9, no. 1 (1998): 209–23. See also Dummitt, *The Manly Modern*; Franca Iacovetta, "The Sexual Politics of Male Citizenship and Containing Dangerous Foreign Men in Cold War Canada, 1950s–1960s," *Histoire sociale / Social History* 33, no. 66 (2000): 361–89; Iacovetta, "Gossip, Contest, and Power in the Making of Suburban Bad Girls: Toronto, 1945–1960,"

Canadian Historical Review 80, no. 4 (1999): 585–623; Iacovetta, *Such Hardworking People: Italian Immigrants in Postwar Toronto* (Montreal and Kingston: McGill–Queen's University Press, 1992); Joy Parr, "Gender History and Historical Practice," *Canadian Historical Review* 76, no. 3 (1995): 354–76. See also Parr, *The Gender of Breadwinners: Women, Men, and Change in Two Industrial Towns, 1880–1950* (Toronto: University of Toronto Press, 1990); Robert Rutherdale, "Fatherhood, Masculinity, and the Good Life during Canada's Baby Boom, 1945–1960," *Journal of Family History* 24, no. 3 (1999): 351–73; Joan W. Scott, "Gender: A Useful Category of Historical Analysis," *American Historical Review* 91 (1986): 1053–75; John Tosh, *Manful Assertions: Masculinities in Britain since 1800* (London: Routledge, 1991). See also Tosh, "What Should Historians Do with Masculinity? Reflections on Nineteenth-century Britain," *History Workshop* 38, no. 1: 179–202; Tosh, "The History of Masculinity: An Outdated Concept," in John H. Arnold and Sean Brady, eds., *What Is Masculinity?: Historical Dynamics from Antiquity to the Contemporary World* (London: Palgrave Macmillan, 2011), 17–34.

17 Franca Iacovetta, Molly Ladd-Taylor, Edmund Abaka, Lykke de la Cour, Lisa Dillon, Stephen Heathorn, Lorraine O'Donnell, and Adele Perry, *Becoming a Historian: A Canadian Manual for Women and Men* (Ottawa: Co-ordinating Committee on Women Historians, American Historical Association, Canadian Committee on Women's History, and Canadian Historical Association, 1999), 199.

18 R.W. Connell, *Masculinities* (Berkeley: University of California Press, 1995).

19 Connell, *Masculinities*.

20 Demetrakis Z. Demetriou, "Connell's Concept of Hegemonic Masculinity: A Critique," *Theory and Society* 30 (2001): 337–61 at 342.

21 Jane Scott, "Contrasts Studied at Gardens," *Globe and Mail*, 20 October 1951. Some men's memories of their postwar boyhood demonstrate how closely hockey skills, masculinity, and nationhood were intertwined. In a recent segment on CBC's *The Sunday Edition*, radio host Michael Enright recalled how, as a boy growing up in the 1950s, he felt "less of a guy, less of a Canadian because I could not skate." See Michael Enright, Sunday, 19 December 2010, available at http://www.cbc.ca/thesunday edition/shows/2010/12/19/december-19-2010. Similarly, in his recent memoir, former professional hockey player Derek Sanderson writes that when growing up in Niagara Falls, Ontario, during the postwar years, learning to skate and play hockey was "a rite of passage for most Canadian boys." See Sanderson, *Crossing the Line: The Outrageous Story of a Hockey Original* (Toronto: HarperCollins, 2012), 26.

22 According to Rutherdale, *Maclean's* was "Canada's most popular English-language weekly during the postwar era." See Rutherdale, "Fatherhood, Masculinity, and the Good Life," 354.

23 *Canadian Almanac and Legal and Court Directory for the Year 1945*, ed. Horace C. Corner (Toronto: Copp Clark, 1945), 734.

24 *Canadian Almanac & Directory for 1954*, ed. Beatrice Logan (Toronto: Copp Clark, 1954), 811.

25 In 1947, the *United Church Observer* had a circulation rate in Ontario of 58,200, while the circulation rate for *The Canadian Baptist* was 6,000. See Corner, *Canadian Almanac*, 765, 763. The circulation rate for the *Church Times* was not available.

26 Dummitt, *The Manly Modern*, 4.

27 Dummitt, *The Manly Modern*, 4.

28 Lara Campbell, *Respectable Citizens: Gender, Family, and Unemployment in Ontario's Great Depression* (Toronto: University of Toronto Press, 2009), 83.

29 Strong-Boag, "Canada's Wage Earning Wives," 6. See also Pierson, *"They're Still Women after All,"* 103–23.

30 Dummitt, *The Manly Modern*, 6.

31 Lewis Milligan, "Should Mothers Go Out to Work," *Leamington Post and News*, 12 April 1945.

32 Kenneth Rogers, *Boys Are Worth It* (Toronto: Ryerson, 1944), 4. George Isaac Harvey, a member of the Ontario legislature, cited "moral laxity" as a cause of social disorder as it contributed to an increase in "illegitimate children." See Harvey, letter to the editor, *Toronto Daily Star*, 1 September 1947. Related to this, some commentators blamed women, in particular women who adopted the "feminine impression of liberty," for the rise in the number of illegitimate children. See "Psychologists, Officials Said 'Lords of Education,'" *Toronto Daily Star*, 31 March 1948.

33 Neil Sutherland, *Children in English-Canadian Society: Framing the Twentieth-Century Consensus* (Toronto: University of Toronto Press, 1976), 14.

34 "London Boys Interested in Sports Welcome at Labor Council's Club," *London Free Press*, 13 May 1946 (London Public Library Archives, London Room Vertical Files# London-Boys).

35 Susan Faludi, *Stiffed: The Betrayal of the American Man* (New York: William Morrow, 1999), 24.

36 Editorial, *Essex County Reporter and Lakeshore News*, 23 August 1945.

37 Vincent Massey, *Speaking of Canada* (Toronto: Macmillan of Canada, 1959), 185.

38 "Strength of a Nation," *Acton Free Press*, 21 April 1949.

39 Murray G. Ross, *The Y.M.C.A. in Canada* (Toronto: Ryerson, 1951), 460–61.

40 Joe Holliday, *Dale of the Mounted: Dew Line Duty* (Toronto: Thomas Allen, 1957), cover jacket.

41 See, for example, "World Insecurity," *Leamington Post and News*, 20 May 1954; "The Insecurity of the World," *Kingsville Reporter*, 21 October 1954.

42 Hilda Neatby, *So Little for the Mind* (Toronto: Clarke, Irwin), 12–13.

43 Arthur R.M. Lower, "The Survival of a Soft Nation," *Saturday Night*, 31 October 1953, 7–8.

44 David I. Macleod, *Building Character in the American Boy: The Boy Scouts, YMCA, and Their Forerunners, 1870–1920* (Madison: University of Wisconsin Press, 1983).

45 "Athlone, Dr. Cody Salute Boy Scouts," *Globe and Mail*, 5 February 1945.

46 "20,000 Scouts and Wolves 'Howl' at Empire Chieftain," *Toronto Daily Star*, 6 September 1946.

47 Borden Spears, "No Menace Is Greater, Quiet Communist Hunt Is Under Way—Mr. King," *Toronto Daily Star*, 18 March 1948.

48 "The Fight Against Communism," *Essex County Reporter*, 24 April 1947.

49 "Creeping Communism," *Acton Free Press*, 12 May 1955.

50 "Others to Follow Robinson," *Toronto Daily Star*, 7 May 1948.

51 On the Canadian government's persecution of non-heterosexual identities, see Gary Kinsman, *The Regulation of Desire: Homo and Hetero Sexualities* (London: Black Rose, 1996); Gary Kinsman and Patrizia Gentile, *The Canadian War on Queers: National Security as Sexual Regulation* (Toronto: UBC Press, 2010).

52 "Laws Promote Tolerance," letter to the editor, *Globe and Mail*, 16 September 1948.

53 "Strategy for America," *Kingsville Reporter*, 9 September 1948.

54 Lewis Milligan, "Labour Struggle for Power," *Essex Free Press*, 5 April 1946.

55 Ontario, Department of Treasury and Economics, *Corporation Growth in Ontario, 1946–1969*, Ontario Statistical Centre, 1970, 9.

56 Campbell McFarlane, "The White Collar Man," *Calgary Herald*, 13 December 1946.

57 "The Problem of Leisure," *Leamington Post*, 26 April 1951.

58 Concerns over the rise of corporations in postwar Ontario generated a May 1949 editorial, which argued that the growth of "giant corporations" in Ontario was "crushing out the small businessman and the small independent farmer." See "The Dignity of Man," *Kingsville Reporter*, 5 May 1949.

59 John Thomas Phair and Norman Raeburn Speirs, *Good Health* (Toronto: Ginn, 1955), 8.

60 "Health of Workers Vital to Industry," *Leamington Post*, 17 June 1948.

61 "Say Communism Breeds as Health Standards Low," *Leamington Post*, 6 May 1954.

62 Sharon Wall, "Totem Poles, Teepees, and Token Traditions: 'Playing Indian' at Ontario Summer Camps, 1920–1955," *Canadian Historical Review* 86 (2005): 513–44 at 544.

63 Mark Moss, *Manliness and Militarism: Educating Young Boys in Ontario for War* (Toronto: Oxford University Press, 2001). For primary sources, see also William Byron Forbush, *The Boy Problem* (New York: Pilgrim, 1901); H.W. Gibson, *Boyology or Boy Analysis* (New York: Association Press, 1922).

64 See, for example, Edward A. Strecker, *Their Mothers' Sons* (New York: J.B. Lippincott, 1947). When reflecting on her gendered experiences growing up during the postwar period in the suburbs, one American writer recently put it this way: "The postwar suburbs were either heaven or hell for their inhabitants—endless stretches of brand-new houses on quarter-acre lots, occupied, during weekday hours, entirely by women and children. I grew up in one ... where the dads drove off to work every morning in what was then the only family car, leaving behind a land in which the only adult males were Tommy the milkman and Art, who drove an old bus outfitted with shelves of groceries that he sold to the stranded housewives." See Gail Collins, "'The Feminine Mystique' at 50," *New York Times Magazine*, 23 January 2013.

65 Whitaker and Marcuse, *Cold War Canada*; Robert J. Corber, *Homosexuality in Cold War America: Resistance and the Crisis of Masculinity* (Durham: Duke University Press, 1997).

66 "Battle of the Sexes," *Globe and Mail*, 17 April 1958.

67 James Bannerman, "Our Men Are Mice," *Maclean's*, January 1, 1948, 8.

68 Fred Bodsworth, "Man the Vanishing Sex," *Chatelaine*, May 1950, 34, 44.

69 Gordon Sinclair, "Help! Equal Rights for Men," *Chatelaine*, July 1950, 43. Similarly, sometime between 1952 and 1953, popular science fiction writer Philip K. Dick wrote *Voices from the Street*, a novel that reflected concerns over the fate and fitness of men's masculinity. See Dick, *Voices From the Street* (New York: Tom Doherty, 2007).

70 Irving Layton, *A Red Carpet for the Sun* (Toronto: McClelland and Stewart, 1959), 3.

71 "Age of Man Said Waning," *Globe and Mail*, 24 March 1956.

72 Samuel R. Laycock, "You Can't Get Away from Discipline," *Educational Review of the New Brunswick Teachers' Federation*, 60, no. 7 (1946): 7.

73 Henry G. Borchardt, "A Teacher Looks at His Job," *Life*, 6 January 1947, 78.

74 Michael Kimmel, *Manhood in America* (New York: Free Press, 1996). See also Kimmel, "The Contemporary 'Crisis' of Masculinity in Historical Perspective," in Harry Brod ed., *The Making of Masculinities: The New Men Studies* (Boston: Allen and Unwin, 1987), 121–54.

75 It is not surprising to find that today the changing nature of the post-industrial neoliberal capitalist economy, the increased movement of women into the labour force, the proliferation of queer identities, and challenges to the traditional definition of marriage have all come together to once again incite anxieties over the status of men's masculinity and have once again raised concerns over the fate of boyhood, a topic further explored in Chapter 5.

76 See Kinsman and Gentile, *The Canadian War on Queers*. See also David K. Johnson, *The Lavender Scare: The Cold War Persecution of Gays and Lesbians in the Federal Government* (Chicago: University of Chicago Press, 2004); Corber, *Homosexuality in Cold War America*.

77 See Elise Chenier, *Strangers in Our Midst: Sexual Deviancy in Postwar Ontario* (Toronto: University of Toronto Press, 2008).

78 Kinsman, *The Regulation of Desire*, 158.

79 J.V. McAree, "An Epoch-Marking Study of Sex," *Globe and Mail*, 13 January 1948.

80 Alfred C. Kinsey, Wardell B. Pomeroy, and Clyde E. Martin, *Sexual Behaviour in the Human Male* (Philadelphia and London: W.B. Saunders), 618–66.

81 Kinsey et al., *Sexual Behaviour*, 650.

82 Ontario, *Report of the Select Committee Appointed by the Legislative Assemble of the Province of Ontario, To Study and Report Upon Problems of Delinquent Individuals and Custodial Questions, and the Place of Reform Institutions Therein*, 8 March 1954, Toronto, 312.

83 "Forum on Sex Offenders," *Toronto Daily Star*, 30 January 1956. See also Frank S. Caprio, "Neurotics Blame Their Parents," *Toronto Daily Star*, 19 December 1957.

84 "Society Studies Pervert Problem," *Globe and Mail*, 28 November 1947.

85 See, for example, Mona Gleason, *Normalizing the Ideal: Psychology, Schooling, and the Family in Postwar Canada* (Toronto: University of Toronto Press, 1999); Mary Louise Adams, *The Trouble with Normal: Postwar Youth and the Making of Heterosexuality* (Toronto: University of Toronto Press, 1997).

86 Chenier, *Strangers in Our Midst*, 29.

87 "Psychologists, Officials Said 'Lords of Education,'" *Toronto Daily Star*, 31 March 1948.

88 "Successful Parenthood," *Kingsville Reporter*, 2 February 1950.

89 Frank Tumpane, "Bill and Psychiatry," *Globe and Mail*, 6 July 1946.

90 Ontario, Budget Statement of the Honourable James N. Allan, Treasurer of Ontario, 1961 (Toronto: Frank Fogg, Queen's Printer, 1961), 95.

91 Ontario, Budget Statement of the Honourable Leslie M. Frost, Prime Minister and Treasurer of the Province of Ontario, 1955 (Toronto: Baptist Johnston, Queen's Printer, 1955), 89.

92 Ontario, Budget Statement of the Honourable Dana Porter, Treasurer of the Province of Ontario, 1956 (Toronto: Baptist Johnston, Queen's Printer, 1956), 99.

93 Iacovetta, *Gatekeepers*, 1–19.

94 Cynthia Comacchio has noted that concerns over modern youth were typically associated with working-class and immigrant youth. In the eyes of "their largely

middle-class, white, Canadian born observers," it was these youths who were "inherently problematic" for the social order. For more on this, see Comacchio, *The Dominion of Youth*, 212.

95 John Porter, *The Vertical Mosaic: An Analysis of Social Class and Power in Canada* (Toronto: University of Toronto Press, 1965), 3.

96 See Iacovetta, "The Making of Suburban Bad Girls." See also Gleason, *Normalizing the Ideal*; Joy Parr, ed., *A Diversity of Women: Ontario, 1945–1980* (Toronto: University of Toronto Press, 1995).

97 J.V. McAree, "Delinquent Children in Great Britain," *Globe and Mail*, 9 June 1949.

98 William H. Whyte, *The Organization Man* (New York: Simon and Schuster, 1956), 75.

99 Joseph Pleck's point is that during the postwar era, women's influence on boys and men's difficulties in their role were formulated in terms of "feminization." See William Pleck, "The Theory of Male Sex-Role Identity," in Brod, ed., *The Making of Masculinities* (Boston: Allen and Unwin, 1987), 35.

100 "Boys in Trouble: Fruit of Unspeakable Homes," *Church Times*, 14 January 1955, 9.

101 "Can You Answer These Questions about Your Welfare Chest?" *Globe and Mail*, 11 October 1946.

102 See Wayne Martino and Maria Pallotta-Chiarolli, *So What's a Boy? Addressing Issues of Masculinity and Schooling* (Philadelphia: Open University Press, 2003); see also Michael Atkinson, *Deconstructing Men & Masculinities* (Toronto: Oxford University Press, 2011).

Notes to Chapter 1

1 On familialist ideology, see also Lynn Segal, *What Is to Be Done about the Family?* (Harmondsworth: Penguin, 1983).

2 "Delinquency: Working Mothers Share the Blame," *Toronto Daily Star*, 6 August 1955.

3 Interestingly, Ferdinand Lundberg and Marynia Farnham, in their 1947 book, *Modern Woman: The Lost Sex*, in their efforts to reconstruct the patriarchal family and to usher women back into the home, seemed disappointed that they could not simply follow the straightforward method of the Nazis: "The Nazis got women back in the home; they ordered them there" (364).

4 For a good example of postwar discourse about the "problem" of unmarried mothers, see Leontine Young, *Out of Wedlock: A Study of the Problems of the Unmarried Mother and Her Child* (Toronto: McGraw-Hill, 1954).

5 Editorial, *Toronto Daily Star*, 23 February 1946.

6 Marian E. Breckenridge and Elizabeth Lee Vincent, *Child Development: Physical and Psychological Growth Through the School Years* (Philadelphia: W.B. Saunders, 1949), 227, 229.

7 Franca Iacovetta, "Gossip, Contest, and Power in the Making of Suburban Bad Girls: Toronto, 1945–1960," *Canadian Historical Review* 80, no. 4 (1999): 585–623 at 598.

8 Robert M. Goldenson, "Why Boys and Girls Go Wrong or Right," *Parents' Magazine*, May 1951, 83.

9 Franca Iacovetta, *Gatekeepers: Reshaping Immigrant Lives in Cold War Canada* (Toronto: Between the Lines, 2006), 203.

10 Frank S. Caprio, "Neurotics Blame Their Parents," *Toronto Daily Star*, 19 December 1957.

11 "Babe Ruth Prays for Hour Then Passes in His Sleep," *Toronto Daily Star,* 17 August 1948.

12 "'The Good Samaritan,' Scott Mission Co.," *Globe and Mail,* 14 April 1945.

13 Editorial, *Toronto Daily Star,* 31 October 1946.

14 "Good Parents Make Nation Great," *Globe and Mail,* 4 July 1947.

15 For a detailed discussion of postwar fathers and masculine domesticity, see Robert Rutherdale, "Fatherhood, Masculinity, and the Good Life During Canada's Baby Boom, 1945–1965," *Journal of Family History* 24, no. 3 (1999): 351–73; and Rutherdale, "Fathers in Multiple Roles: Assessing Modern Canadian Fatherhood as a Masculine Category," in Christopher J. Greig and Wayne J. Martino, eds., *Canadian Men and Masculinities: Historical and Contemporary Perspectives* (Toronto: Canadian Scholars' Press, 2012). On interwar and postwar fatherhood, see also Cynthia Comacchio, "'A Postscript for Father': Defining a New Fatherhood in Interwar Canada," *Canadian Historical Review* 78, no. 3 (September 1997): 478–511; and Christopher Dummitt, "Finding a Place for Father: Selling the Barbeque in Postwar Canada," *Journal of the Canadian Historical Association* 9, no. 1 (1998): 209–23.

16 Dummitt, "Finding a Place for Father."

17 Benjamin Spock, *Baby and Child Care* (Montreal: Pocket Books of Canada, 1946, 1965), 314.

18 Rutherdale, "Fatherhood, Masculinity, and the Good Life," 369.

19 Benjamin Spock, *Dr. Spock Talks with Mothers: Growth and Guidance* (New York: Fawcett, 1961), 114.

20 Spock, *Dr. Spock Talks with Mothers.*

21 Nancy Cleaver, "A Self-Reliant Child," *Stouffville Sun-Tribune,* 14 June 1951.

22 Joan Morris, "Was the Victorian Father So Bad After All?", *Chatelaine,* April 1960, 44–52.

23 Ruth E. Hartley, "Some Implications of Current Changes in Sex Role Patterns," *Merrill-Palmer Quarterly of Behaviour and Development* 6, no. 3 (April 1960): 159.

24 Owram reports that *Father Knows Best* was the most famous of these shows and that it had an essential role in shaping middle-class expectations as to what families should be. See Owram, *Born at the Right Time: A History of the Baby-Boom Generation* (Toronto: University of Toronto Press, 1996), 91.

25 Marilyn Coleman et al., *Family Life in 20th Century America* (London: Greenwood, 2007), 168.

26 Ibid.

27 Mary Louise Adams, *The Trouble with Normal: Postwar Youth and the Making of Heterosexuality* (Toronto: University of Toronto Press, 1997), 30.

28 Pierre Berton and C.G. Gifford, "The Beanery Gang," *Maclean's,* 15 December 1948, 12.

29 "Today's Father Plays a New Role," *Globe and Mail,* 12 June 1958.

30 Norman Kelman, "Father's Part in Sex Education," *Parents' Magazine,* March 1949, 22.

31 Edward A. Strecker, "Pops and Popism," *Parents' Magazine,* May 1947, 102.

32 Spock, *Book of Baby and Child Care,* 18.

33 Kelman, "Father's Part in Sex Education," 20.

34 Kelman, "Father's Part in Sex Education," 22.

NOTES TO CHAPTER 1 137

35 Angelo Patri was a New York City public school principal and author of a widely syndicated newspaper column offering advice to parents in the 1920s and 1930s. His columns were republished in the postwar era. Patri, historian Julia Grant notes, focused his column's attention on school-aged boys. His advice, grounded in the work of G. Stanley Hall and a model of boyhood that accepted the idea of the boy-savage, often exemplified ideas about boyhood shared by many boy workers and educators. He believed that education and society, in general, should be modified to meet the demands of "boy-nature." See Grant, "A 'Real Boy' and Not a Sissy: Gender, Childhood, and Masculinity, 1890–1940," *Journal of Social History* (2004): 829–51. For Ontario readers, Patri's syndicated column *Our Children* ran almost daily in the *Globe and Mail* from 25 January 1937 to 16 January 1959. He was often cited by postwar boy experts. See, for example, this book by the General Secretary of the Big Brother Movement of Toronto: Kenneth Rogers, *Boys Are Worth It* (Toronto: Ryerson, December 1944). It seems that Patri's "boy-expertise" was useful with "boys" of any age. In January 1933, Patri was consulted by Toronto Maple Leafs manager Conn Smythe about the poor play of popular Maple Leaf hockey star and "Boy Phenom" Harvey Jackson. See "3 Stars of Saturday's Game," *Globe and Mail*, 30 January 1933.

36 Angelo Patri, "Our Children," *Globe and Mail*, 21 July 1945.

37 Spurgeon English, "How to Be a Good Father," *Parents' Magazine*, June 1950, 87.

38 "The House of Seagram," *Globe and Mail*, 19 June 1959.

39 Patri, "Our Children," *Globe and Mail*, 21 July 1945.

40 Spock, *Book of Baby and Child Care*, 315.

41 Laura C. Reynolds, "Calling All Fathers," *Parents' Magazine*, March 1945, 33.

42 English, "How to Be a Good Father," 87.

43 Frederick Elkin, *The Child and Society: The Process of Socialization* (New York: Random House, 1960), 55.

44 Paul Mussen and Luther Distler, "Child-Rearing Antecedents of Masculine Identification in Kindergarten Boys," *Child Development* 30, no. 1 (1960): 97.

45 Frances L. Ilg and Lousie Bates Ames, *The Gesell Institute's Child Behavior from Birth to Ten* (New York: Perennial Library, 1955), 223.

46 Herschel Alt, "In Defense of Mothers," *Parents' Magazine*, February 1950, 26.

47 Joan Morris, "Was the Victorian Father So Bad After All?", *Chatelaine*, April 1960, 44.

48 "Today's Father Plays a New Role," *Globe and Mail*, 12 June 1958.

49 Strecker, "Pops and Popism," 20.

50 Reginald Whitaker and Gary Marcuse, *Cold War Canada: The Making of a National Insecurity State, 1945–1957* (Toronto: University of Toronto Press, 1994), 22.

51 Joseph Pleck, "The Theory of Male Sex-Role Identity," in Harry Brod, ed., *The Making of Masculinities: The New Men Studies* (Boston: Allen and Unwin, 1987), 35.

52 See, for example, Hugh MacLennan, *Each Man's Son* (Toronto: Macmillan, 1951).

53 Joyce W. Knowles, "Some Personality Characteristics of Fatherless Boys," *Educational Review* 9, no. 3 (June 1957): 203.

54 Spock, *Baby and Child Care*, 577.

55 Robert Coughlan, "Changing Roles in Modern Marriage," *Life*, 24 December 1956, 110.

56 David Spurgeon, "Sex Role Disturbed by Industry," *Globe and Mail*, 7 November 1958.

57 Spurgeon, "Sex Role Disturbed."

58 "High Handed Wife Unhappy," *Globe and Mail*, 25 March 1960.

59 Paul S. Ullman, "Parental Participation in Childrearing as Evaluated by Male Social Deviates," *Pacific Sociological Review* 3, no. 2 (1960): 89–95 at 95.

60 Otto Fenichel, *The Pyschoanalytical Theory of Neurosis* (New York: W.W. Norton, 1945), 331.

61 "Gay Men Hounded in 60s by RCMP, Files Show," *Toronto Star*, 24 April 1992.

62 Whitaker and Marcuse, *Cold War Canada*, 184.

63 "RCMP Kept Files on 8,200 Gays," *Globe and Mail*, 24 April 1992.

64 Maurice Leznoff and William A. Westley, "The Homosexual Community," *Social Problems* 3, no. 4 (1956): 257–63 at 258.

65 Daniel J. Robinson and David Kimmel, "The Queer Career of Homosexual Security Vetting in Cold War Canada," *Canadian Historical Review* 75, no. 3 (1994): 319.

66 James C. Anderson, "Father Was a Gambler," *Maclean's*, 1 January 1949, 36.

67 Anderson, "Father Was a Gambler," 19.

68 Anderson, "Father Was a Gambler," 36.

69 Ernest Havemann, "What Makes a Criminal?", *Life*, 7 October 1957, 145, 152–58, 165–70.

70 Norman Kelman, "Social and Psychoanalytical Reflections on the Father," *American Scholar* 29, no. 3 (Summer, 1960): 335–58 at 342.

71 See, for example, Daniel G. Brown, "Psychosexual Disturbances: Transvestism and Sex-Role Inversion," *Marriage and Family Living* 22, no. 3 (August, 1960): 218–27.

72 Jennifer A. Stephen, *Pick One Intelligent Girl: Employability, Domesticity, and the Gendering of Canada's Welfare State, 1939–1947* (Toronto: University of Toronto Press, 2007), 99.

73 Wilfrid L. Cozens, letter to the editor, *Globe and Mail*, 5 August 1950.

74 Mercedes Steedman, "The Red Petticoat Brigade: Mine Mill Women's Auxiliaries and the Threat from Within, 1940s–1970s," in Gary Kinsman, Dieter K. Buse, and Mercedes Steedman, eds., *Whose National Security?: Canadian State Surveillance and the Creation of Enemies* (Toronto: Between the Lines, 2000), 57.

75 Robert Thom, letter to the editor, *Globe and Mail*, 4 July 1947.

76 Stephen, *Pick One Intelligent Girl,* 107.

77 Elijah Adlow, "Delinquency: Working Mothers Share the Blame," *Toronto Daily Star*, 6 August 1955.

78 "Parent's Greed for Money Seen Boy's Downfall," *Evening Telegram*, 2 March 1946.

79 Brock Chisholm, "Do Women Make War?", *Chatelaine*, 7 July 1948, 6–7, 36–37.

80 "Homelife Causes Maladjustments, Psychiatrist Says," *Globe and Mail*, 9 May 1946.

81 Brigadier J.R. Rees, "What War Taught Us about Human Nature," *New York Times*, 17 March 1946.

82 "Home and School Clubs Survey Urgent Problems," *Globe and Mail*, 22 January 1947.

83 "Good Parents Make Nation Great," *Globe and Mail*, 4 July 1947.

84 Coughlin, "Changing Roles in Modern Marriage," 114.

85 Janet Powers, "Stan Was Too Cautious," *Chatelaine*, 1 May 1946, 102.

86 Frances L. Ilg and Louisie Bates Ames, "Child Behaviour: Don't Call Him 'Sweetheart Son," *Toronto Daily Star*, 29 November 1960.

87 Dorothy Muir Bowman, "Didn't Want to Be a Sissy," *Newmarket Era*, 4 January 1951.

88 Bowman, "Didn't Want to Be a Sissy."

89 Bowman, "Didn't Want to Be a Sissy."

90 In their 1947 work *Modern Woman*, Lunderberg and Farnham asserted that homosexuals are "mother fixated" or are the products of overprotective mothers (349). See also Ullman, "Parental Participation in Childrearing."

91 For more on this, see Gary Kinsman and Patrizia Gentile, *The Canadian War on Queers: National Security as Sexual Regulation* (Vancouver: UBC Press, 2010).

92 Samuel Laycock, "Your Child's Love Life," *Maclean's*, 15 November 1946, 8.

93 Samuel Laycock, "How to Protect Your Child from Sex Deviates," *Chatelaine*, April 1956, 11.

94 Elkin, *The Child and Society*, 54.

95 "Threat of Feminine Identity: Car Called Masculinity Symbol to Accident Repeaters," *Globe and Mail*, 8 June 1961.

96 Ilg and Ames, "Child Behaviour."

97 Deborah C. Stearns, "Anger and Aggression," in Paula S. Fass, ed., *Encyclopedia of Children and Childhood in History and Society*, vol. 1 (New York: Macmillan Reference USA, 2004), 61.

98 Eve Burkhardt, "The Soda Set," *Maclean's*, 15 December 1946, 20.

99 William J. Meyer and George G. Thompson, "Sex Differences in the Distribution of Teacher Approval and Disapproval among Sixth Grade Children," *Journal of Educational Psychology* 47, no. 7 (1956): 393.

100 Meyer and Thompson, "Sex Differences," 386.

101 George Kisker, "Men Are Men—or Are They?" *Maclean's*, 1 April 1948, 16.

102 Nancy Cleaver, "Don't Be a Coward," *Stouffville Tribune*, 15 February 1951.

103 Powers, "Stan Was Too Cautious," 102.

104 Powers, "Stan Was Too Cautious"; emphasis in the original.

105 Ilg and Ames, "Child Behaviour," *Toronto Daily Star*, 29 November 1960.

106 Ilg and Ames, "Child Behaviour."

107 Sophie Drinker and Josephine Schreier, "Patriarchal Values in Women's Education," *Journal of Higher Education* 25, no. 3 (1954): 115–21, 171.

Notes to Chapter 2

1 "Jamboree of New Horizons," *Toronto Daily Star*, 17 August 1955.

2 William H. Whyte, *The Organization Man* (New York: Simon and Schuster, 1956), 75.

3 Peter S. McInnis, "Teamwork for Harmony: Labour-Management Production Committees and the Postwar Settlement in Canada," *Canadian Historical Review* 77, no. 33 (1996): 317.

4 McInnis, "Teamwork for Harmony."

5 McInnis, "Teamwork for Harmony."

6 Craig Heron and Steve Penfold, *The Workers' Festival: A History of Labour Day in Canada* (Toronto: University of Toronto Press, 2005), 197.

7 "Canada's Industrial Peace," *Essex Free Press*, 23 September 1949.

8 Angered by the nation's first mass strike of the railway unions in 1950, which caused some concern that big cities would not be fed and businesses would shut down from coast to coast, one author of a letter to the editor expressed the idea that the trade unions should stop trying to settle the issue at "gun point," but should attempt to do so on the basis of "fair play." See "Finds Safeguards Are Lacking," letter to the editor, *Globe and Mail*, 31 August 1950.

9 "Industry Hold Key Place in Future Battle," *Globe and Mail*, 22 September 1945.

10 "Doolittle Plans to Crush Japan by Air Assaults," *Globe and Mail*, 12 May 1945.

11 "Key Nurses Being Trained to Teach Civil Defense," *Globe and Mail*, 16 November 1951.

12 Lewis Milligan, "The Mightiest Ally of Russia," *Essex Free Press*, 27 September 1946.

13 "Battle Line No. 2," *Acton Free Press*, 27 March 1947.

14 Editorial, "The Same Answer," *Acton Free Press*, 15 August 1946.

15 "Labour and Management Try Teamwork," *Globe and Mail*, 26 April 1946.

16 "Finance at Large," *Globe and Mail*, 20 February 1947.

17 "Need Top Efficiency to Compete," *Teamwork in Industry*, October 1960, 3.

18 "Do We Look High Enough in Seeking Formula for Effective Postwar Teamwork in Industry?" *Globe and Mail*, 15 September 1945.

19 "Mounties Staged a Massive Hunt for Gay Males in Civil Service," *Globe and Mail*, 24 April 1992; "PM Denounces 1960s Purge of Homosexual Civil Servants," *Globe and Mail*, 28 April 1992.

20 "Service Clubs Fete Local Hockey Teams," *Toronto Daily Star*, 6 May 1946.

21 Kimball McIlroy, "Shall I Let My Son Play Hockey?", *Saturday Night*, 18 January 1949, 16.

22 "Father Flannigan Guest Speaker at Unionville Hockey Banquet," *Stouffville Tribune*, 10 May 1951.

23 McIlroy, "Shall I Let My Son Play Hockey?", 16.

24 Angelo Patri, "Must Take Bumps, Lumps during Play and in Life," *Globe and Mail*, 14 June 1950.

25 "School Without Bars Reclaims Delinquents," *Telegram*, 19 March 1949.

26 "Childhood Problems," *Parents' Magazine*, September 1946, 34.

27 Samuel Bowles and Herbert Gintis, *Democracy and Capitalism: Property, Community, and the Contradictions of Modern Social Thought* (New York: Basic, 1986), 96–98.

28 Ray O. Duncan, "The Contribution of School Athletics to the Growing Boy," *Journal of Educational Sociology* 28, no. 6 (February 1955): 274.

29 *The Man in the Gray Flannel Suit*, DVD, dir. Nunnally Johnson (1956; Twentieth Century Fox, 2005). The film played at Toronto's Shea's Theatre in May 1946 and was reviewed by *Star* critic Jack Karr, who praised the film for being an "intelligent and sensitive piece of work." See "Showplace," *Toronto Daily Star*, 16 May 1956.

30 "Children of the World Might Help to Bring Differing Peoples Together," *Globe and Mail*, 2 March 1946.

31 "Boss–Employee Partnership Importance Told to Jaycees," *Leamington Post*, 13 March 1958.

32 Colin D. Howell, *Blood, Sweat, and Cheers: Sport and the Making of Modern Canada* (Toronto: University of Toronto Press, 2001), 51.

33 "Today's Father Plays a New Role," *Globe and Mail*, 12 June 1958.

34 Benjamin Spock, *Baby and Child Care* (Montreal: Pocket Books of Canada, 1946, 1965), 310.

35 Spock, *Baby and Child Care*, 311.

36 B.E.N, review of *Safe on Second Base* by Ed Winfield, *Saturday Night*, 2 May 1953, 16.

37 Scott Young, *Boy on Defense* (Toronto: McClelland and Stewart, 1953).

38 Louisa Matthews, review of *Boy on Defence* by Scott Young, *Saturday Night*, 28 November 1953, 32.

39 William Arthur Deacon, review of *Scrubs on Skates* by Scott Young, *Globe and Mail*, 1 November 1952.

40 J.L. Charlesworth, review of *Scrubs on Skates* by Scott Young, *Saturday Night*, 22 November 1952, 42.

41 Deacon, review of *Scrubs on Skates*.

42 Deacon, review of *Scrubs on Skates*.

43 Charlesworth, review of *Scrubs on Skates*.

44 Brian Cahill, "Backfire of the Neighbourhood Spirit," *Saturday Night*, 1 September 1956, 10–11, 42.

45 McIlroy, "Shall I Let My Son Play Hockey?"

46 McIlroy, "Shall I Let My Son Play Hockey?"

47 Carol Dyhouse, "Women Students and the London Medical Schools, 1914–39: The Anatomy of a Masculine Culture," *Gender and History* 10, no. 1 (April 1998): 110–32.

48 Adrian Bingham, *Gender, Modernity, and the Popular Press in Inter-War Britain* (Oxford: Oxford University Press, 2004), 220.

49 "Look Here, Mr. Childs," *Globe and Mail*, 25 January 1946.

50 "A Helping Hand," *Globe and Mail*, 8 January 1945.

51 "Nonchalant, Eh," *Globe and Mail*, 22 January 1946.

52 "School Boy Softballers Play Exciting Games," *Globe and Mail*, 12 June 1946.

53 During the postwar period, for example, companies such as Canadian Comstock, United Suburban Gas Company, and O'Keefe's Brewery Company often employed the concept of teamwork as a key part of their advertising campaigns. For example, one advertisement, found in the 4 November 1952 edition of the *Globe and Mail* for the engineering construction firm Canadian Comstock, started with the caption, "The Teamwork That Counts." Likewise, Statham's Drug Store in Kingsville, Ontario, used the slogan "The Teamwork Behind Your Medicine" as the head caption in one of their newspaper ad campaigns. See "Statham's [advertisement]," *Kingsville Reporter*, 20 October 1949. Community organizations such as the Lions Club also employed the concept of teamwork in their ad campaigns to solicit donations from the public. See "Leamington Lion's Club [advertisement]," *Leamington Post and News*, 21 April 1949. For other examples, see "United Suburban Gas Company [advertisement]," *Georgetown Herald*, 20 June 1956; and "O'Keefe's [advertisement]," *Georgetown Herald*, 21 December 1949.

54 Ontario, Royal Commission on Education in Ontario, *Report* (Toronto: Baptist Johnston, King's Printer, 1950), 29.

55 "Teamwork Pays in Air as in Hockey, Says Ace," *Globe and Mail*, 15 October 1947.

56 Varda Burstyn, *The Rites of Men: Manhood, Politics, and the Culture of Sport* (Toronto: University of Toronto Press, 2000), 120.

57 Burstyn, *The Rites of Men*.

58 Geoffrey S. Smith, "National Security and Personal Isolation: Sex, Gender, and Disease in the Cold-War United States," *International History Review* 14 (May 1992): 307–37 at 332.

59 Jim Vipond, "Sports Digest," *Globe and Mail*, 8 February 1956.

60 Canada, Parliament of Canada, House of Commons, *Official Reports of the Debates of the House of Commons of the Dominion of Canada*, June 1950 (Ottawa: Queen's Printer), IV:3363.

61 Burstyn, *The Rites of Men*, 74.

62 Bingham, *Gender, Modernity*, 219.

63 "They Loved It," *Globe and Mail*, 2 November 1948.

64 "They Loved It," *Globe and Mail*, 2 November 1948.

65 Bruce Kidd, "Sports and Masculinity," in Michael Kaufman, ed., *Beyond Patriarchy* (Toronto: Oxford University Press, 1987), 255.

66 Foster Hewitt, *Along Olympic Road* (Toronto: Ryerson, 1951), 21.

67 "The Siberia Treatment," *Acton Free Press*, 26 February 1959.

68 "Pro Hockey Is Every Kid's Dream," *Globe and Mail*, 9 January 1950.

69 Michael Kimmel, "Men's Responses to Feminism at the Turn of the Century," *Gender and Society* 1, no. 3 (September 1987): 261.

70 Hiram Walker, advertisement, *Maclean's*, 15 April 1946, 5.

71 "Preston Boy Is Stabbed in School "Gang" Battle," *Toronto Evening Telegram*, 13 March 1946.

72 Brigadier J.R. Rees, "What War Taught Us about Human Nature," *New York Times*, 17 March 1946.

73 R.D. Gidney, *From Hope to Harris: The Reshaping of Ontario's Schools* (Toronto: University of Toronto Press, 1999), 25.

74 John Thomas Phair and Norman Raeburn Speirs, *Good Health* (Toronto: Ginn, 1945), 8.

75 "Job Problem," *Kingsville Reporter*, 20 March 1952.

76 Phair and Speirs, *Good Health*, 8.

77 "Disgraceful Absenteeism," *Globe and Mail*, 17 February 1947. See also Robert Kahn and Susan Radius, "Two Roads to Health Care: U.S. and Canadian Policies 1945–1975," *Medical Care* 12, no. 3 (March 1974): 189–201 at 193. Worker absenteeism and the costs this brought to Canadian industry remained a concern from the postwar era well into the late 1970s. See, for example, W.D. Wood and Pradeep Kumar, *The Current Industrial Relations Scene in Canada 1979* (Kingston: Industrial Relations Centre, 1979), 110.

78 "Absenteeism: The New National Malady," *Fortune* 27 (March 1943): 104–5.

79 "Absenteeism Costs Business 500 Million Dollars a Year," *Teamwork in Industry* (July–August 1959), 3.

80 Marian E. Breckenridge and Elizabeth Lee Vincent, *Child Development: Physical and Psychological Growth Through the School Years* (Philadelphia: W.B. Saunders, 1949), 24.

81 Breckenridge and Vincent, *Child Development*, 25.

82 Breckenridge and Vincent, *Child Development*, 25.

83 Pauline Beery Maek, "Do Children Need Sweets," *Parents' Magazine*, March 1950, 51.

84 On "thin" children as a problem, see, for example, Spock, *Baby and Child Care*, 421.

85 John K. McCreary, "Psychopathia Homosexualis," *Canadian Journal of Psychology* 4 (1950): 63–74 at 64.

86 McCreary, "Psychopathia Homosexualis," 67.

87 Frances L. Ilg and Lousie Bates Ames, *The Gesell Institute's Child Behavior from Birth to Ten* (New York: Perennial Library, 1955), 45.

88 Breckenridge and Vincent, *Child Development*, 28.

89 Breckenridge and Vincent, *Child Development*, 29.

90 "The Doctor Made a Boy of Bill," *Parents' Magazine*, September 1945.

91 "The Doctor Made a Boy of Bill," *Parents' Magazine*.

92 "The Doctor Made a Boy of Bill," *Parents' Magazine*.

93 "The Doctor Made a Boy of Bill," *Parents' Magazine*.

94 Whyte, *The Organization Man*, 152.

95 D. Sangster, "What Do Our Children Think About?", *Chatelaine*, March 1959, 17–19, 48–50.

96 Royal Commission on Education in Ontario, *Report*, 70.

97 Royal Commission on Education in Ontario, *Report*, 70.

98 "Voyageurs of the 20th Century, 27 Boys of Muskoka Camp Plan to Paddle Their Way to Exhibition," *Toronto Daily Star*, 22 August 1958.

99 "Boys Enjoy Jaunts to Canadian Wilds," *Toronto Daily Star*, 18 June 1960.

100 Whyte, *The Organization Man*, 148.

101 "Chain of Pals Saves Youth from River," *Telegram*, 28 January 1950.

102 Whyte, *The Organization Man*, 4.

103 Whyte, *The Organization Man*, 179.

104 Robert Bothwell, Ian Drummond, and John English, *Canada since 1945: Power, Politics, and Provincialism* (Toronto: University of Toronto Press, 1981), 19.

105 Spock, *Baby and Child Care*, 577.

106 Frank Tumpane, "How to Understand Women," *Chatelaine*, November 1950, 19.

107 Tumpane, "How to Understand Women."

108 W.H. Gibson, *Boyology or Boy Analysis* (New York: Association Press, 1922), 82.

109 "United Appeal Fund Aids Boy Scout Work Asset to Community," *Toronto Daily Star*, 5 September 1956.

110 David Macleod notes that many boy-workers at the turn of the twentieth century in the United States assumed it began closer to the age of twelve. See David I. Macleod, *Building Character in the American Boy: The Boy Scouts, YMCA, and Their Forerunners, 1870–1920* (Madison: University of Wisconsin Press, 1983), 106.

111 Royal Commission on Education in Ontario, *Report*, 50.

112 Breckenridge and Vincent, *Child Development*, 464.

113 A.R. Crane, "Pre-Adolescent Gangs: A Topological Interpretation," *Journal of Genetic Psychology* 81, no. 1 (1952): 113–23 at 118.

114 Charles E. Hendry, "Adolescence," *The School*, June 1948, 588.

115 Editorial, *Globe and Mail*, 12 July 1948.

116 Breckenridge and Vincent, *Child Development*, 519.

117 See, for example, 'Gangs Are Unnecessary," *Globe and Mail*, 4 September 1948.

118 John Hagedorn, "Gangs," in *Encyclopedia of Community: From Village to the Virtual World*, ed. Karen Christenson and David Levison (Thousand Oaks: Sage, 2003), 517.

119 Joan Sangster, *Girl Trouble: Female Delinquency in English Canada* (Toronto: Between the Lines, 2002), 31.

120 Lewis Yablonsky, "The Delinquent Gang as a Near-Group," *Social Problems* 17, no. 2 (1959): 108–17 at 108.

121 Albert Cohen, *Delinquent Boys: The Culture of the Gang* (Glencoe: Free Press, 1955).

122 Herbert Bloch and Arthur Niederhoffer, *The Gang: A Study in Adolescent Behavior* (New York: Philosophical Library, 1958).

123 See, for example, "Gangs Are Unnecessary," *Globe and Mail*, 4 September 1948.

124 "Can Get Results with Gangs, View of Worker," *Toronto Daily Star*, 24 January 1946.

125 "New Y Approach to Boys Ends Police Headaches," *Globe and Mail*, 29 April 1947.

126 "Can Get Results with Gangs, View of Worker," *Toronto Daily Star*.

127 "Can Get Results with Gangs, View of Worker," *Toronto Daily Star*.

128 "Can Get Results with Gangs, View of Worker," *Toronto Daily Star*.

129 "Can Get Results with Gangs, View of Worker," *Toronto Daily Star*.

130 Julia Grant, "A 'Real Boy' and Not a Sissy: Gender, Childhood, and Masculinity, 1890–1940," *Journal of Social History* 37, no. 4 (2004): 829–51 at 835.

131 Grant, "A 'Real Boy' and Not a Sissy."

132 Gang instinct as a natural feature of boyhood was first theorized as part of recapitulation theory. The recapitulation theory, reformulated in the 1920s by psychologist and educational reformer G. Stanley Hall, posited that each successive stage of an individual's development represented one of the adult forms that appeared in its evolutionary history. Green offers a useful summary. The "Law of Recapitulation," born out of the scientific optimism of the Progressive Era, was the first modern theory of child development. It held that as the child progressed from infancy to adolescence, it recapitulated each stage of human evolution, beginning with the ape, ascending toward the savage, and climaxing with civilized man. See Amy Susan Green, "Savage Childhood: The Scientific Construction of Girlhood and Boyhood in the Progressive Era," Ph.D. diss., Yale University, 1995, 75.

133 "Don't Smash That Boy Gang, Harness It—Expert," *Toronto Daily Star*, 21 January 1946.

134 "Don't Smash That Boy Gang, Harness It—Expert," *Toronto Daily Star*.

135 "Teach Parents First Kitchener Youth Plan," *Toronto Daily Star*, 27 February 1946.

136 Editorial, *Globe and Mail*, 12 July 1948.

137 "United Appeal Fund Aids Boy Scout Work," *Toronto Daily Star*, 5 September 1956.

138 "United Appeal Fund Aids Boy Scout Work," *Toronto Daily Star*.

139 "Use Gang Instinct in Boys' Work—Pastor," *Toronto Daily Star*, 7 June 1951.

140 "Use Gang Instinct in Boys' Work—Pastor," *Toronto Daily Star*.

141 Editorial, *Globe and Mail*, 12 July 1948.

142 Breckenridge and Vincent, *Child Development*, 467.

143 "Childhood Problems," *Parents' Magazine*, February 1950, 46.

144 Charles Morris, "The Child Who Walks Alone," *Parents' Magazine*, September 1950, 142.

145 Bowles and Gintis, *Democracy and Capitalism*, 112.

Notes to Chapter 3

1 Joseph A. Schumpeter, *The Theory of Economic Development: An Inquiry into Profits, Capital, Credit, Interest, and the Business Cycle* (New Brunswick: Transaction, 1934/1983), 93–94.

2 Lois Stevenson, "Against All Odds: The Entrepreneurship of Women," *Journal of Small Business Management* 24 no. 4 (1986): 30–36 at 36.

3 Attila Bruni et al., "Doing Gender, Doing Entrepreneurship: An Ethnographic Account of Intertwined Practices," *Gender, Work and Organization* 11, no. 4 (July 2004): 406–29 at 407.

4 R.W. Connell, "The Big Picture: Masculinities in Recent World History," *Theory and Society* 22 (1993): 614.

5 C. Wright Mills, *White Collar: The American Middle Classes* (New York: Oxford University Press, 1951), xiv.

6 Schumpeter, *The Theory of Economic Development*, 93–94.
7 Schumpeter, *Business Cycles: A Theoretical, Historical and Statistical Analysis of the Capitalist Process* (New York: McGraw-Hill, 1939), 82.
8 William H. Whyte, *The Organization Man* (New York: Simon and Schuster, 1956), 75-77.
9 Called to mind here, for me, are the powerful visual images found in King Vidor's 1949 adaption of Ayn Rand's 1943 book *The Fountainhead*. The film starred Gary Cooper playing the role of Howard Roark, the virile quintessential entrepreneurial architect and the embodiment of hegemonic masculinity. See *The Fountainhead*, DVD, dir. King Vidor (1949; Warner Brothers, 2006).
10 Heinz Hartmann, "Managers and Entrepreneurs: A Useful Distinction?" *Administrative Science Quarterly* 3, no. 4 (March 1959): 429–51 at 431.
11 "Canada Can Do Big Trade with China," *Globe and Mail*, 30 May 1950.
12 "Boy's Quick Action Helps Save Eight," *Evening Telegram*, 3 January 1946.
13 "Boy Hero," *Globe and Mail*, 13 January 1945.
14 "Boy in Sunday Pants, Taught by 'Y,' Makes 4th Rescue," *Toronto Daily Star*, 5 March 1948.
15 Kate Mulholland, "Entrepreneurialism, Masculinities and the Self-Made Man," in David L. Collinson and Jeff Hearn, eds., *Men as Managers, Managers as Men: Critical Perspectives on Men, Masculinities, and Managements* (London: Sage, 1996), 143.
16 "Admiration for a Hero, 11 Years Old," *Toronto Evening Telegram*, 10 November 1948.
17 "Boy, 13, Gets Medal for Saving Sailors," *Toronto Daily Star*, 18 March 1948.
18 "31 Decorated: George Medal to Boy Investiture High Point," *Globe and Mail*, 24 May 1954.
19 Deborah Kerfoot and David Knights, "'The Best Is Yet to Come?': The Quest for Embodiment in Managerial Work," in Collinson and Hearn, eds., *Men and Managers, Managers as Men*, 91.
20 Robert Von der Osten, "Four Generations of Tom Swift: Ideology in Juvenile Science Fiction," *The Lion and the Unicorn* 28, no. 2 (2004): 268–83 at 271.
21 "Hate to Tell Boy Baby Brother Died," *Evening Telegram*, 28 January 1946.
22 "Boy, 6, Carries Pal, 5 Quarter Mile to Aid," *Toronto Daily Star*, 24 August 1946.
23 Mulholland, "Entrepreneurialism, Masculinities," 126.
24 "Boy, 7, Saves Sisters on Rail Bridge," *Globe and Mail*, 10 July 1954.
25 "Boy Who Can't Run," *Globe and Mail*, 11 July 1954.
26 "Boys, 7, Save Little Girl from Spadina Rd. Creek," *Globe and Mail*, 21 May 1945.
27 "Boy, 13, Jumps into Lake Rescues Scarboro Girl, 4," *Evening Telegram*, 2 July 1946.
28 "Boy, 11, Saves Mom from Chilly Lake Water," *Globe and Mail*, 2 May 1952.
29 "11-year-Old Boy Pulls Mother from Flames," *Globe and Mail*, 13 September 1948.
30 "Boy, 14, Saves Mother," *Globe and Mail*, 3 June 1950.
31 "Mother Saved from Flames by Son, Age 11," *Evening Telegram*, 13 September 1948.
32 "Boy Leads Way as 3 Escape Blazing Cottage," *Toronto Telegram*, 7 January 1950.
33 "Boy Leads Way as 3 Escape Blazing Cottage," *Toronto Telegram*.
34 "Announcing the Inauguration of the Dow Award," *Toronto Daily Star*, 15 April 1946; "The Dow Award," *Evening Telegram*, 19 July 1946. The award was given out for only a short time. Dow Brewery discontinued the award in 1951.

35 "Boy Dies after Heroically Saving Grandmother's Life," *Globe and Mail*, 30 April 1951. Like other awards, this particular award was also published in *Maclean's* magazine. See "Dow Brewery Boy Dies after Heroically Saving Grandmother's Life," *Maclean's*, 15 June 1951, 50.

36 "Boy Dies after Heroically."

37 Beverly Pennell, "Redeeming Masculinity at the End of the Second Millennium," in John Stephens, ed., *Ways of Being Male: Representing Masculinity in Children's Literature and Film* (New York: Routledge, 2002), 60.

38 Veronica Strong-Boag, "Home Dreams: Women and the Suburban Experiment in Canada, 1945–60," *Canadian Historical Review* 72, no. 4 (1991): 471–505 at 477.

39 "Let Men Be Boss, You've Botched It, Women Told," *Toronto Daily Star*, 25 June 1946.

40 "Can You Help a Boy Own a Bike," *Toronto Daily Star*, 14 April 1955.

41 Although made in 1940, I have included *The Biscuit Eater* because in 1948 it was one of the films chosen by the Canadian Motion Picture Distributors Association as an appropriate movie to include in a children's film library. See "If the Youngsters Wiggle Movie No Good, Say Test," *Toronto Daily Star*, 21 September 1948.

42 "Joe E. Brown Is Parson in Film of Boy and His Dog," *Toronto Daily Star*, 20 February 1948.

43 Pierre Berton, "This Column Is Strictly for Lassie Fans," *Toronto Daily Star*, 25 August 1959.

44 Leland Sillman, *The Daredevil* (Philadelphia: John C. Winston, 1948). This boy–dog book was recommended to Ontario parents for their boys. See "The Bookshelf," *Saturday Night*, 22 May 1948, 22.

45 Catherine Anthony Clark, *The Golden Pine Cone* (Toronto: Macmillan of Canada, 1950).

46 Lois Lanski, *Davy and His Dog* (Oxford: Oxford University Press, 1956).

47 Louise Rorke, *Lefty's Adventure* (Toronto: Thomas Nelson, 1945).

48 "The Rendezvous Book Shop," *Globe and Mail*, 15 December 1945.

49 Morley Callaghan, *Luke Baldwin's Vow* (Toronto: Macmillan of Canada, 1948).

50 Farley Mowat, *The Dog Who Wouldn't Be* (Boston: Little, Brown, 1957).

51 Sally Townsend, "Tender Boy and Dog Story Study of Unfolding Youth," *Globe and Mail*, 30 October 1948.

52 Helen O'Reilly, Review of *Good-Bye, My Lady* by James Street, *Globe and Mail*, 20 November 1954.

53 Lotta Dempsey, "Mr. Orpen Likes Horses and His Grand Piano," *Globe and Mail*, 31 December 1949.

54 Helene Ahl, "Why Research on Women Entrepreneurs Needs New Directions," *Entrepeneurship Theory and Practice* 30, no. 5 (2006): 595–621 at 601.

55 "Boy with His Dog," *Toronto Daily Star*, 2 July 1947.

56 Edna Jaques, "There Is a Strange Serenity," *Toronto Daily Star*, 30 January 1954.

57 Maunsell B. Jackson, "A Boy and a Dog Journey to Far Places," *Globe and Mail*, 17 April 1954.

58 Angelo Patri, "Our Children: Grave Injustice Done Child if Parents Object to Dog," *Globe and Mail*, 24 February 1947.

59 Harvey Caulfield, "A Boy and His Dog," *Toronto Daily Star*, 30 April 1952.

60 "Underground Dog Shares Homeless Dutch Boy's Lot," *Toronto Daily Star*, 6 January 1945.

61 "Boy, 13, Going to Spend $140.00 on Funeral for His Pet Dog," *Toronto Daily Star*, 7 June 1956.

62 "Boy, 13, Going to Spend $140.00," *Toronto Daily Star*.

63 "Boy, 13, Going to Spend $140.00," *Toronto Daily Star*.

64 "J.P. Has His dog, May Discard Braces," *Globe and Mail*, 28 November 1952.

65 "Dog Pulls Clothes, but Pal, 5, Burns," *Toronto Daily Star*, 7 June 1951.

66 "Rescue Dog First, Boy of 14 Insists," *Toronto Daily Star*, 30 March 1948.

67 "Boy, 13, Saves Dog from Speed River," *Toronto Daily Star*, 23 March 1949.

68 "Boy, 13, Saves Dog," *Toronto Daily Star*.

69 "Boy and Dog Saved from Hamilton Bay," *Globe and Mail*, 30 March 1948.

70 "Boy and Dog Saved from Hamilton Bay," *Globe and Mail*.

71 "Boy, 14, Kills Wolf Attacking His Dog," *Evening Telegram*, 9 October 1948.

72 R.K. Mitchell, "Oral History and Expert Scripts: Demystifying the Entrepreneurial Experience," *International Journal of Entrepreneurial Behaviour and Research* 3, no. 2 (1997): 122–39.

73 "Saved Dog in Canyon, Gets Award," *Globe and Mail*, 21 July 1953.

74 "Saved Dog in Canyon," *Globe and Mail*.

75 Mowat, *The Dog Who Wouldn't Be*.

76 Mowat, *The Dog Who Wouldn't Be*, 10, 11.

77 Mowat, *The Dog Who Wouldn't Be*, 6, 10.

78 Marion Swartz, *A History of Dogs in the Early Americas* (New Haven: Yale University Press, 1997), 3.

79 Mulholland, "Entrepreneurialism, Masculinities," 132.

80 Mulholland, "Entrepreneurialism, Masculinities," 131.

81 Edmund W. Vaz, "Delinquency and the Youth Culture: Upper and Middle-Class Boys," *Journal of Criminal Law, Criminology, and Police Science* 60, no. 1 (1969): 33–46 at 37.

82 David MacDonald, "Why Have the Boy Scouts Survived?", *Maclean's*, 20 August 1955, 52–57.

83 "Drew Applauds Leadership Given by Scout Groups," *Globe and Mail*, 26 February 1945.

84 "Drew Applauds Leadership," *Globe and Mail*.

85 "20,000 Scouts and Wolves 'Howl' at Empire Chieftain," *Toronto Daily Star*, 6 September 1946.

86 "20,000 Scouts and Wolves," *Toronto Daily Star*.

87 "Athlone, Dr. Cody Salute Boy Scouts," *Globe and Mail*, 5 February 1945.

88 "Alexander Gladly Accepts Office of Chief Scout," *Globe and Mail*, 1 May 1946.

89 "Alexander Gladly Accepts," *Globe and Mail*.

90 "Saunders Accepts Post as Boy Scout Deputy," *Globe and Mail*, 1 March 1948.

91 Editorial, *Globe and Mail*, 2 February 1953.

92 "Canada's Future … in Training," *Globe and Mail*, 17 February 1945.

93 "48,469 in Boy Scouts Up 10,000 in 5 years," *Toronto Daily Star*, 10 February 1947.

94 "Scouts Need Assistance," *Newmarket Era and Express*, 12 March 1953.

95 See, for example, "$125,000 Sought in Toronto Drive," *Globe and Mail*, 31 January 1950.

96 Doug Owram, *Born at the Right Time: A History of the Baby-Boom Generation* (Toronto: University of Toronto Press, 1996), 102.

97 "Our Good Citizens," *Globe and Mail*, 2 February 1953.

98 "Scout–Guide Week Is Observed by Local Groups," *Newmarket Era and Express*, 17 February 1955.

99 Robert B. Pierce, "Reading *Paradise Regained* Ethically," *Philosophy and Literature* 30 (2006): 208–22 at 216.

100 Mark Moss, *Manliness and Militarism: Educating Young Boys in Ontario for War* (Toronto: Oxford University Press, 2001).

101 "Terms Scouting Influence to End Toronto Gangs," *Globe and Mail*, 11 December 1948.

102 Mariana Valverde notes that urban environments have been considered morally problematic at least since Jean-Jacques Rousseau and the English Romantics. On the "City" as a moral problem, 1885–1925, see Valverde, *The Age of Light, Soap, and Water: Moral Reform in English Canada, 1885–1925* (Toronto: McClelland & Stewart, 1991).

103 R.J. Renison, "Education," *Globe and Mail*, 14 November 1945.

104 Renison, "Education."

105 "They Will Be Men," *Globe and Mail*, 12 February 1958.

106 "Help a Boy Become a Man," *Toronto Daily Star*, 25 February 1947.

107 "The Boy Scout Association," *Globe and Mail*, 22 February 1947.

108 "The Boy Scout Association," *Globe and Mail*.

109 "The Boy Scout Association," *Globe and Mail*.

110 MacDonald, "Why Have the Boy Scouts Survived?", 57.

111 "Salvationist Chief Lauds Boy Scouts," *Evening Telegram*, 19 June 1946.

112 Herbert S. Lewin, "The Way of the Boy Scout," *Journal of Educational Sociology* 21, 3 (November 1947), 169–76 at 169.

113 "$2,500 for Boys, $1,000 for Girls, Riles Woman MPP," *Globe and Mail*, 25 March 1950.

114 See, for example, Irving Layton, *A Red Carpet for the Sun* (Toronto: McClelland and Stewart, 1959), Foreword.

Notes to Chapter 4

1 "Rural Living," *Stouffville Tribune*, 15 April 1951.

2 "New Light on Juvenile Delinquency," *Kingsville Reporter*, 23 November 1950.

3 Sangster notes that by the early 1950s, studies of male gangs had proliferated, with middle-class investigators betraying an almost voyeuristic fascination with the contours of "underclass" boy life. See Joan Sangster, "Creating Social and Moral Citizens: Defining and Treating Delinquent Boys and Girls in English Canada, 1920–65," in Dorothy E. Chunn, Robert J. Menzies, and Robert L. Adamoski, eds., *Contesting Canadian Citizenship: Historical Readings* (Peterborough: Broadview, 2002), 348.

4 D. Owen Carrigan, *Juvenile Delinquency in Canada: A History* (Concord: Irwin, 1998), 163.

5 Canada, Dominion Bureau of Statistics, *Juvenile Delinquents for the Year Ended September 30, 1945* (Ottawa: Edmond Cloutier, 1947), iii.

6 Ontario, Royal Commission on Education in Ontario, *Report* (Toronto: Baptist Johnston, King's Printer, 1950), 365.

7 Sangster, "Creating Social and Moral Citizens," 345.

8 In a report issued in 1949 by Ontario judge Hedley S. Mott, which examined the causes of juvenile delinquency, it was noted that in 1948, for example, 164 boys and

28 girls appeared in juvenile court. See "Finding Delinquency Among Juveniles Is Under Control," *Globe and Mail*, 3 February 1949.

9 Franca Iacovetta notes that Ontario courts displayed "a propensity for punishing and incarcerating working-class and poor children." See Iacovetta, "Gossip, Contest, and Power in the Making of Suburban Bad Girls: Toronto, 1945–1960," *Canadian Historical Review* 80, no. 4 (1999): 585–623 at 586.

10 "Boys Home Is Named 'Clifton House,'" *Toronto Daily Star*, 10 May 1958.

11 "Teaching St. John Cadets Thrills Mountie," *Toronto Daily Star*, 21 February 1952.

12 W.E. Blatz, "Your Child Can Go Wrong," *Maclean's*, 1 March 1946, 10.

13 "Delinquency and Its Cure," *Globe and Mail*, 14 January 1954.

14 Sidney Katz, "It's a Tough Time to Be a Kid," *Maclean's*, 15 January 1951, 14–15.

15 Ontario, *Report of the Select Committee Appointed by the Legislative Assemble of the Province of Ontario, To Study and Report Upon Problems of Delinquent Individuals and Custodial Questions, and the Place of Reform Institutions Therein*. 8 March 1954, 10. Hereafter *Delinquency Report*.

16 Bryan Hogeveen, "'The Evils with Which We Are Called to Grapple': Elite Reformers, Eugenicists, Environmental Psychologists, and the Construction of Toronto's Working-Class Boy Problem, 1860–1930," *Labour/Le Travail* 55 (Spring 2005), 37–68 at 39.

17 Hogeveen, "'The Evils.'"

18 "Boys from 'Bad District' Start Afresh with Club," *Globe and Mail*, 19 January 1946.

19 "Boys from 'Bad District.'"

20 "Boys from 'Bad District.'"

21 June Callwood, "Will Your Youngster Turn to Crime?", *Maclean's*, 15 September 1954, 101–3.

22 Callwood, "Will Your Youngster Turn to Crime?", 16.

23 Callwood, "Will Your Youngster Turn to Crime?", 102.

24 Callwood, "Will Your Youngster Turn to Crime?"

25 Callwood, "Will Your Youngster Turn to Crime?", 102.

26 "Mama's Pet Most Difficult of Delinquents," *Globe and Mail*, 12 February 1947.

27 "New Light on Juvenile Delinquency," *Kingsville Reporter*, 23 November 1950.

28 "New Light on Juvenile Delinquency," *Kingsville Reporter*.

29 "Mama's Pet Most Difficult of Delinquents," *Globe and Mail*, 12 February 1947.

30 Louis A. D'Amico and Beeman N. Phillips, "Problem Behaviour in School," *Journal of Educational Psychology* 47 (1956): 350.

31 Sheldon Glueck and Eleanor Glueck, *Delinquents in the Making* (New York: Harper, 1952), 7.

32 "Right and Wrong and 'Shook Up' Youth," *Toronto Daily Star*, 1 September 1959.

33 "Study of Sex Perverts in Prisons Reveals Present Penal Treatment Contributes to Their Degeneration," *Globe and Mail*, 22 April 1948.

34 "The biggest cause of juvenile delinquency is parent delinquency," declared one postwar expert. See "Clubs Will Take Lads Off Corners, McCleary Sure," *Globe and Mail*, 29 September 1948. See also "Can't Trust State with Child Aid, Dr. Whitton Warns," *Globe and Mail*, 4 October 1948. On ineffective schools as a cause of delinquency, see "Survey the Resources," *Globe and Mail*, 25 January 1949. See also *Delinquency Report*, 270. A 1949 editorial published in *Stouffville Tribune* wondered aloud if toy guns were contributing to boy delinquency in Ontario. See "The Wrong Toys," 15 December 1949. On film as a cause for delinquency, see

"Thrill Movies Bad for Child Minds—Big Brothers," *Toronto Daily Star*, 29 January 1946; "Do the Movies Really Make Delinquents," *Saturday Night*, 16 February 1946. On comic books and delinquency, see "Gun-Totin' Comic Characters Rapped by Dufferin Delegate," *Globe and Mail*, 27 February 1946; "Boy, 6, Kills Brother, 10, After Comic Book Dispute," *Telegram*, 4 October 1948; "Sponsor Campaign Against Sale of Crime Comics Here," *Newmarket Era and Express*, 16 December 1953; "Comics, Radio, TV Held Responsible for Delinquency," *Globe and Mail*, 9 March 1954.

35 "Delinquent Parents," *Essex Free Press*, 1 August 1947.

36 Kenneth H. Rogers, *Boys Are Worth It* (Toronto: Ryerson, 1944).

37 Peter Bryce, "The Children and the Church," *Toronto Daily Star*, 29 June 1946.

38 Rogers, *Boys Are Worth It*, 31.

39 Mona Gleason, *Normalizing the Ideal: Psychology, Schooling, and the Family in Postwar Canada* (Toronto: University of Toronto Press, 1999), 87.

40 "Boys in Trouble: Fruit of Unspeakable Homes," *Church Times*, 14 January 1955, 9.

41 "Misdeeds of Youth Pose Hard Problem," *Toronto Telegram*, 14 January 1946.

42 Bobbie Rosenfeld, "Fred Bell Fights Delinquency in Practical Way," *Globe and Mail*, 7 May 1946.

43 "Boys', Girls' Clubs Seen Major Need," *Globe and Mail*, 19 February 1946.

44 Hogeveen, "'The Evils,'" 41.

45 "Mama's Pet Most Difficult of Delinquents," *Globe and Mail*.

46 "Danny Boy: Saving of Young Truant from Across the Tracks Illustrates Need of Chest Fund," *Globe and Mail*, 22 September 1945.

47 "Danny Boy," *Globe and Mail*.

48 "Danny Boy," *Globe and Mail*.

49 "It's Your Job," *Kingsville Reporter*, 27 August 1953.

50 "Case Histories," *Globe and Mail*, 10 January 1946.

51 "Danny Boy," *Globe and Mail*.

52 "Danny Boy," *Globe and Mail*.

53 "Probation Officer Discusses 'Juvenile Delinquency' at Local Home and School Club Meeting," *Stouffville Sun-Tribune*, 24 January 1957.

54 "Boys in Trouble," *Church Times*.

55 "Delinquent Often Has Broken Home," *Globe and Mail*, 26 January 1956.

56 "Delinquent Often Has Broken Home," *Globe and Mail*. Writing in a 1959 edition of the *Stouffville Tribune*, child advice expert Nancy Cleaver argued that children who "get into trouble with the law" typically have no church connection. See Cleaver, "Parents and the Church," *Stouffville Tribune*, 22 January 1959.

57 "Teach Parents First Kitchener Youth Plan," *Toronto Daily Star*, 27 February 1946.

58 "Delinquency Rate Rises as Parental Neglect of Children Grows," *Globe and Mail*, 13 April 1946.

59 "Who's to Blame?", *Stouffville Tribune*, 24 November 1960.

60 For a historical discussion on permissive parenting and other approaches to child care, see Peter N. Stearns, *A History of Modern Childrearing in America: Anxious Parents* (New York: NYU Press, 2003). See also Ann Hulbert, *Raising America: Experts, Parents, and a Century of Advice about Children* (New York: Alfred A. Knopf, 2003)

61 "Raising Delinquents," *Acton Free Press*, 26 November 1959.

62 Louise Baker, *Snips and Snails* (Toronto: McGraw-Hill, 1953), 48.

63 "Curb Delinquency with Spanking Group Suggests," *Globe and Mail*, 9 March 1954.

64 "Curb Delinquency," *Globe and Mail*.

65 "A Little of Everything," *Toronto Daily Star*, 5 March 1954.

66 "Crime and Punishment," *Globe and Mail*, 12 March 1946.

67 *Delinquency Report*, 1–3. See also Paul Axelrod, "No Longer a 'Last Resort': The End of Corporal Punishment in the Schools of Toronto," *Canadian Historical Review* 91, no. 2 (2010): 262–85 at 271.

68 Christopher Dummitt, *The Manly Modern: Masculinity in Postwar Canada* (Vancouver: UBC Press, 2007), 103.

69 "Not Gangs, but Teams, as East York Beats Delinquency Problem," *Globe and Mail*, 12 January 1949. Additionally, in order to prevent further boy trouble and avoid creating another "Regent Park scheme" with "its heavy drain on the taxpayer," Rev. Ray McCleary recommended to the Toronto Board of Trade creating a "planned program of recreation" for boys. See "Clubs Will Take Lads Off Corners, McCleary Sure," *Globe and Mail*, 29 September 1948.

70 "Community Centers an Answer," *Globe and Mail*, 3 January 1946.

71 "Delinquency At 9-Year Low Big Brothers Assn. Reports," *Toronto Daily Star*, 2 March 1946.

72 "Judge Recommends Strap for Juvenile Delinquents," *Toronto Daily Star*, 16 January 1946.

73 "Judge Recommends Strap," *Toronto Daily Star*.

74 Rogers, *Boys Are Worth It*, 29.

75 Rogers, *Boys Are Worth It*.

76 "Fruitless Task," *Globe and Mail*, 15 November 1952.

77 Edgar Guest, "Boys," *Toronto Evening Telegram*, 5 January 1946.

78 Cynthia R. Comacchio, *The Dominion of Youth: Adolescence and the Making of a Modern Canada, 1920–1950* (Waterloo: Wilfrid Laurier University Press, 2006), 194.

79 "Coal Bin Clubs' Scheme Booms North Toronto 'Y,'" *Globe and Mail*, 25 September 1945.

80 "Coal Bin Clubs' Scheme," *Globe and Mail*.

81 "Coal Bin Clubs' Scheme," *Globe and Mail*.

82 "Brothers Available," *Globe and Mail*, 9 January 1956.

83 Although activities were directed toward boys, girls were "invited" to share the clubs. See "$350,000 Youth Centre for Dovercourt Park Approved by Council," *Globe and Mail*, 11 January 1957.

84 "New Club for Boys Dovercourt Centre Drives for $350,000," *Toronto Telegram*, 1 June 1946.

85 "Started in Room over Chinese Laundry," *Globe and Mail*, 6 May 1954.

86 "Church's Many Activities Tend to Curb Delinquency," *Toronto Daily Star*, 10 January 1946.

87 "Clubs Build Character," *Globe and Mail*, 17 September 1957.

88 "New Club for Boys Dovercourt Centre Drives for $350,000," *Toronto Telegram*, 1 June 1946.

89 "Pupils and Parents Are All Good Neighbors," *Globe and Mail*, 21 December 1950.

90 "Doing Great Boys' Work," *London Free Press*, 13 July 1946.

91 "Boys Club Opened Officially and Noisily," *Globe and Mail*, 24 April 1958.

92 "Lions, 'Y' Sponsor New Boys Groups," *London Free Press*, 1946.

93 "Lions, 'Y'," *London Free Press*.

94 *Police Club for Boys*, VHS, dir. by Allen Stark (1954; Ottawa, National Film Board).

95 *Police Club for Boys*.

96 Miriam Chapin, "Boys Clubs Run by Police Cut Down Delinquency," *Saturday Night*, 5 April 1949, 14.

97 Chapin, "Boys Clubs Run by Police."

98 Chapin, "Boys Clubs Run by Police."

99 "Boys Club Opened Officially and Noisily," *Globe and Mail*, 24 April 1958.

100 Ferdinand Lundberg and Marynia L. Foot Farnham, *Modern Woman: The Lost Sex* (New York: Harper, 1947), 65.

101 "Boys Made Good Citizens with Red Feather Aid," *Toronto Daily Star*, 14 October 1953.

102 "St. Albans Boys Speed Drive to Complete New Club," *Globe and Mail*, 13 May 1960.

103 "Hockey Sticks, Bass Drums End Delinquency in Dundas," *Toronto Daily Star*, 27 February 1946.

104 "Hockey Sticks, Bass Drums," *Toronto Daily Star*.

105 Fran Archer, "The Cat's Miaou," *Newmarket Era and Express*, 3 March 1960.

106 "Boy Proud of Distinction, 'Worst in Neighbourhood,'" *Globe and Mail*, 22 October 1946.

107 "Boy Proud," *Globe and Mail*.

108 "Boys Made Good Citizens," *Toronto Daily Star*.

109 "Boys Made Good Citizens," *Toronto Daily Star*.

110 "Boxing Bouts Feature Boys' Work Display," *London Free Press*, 1945 (London Public Library Archives, London Room Vertical Files# London-Boys).

111 "Lions, 'Y'," *London Free Press*, 1946 (London Public Library Archives, London Room Vertical Files# London-Boys).

112 "Athletic Army," *Globe and Mail*, 13 March 1954.

113 "Athletic Army," *Globe and Mail*.

114 "Assistant Y.M.C.A. Secretary," *Toronto Daily Star*, 26 January 1946.

115 Frank E. Jones and Wallace E. Lambert, "Attitudes Toward Immigrants in a Canadian Community," *Public Opinion Quarterly* 23, no. 4 (1959–1960): 537–46 at 537.

116 "Model Youth Wins Y.M.C.A. 'Family Prize,'" *Toronto Telegram*, 14 January 1950.

117 "Model Youth," *Toronto Telegram*.

118 "3,000 Children See 'K' Club Good Life," *Toronto Daily Star*, 30 December 1954.

119 "Summer Classes Draw Children from the Street," *Globe and Mail*, 16 July 1946.

120 "Summer Classes," *Globe and Mail*.

121 "Whitby Chief Has Boys on Ice—for Hockey, Not Hookey," *Evening Telegram*, 2 March 1946.

122 "Whitby Chief," *Toronto Evening Telegram*.

123 "Whitby Chief," *Toronto Evening Telegram*.

124 "Clubs Build Character," *Globe and Mail*, 17 September 1957.

125 Peter Bryce, "The Children of the City Streets," *Globe and Mail*, 6 July 1946.

126 "Clubs Build Character," *Globe and Mail*, 17 September 1957.

127 David I. Macleod, *Building Character in the American Boy: The Boy Scouts, YMCA, and Their Forerunners, 1870–1920* (Madison: University of Wisconsin Press, 1983).

128 "Hobbycrafts Gave Boys 'Something to Do,'" *Toronto Evening Telegram*, 12 March 1946.

129 "Boys Club a Success," *Globe and Mail*, 7 June 1957.

130 "Church Sponsored Hobby Shop Keeps Brampton Youths Busy," *Toronto Daily Star*, 22 March 1948.

131 "Hobbycrafts," *Toronto Evening Telegram*.

132 "2,900 Men Fell Ask U.S Probe of Rapido Fight," *Toronto Daily Star*, 21 January 1946.

133 Lucie I. Huxtable, "Home Forum," *Globe and Mail*, 7 September 1945.

134 "Hockey Sticks, Bass Drums," *Toronto Daily Star*.

135 Gordon Allison, "A Week of Gangland: Tough Talk, Obscenity, Mark of Beanery Boys Seeking Liquor, Girls," *Globe and Mail*, 6 September 1948.

136 "Fathers and Sons of West End Y.M.C.A Have Week-End Outing at Camp Norval Near Brampton," *Toronto Daily Star*, 21 February 1951.

137 "Fathers and Sons," *Toronto Daily Star*.

138 Michael Messner, *The Politics of Masculinities: Men in Movements* (Thousand Oaks: Sage, 1997), 17.

139 Messner, *The Politics of Masculinities*.

140 Angelo Patri, "Our Children," *Globe and Mail*, 7 April 1945.

141 "Individual Champs," *Globe and Mail*, 26 April 1946.

142 "Bud Poile," *Globe and Mail*, 4 May 1948.

143 "Doing Great Boys' Work," *London Free Press*, 1946 (London Public Library Archives, London Room Vertical Files# London-Boys).

144 "Hobbycrafts," *Toronto Evening Telegram*.

145 "Craft Classes for Boys Important Phase of Work," *London Free Press*, 13 May 1946.

146 "Holds Youth Needs Elders' Experience," *Globe and Mail*, 9 February 1945.

147 "Right Type of Court," *Toronto Evening Telegram*, 10 November 1948.

148 "New Club for Boys Dovercourt Centre," *Toronto Telegram*.

149 "Londoners Give Generously to Police Boys Club," *London Free Press*, 1947 (London Public Library Archives, London Room Vertical Files# London-Boys).

150 "Oxford Street Armoury to Become Youth Centre," *London Free Press*, 1947, (London Public Library Archives, London Room Vertical Files# London-Boys). For prominent men, such as Wallace R. Campbell, president of the Ford Motor Company in Windsor, Ontario, to be publicly declared a "good citizen" they had to be more than a "great industrialist," they also had to be involved with character-building organizations such as the Boy Scouts. See, for example, "A Liberal-Minded Industrialist," *Toronto Daily Star*, 12 August 1947.

151 "Ward 2 Business Men Arranging Carnival," *Toronto Daily Star*, 20 July 1946.

152 "Hoping for Early Start on McGarvey Boys Home," *London Free Press*, 17 January 1946.

153 "London Boys Interested in Sports Welcome at Labor Council's Club," *London Free Press*, May 1946 (London Public Library Archives, London Room Vertical Files# London-Boys).

154 "Globe and Mail Donates Pool to Boys," *Globe and Mail*, 15 June 1956.

155 "Globe and Mail Donates," *Globe and Mail*.

156 "Globe and Mail Donates," *Globe and Mail*.
157 "Murder Trial Juror to Donate Fees to Ottawa Boys Club," *Globe and Mail*, 24 January 1946.
158 "Murder Trial Juror," *Globe and Mail*.
159 "Kiwanis Boys Club Awaits Thrilling True Tales Told by Mounties," *Toronto Evening Telegram*, 29 January 1946.
160 Ibid.
161 "Glamour of Police Duty Told to Boys by RCMP," *Globe and Mail*, 30 January 1946.
162 "Kiwanis Boys Club Awaits Thrilling True Tales Told by Mounties," *Toronto Evening Telegram*, 29 January 1946. See also "Glamour of Police Duty Told to Boys by RCMP," *Globe and Mail*, 30 January 1946.
163 Michael Dawson, *The Mountie from Dime Novel to Disney* (Toronto: Between the Lines, 1998), 36.
164 "Life Easier Before TV-Mike," *Toronto Daily Star*, 9 January 1958.
165 "Illegitimate Girl Asks for Help," *Globe and Mail*, 5 November 1968.
166 "Challenge Called Key to Vitality of Boys Clubs," *Globe and Mail*, 1 May 1965.
167 "Challenge Called Key," *Globe and Mail*.
168 "Kitty Pretty Poor," *Globe and Mail*, 31 May 1969.

Notes to Chapter 5

1 Margret Wente, "Broken Arm or Broken Spirit?" *Globe and Mail*, 5 July 2007.
2 R. White, "Scouting the Future," *Sunday Times Review*, 29 July 2007, 1.
3 Deborah Sussman and Stephanie Bonnell, "Wives as Primary Breadwinners," *Perspectives* (August 2006), 10–17.
4 Hanna Rosin, *The End of Men and the Rise of Women* (New York: Riverhead, 2012); Liza Mundy, *The Richer Sex: How The Majority of Female Breadwinners Is Transforming Sex, Love, and Family* (New York: Simon and Schuster, 2012); Kay Hymowitz, *Manning Up: How the Rise of Women Has Turned Men into Boys* (New York: Basic, 2011).
5 Hymowitz, *Manning Up*, 3.
6 Hymowitz, *Manning Up*, 13.
7 Harvey Mansfield, *Manliness* (New Haven: Yale University Press, 2006); Roy F. Baumeister, *Is There Anything Good about Men? How Cultures Flourish by Exploiting Men* (London: Oxford University Press, 2010); David Benatar, *The Second Sexism: Discrimination Against Men and Boys* (London: Wiley-Blackwell, 2012).
8 Christopher J. Greig and Susan Holloway, "Canadian Manhood(s)," in Christopher J. Greig and Wayne J. Martino, eds., *Canadian Men and Masculinities: Historical and Contemporary Perspectives* (Toronto: Canadian Scholars' Press, 2012), 119–38.
9 Z. Bielski, "Are Men Being Robbed of Their Masculinity?", *Globe and Mail*, 30 September 2009.
10 A. Romano and T. Dokoupil, "Men's Lib," *Newsweek*, 20 September 2010.
11 G. Stoddard, "Is the Alpha Male in Danger of Extinction?", *Women's Health*, September 2009, 136–41.
12 R. Pelling, "Men Are Redundant, but Let's Keep Them Anyway," *Vancouver Sun*, 10 July 2009.
13 D. Zinczenko, "Men of Extinction: Forget the Whales: It's Time to Save the Males," *Men's Health*, 20 December 2009.

14 A. Zerbaris, "Save the Males," *Toronto Star,* 15 July 2008.

15 "World's Males Are Under Siege," *Victoria Times-Colonist,* 14 December 2008.

16 M. Mittelstaedt, "Humanity at Risk: Are the Males Going First?" *Globe and Mail,* 20 September 2008.

17 P. Lee, "Death of the Traditional Man," *Ottawa Citizen,* 4 March 2001.

18 D. Gaughan, "Manly Men Take a Beating," *Edmonton Journal,* 10 November 2001.

19 J. O'Sullivan, "Lament for the Days of Manly Men," *National Post,* 18 July 2000.

20 E. Eakin, "Real Men Reeling: Whether Feminism, the Economy or Other Factors Are Responsible, North American Males Feel the Heat," *The Gazette,* 27 December 2000.

21 R. Highfield, "Macho Man to Become Evolutionary Footnote," *Saskatoon Star-Phoenix,* 28 August 2008.

22 H. Rosin, "The End of Men: How Women Are Taking Control—of Everything," *The Atlantic,* July–August 2010, 56–73.

23 Greig and Holloway, "Canadian Manhood(s)," 120.

24 Christie Blatchford, "Toronto, City of Sissies," *National Post,* 10 December 2011.

25 Greig and Holloway, "Canadian Manhood(s)," 120.

26 D. Eddie, "In Praise of the Strong, Silent Dad," *Globe and Mail,* 20 June 2009.

27 F. Petrick, "Our Descent into Wimpiness," *Kingston Whig-Standard,* 9 October 2009.

28 "What's Wrong with Men Today?", *Hamilton Spectator,* 11 January 2012.

29 "What's Wrong with Men Today?", *Hamilton Spectator.*

30 For a discussion on the rise of the conservative men's movement, see "Men's Movements," in Michael Kimmel and Amy Aronson, eds., *Men and Masculinities: A Social, Cultural, and Historical Encyclopedia,* Vol. 2 (Oxford: ABC-CLIO, 2004), 538–33.

31 Greig and Holloway, "Canadian Manhood(s)," 120.

32 M. Steyn, "The War on Terror Is the Real Women's Issue," *Maclean's,* 9 January 2006. Retrieved from http:www.macleans.ca.

33 Rob Bredin, "A Real Man Would Have Tried to Stop Marc Lepine," *National Post,* 10 December 2011.

34 Raewyn Connell, "Understanding Neoliberalism," in Susan Braedley and Meg Luxton, eds., *Neoliberalism and Everyday Life* (Montreal and Kingston: McGill-Queen's University Press, 2010), 22–36 at 33.

35 This section on neoliberalism has been drawn from a previously published chapter. See Greig and Holloway, "Canadian Manhood(s)."

36 Noam Chomsky, *Profits over People: Neoliberalism and Global Order* (New York: Seven Stories, 1999), 19.

37 Chomsky, *Profits over People,* 20.

38 Michael Apple, *Educating the "Right" Way: Markets, Standards, God, and Inequality* (New York: Routledge, 2001), 65.

39 David Camfield, *Canadian Labour in Crisis: Reinventing the Workers' Movement* (Halifax: Fernwood, 2011).

40 Alan Sears, "Occupy Actions: From Wall Street to a Campus Near You?" New Socialist, 2010. Retrieved from www.newsocialist.org.

41 Connell, "Understanding Neoliberalism," 33.

42 This section draws from a previously published chapter. See Greig and Holloway, "Canadian Manhood(s)."

43 Connell, "Understanding Neoliberalism," 34.

44 Meg Luxton, "Doing Neoliberalism: Perverse Individualism in Personal Life," in Braedley and Luxton, eds., Neoliberalism and Everyday Life, 163–83 at 175.

45 Canadian Feminist Alliance for International Action and Canadian Labour Congress, Reality Check: Women in Canada and the Beijing Declaration and Platform for Action Fifteen Years On, 22 February 2010.

46 See note 43, 2.

47 American Psychological Association, Report of the APA Task Force on the Sexualization of Girls (Washington: 2007).

48 D. Drummond and B. Caranci, Markets Are a Woman's Best Friend, TD Economics: Special Report, 25 September 2007.

49 Leah Eichler, "How to Be the Only Woman in the Room," Globe and Mail, 15 February 2013.

50 Cara Williams, "Economic Well-Being," Statistics Canada, Cat. no. 89-503-X, 2010.

51 Williams, "Economic Well-Being," 16.

52 Janine Brodie and Isabella Bakker, Canada's Social Policy Regime and Women: An Assessment of the Last Decade (Ottawa: Status of Women Canada, 2007).

53 Brodie and Bakker, Canada's Social Policy Regime.

54 Canadian Feminist Alliance for International Action, "No Action: No Progress: Report Prepared by the Canadian Feminist Alliance for International Action Report on Canada's Progress in Implementing Priority Recommendations Made by the United Nations Committee on the Elimination of Discrimination Against Women in 2008," 2010. Research from The DisAbled Women's Network shows "that women with disabilities can be as much as 10 times more likely to victims of violence." See Wayne Peters, "President's Column: Too Little Learned since the Montreal Massacre," CAUT Bulletin (November 2012), A3.

55 Statistics Canada, The Daily (Ottawa: Statistics Canada, 2006). Retrieved from http://statcan.gc.ca.

56 Meg Meeker, Boys Should Be Boys: 7 Secrets to Training Healthy Sons (New York: Random House, 2009), 5.

57 Meeker, Boys Should Be Boys, 7.

58 The idea that society has become feminized has been termed the "pussification" of Canadian society by some. See, for example, Blaque Jacque Shallague, 15 May 2009 (5:01 a.m.), online comment on Haley Mick's "At the Science Fair, Girls Dominate the Class," Globe and Mail, 15 May 2009.

59 Fred Mathews, "The Forgotten Child: The Declining Status of Boys in Canada," Transition (2003): 3–6. In 2002, Mathews, who is a Toronto youth psychologist, organized the First National Conference on the Status of Male Children in Canada.

60 Andrea Mrozek, "The Status of Men: Boys Are Lagging. How Does the Decline of Marriage Play a Role," Institute of Marriage and Family Canada, November 2010.

61 Winston Churchill, 14 February 2013 (10:16 a.m.), online comment on Margaret Wente's "Boys Will Be Boys—Schools Need to Understand That," Globe and Mail, 14 February 2013.

62 Raewyn Connell, Gender (Cambridge: Polity, 2009). See also Susan Braedley and Meg Luxton, eds., Neoliberalism and Everyday Life (Montreal and Kingston: McGill–Queen's University Press, 2010).

63 John Intini, "Are We Raising Our Boys to Be Underachieving Men?", Maclean's, 25 October 2010.

64 *100 Huntley Street* (television program), Crossroads Christian Communications, 5 November 2010.

65 Leonard Sax, "What's Happening to Boys?", *Washington Post,* 31 March 2006.

66 William Brozo and Richard Whitmire, "Boys Aren't Learning to Read—and It's a Global Problem," *NY Daily News,* 20 December 2010.

67 United Nations, *In Pursuit of Justice: 2011–2012 Progress of the World's Women* (United Nations: UN Entity for Gender Equality and the Empowerment of Women, 2011).

68 Statistics Canada, "High-Income Trends Among Canadian Taxfilers, 1982–2010" (2013), Cat. no. 11-001-X.

69 Michael Gurian, *A Fine Young Man: What Parents, Mentors, and Educators Can Do to Shape Adolescent Boys into Exceptional* Men (New York: Putnam, 1999), 4.

70 Emily Senay, *From Boys to Men: A Woman's Guide to the Health of Husbands, Partners, Sons, Fathers, and Brothers* (New York: Simon and Schuster, 2005), 32.

71 Anthony Rao, *The Way of Boys: Promoting the Social and Emotional Development of Young Boys* (New York: Harper, 2009), 149.

72 Rao, *The Way of Boys,* 8.

73 See Rao, *The Way of Boys.* See also Peg Tyre, *The Trouble with Boys: A Surprising Report Card on Our Sons, Their Problems at School, and What Parents and Educators Must Do* (New York: Three Rivers, 2008).

74 Becky Francis, "Heroes or Zeroes? The Discursive Positioning of 'Underachieving Boys' in English Neo-Liberal Education Policy," *Journal of Education Policy* 21 (2006): 187–200. See also Kimberly A. Mahaffy, "Girls' Low Self-Esteem: How Is It Related to Later Socioeconomic Achievements?", *Gender and Society* 18, no. 3 (2004): 309–27; American Association of University Women (AAUW), *Shortchanging Girls, Shortchanging America: A Call to Action* (Washington: 1991).

75 Diane Raey, "'Spice Girls,' 'Nice Girls,' 'Girlies,' and 'Tomboys': Gender Discourses, Girls' Cultures and Feminities in the Primary Classroom," *Gender and Education* 13, no. 2 (2001): 153–66.

76 See, for example, Raewyn Connell, *Masculinities* (Berkeley: University of California Press, 1995); Michael Kimmel, ed., *Changing Men: New Directions in Research on Men and Masculinity* (Newbury Park: Sage, 1987); Michael S. Kimmel, Jeff Hearn, and R.W. Connell, *Handbook of Studies on Men and Masculinities* (London: Sage, 2005); Wayne Martino and Maria Pallotta-Chiarolli, *So What's a Boy?: Addressing Issues of Masculinity and Schooling* (Philadelphia: Open University Press, 2003). See also Judith Butler, *Gender Trouble: Feminism and the Subversion of Identity* (New York: Routledge, 1990).

77 Margaret Wente, "Celebrate Boys' Boyness—and Work with It," *Globe and Mail,* 17 November 2012.

78 Richard L. Provencher, 14 February 2013 (10:27 p.m.), online comment on Margaret Wente's "Boys Will Be Boys—Schools Need to Understand That," *Globe and Mail,* 14 February 2013.

79 Blye Frank, "Growing Up Male: Everyday/Everynight Masculinities," in Joseph A. Kuypers, ed., *Men and Power* (Halifax: Fernwood, 1999), 173–87.

80 Robert Cribb, "It's Time to Man Up and Take Charge," *Toronto Star,* 2 October 2010.

81 Michael Reist, *Raising Boys in a New Kind of World* (Toronto: Dundurn, 2011).

82 Canada, *Parliamentary Debates,* 36th Parliament, 2nd Session, 11 April 2000, vol. 83 (1250).

83 See, for example, Hoff Sommers, *The War Against Boys: How Misguided Feminism Is Harming Our Young Men* (New York: Simon and Schuster, 2000). See also Margaret Wente, "How the Schools Wage War on Boys," *Globe and Mail,* 27 February 2003; Mark Richardson, "Hormones Can Be a Teacher's Best Friend," *London Free Press,* 10 July 2002.

84 Terrence O. Moore, "Wimps and Barbarians: The Sons of Murphy Brown," *Claremont Review of Books* 4, no. 1 (2003).

85 WeWill, 16 December 2010 (9:06 a.m.), online comment on Keynon Wallace's "A Class of Their Own: Schools Hope Single-Sex Education Will Help Boys Excel," *National Post,* 17 October 2010.

86 In *The Way of Boys,* Anthony Rao suggests that to address the "crisis in young boyhood," we should be hiring more male teachers. Here, Rao is aligned with a long list of other "boy crisis" proponents who see the need to hire more male teachers as a way to create more "boy-friendly learning environments." For Rao and others, more male teachers should be hired in order to counter the assumed negative influence of female teachers on the welfare of boys. See Rao, *The Way of Boys,* 165.

87 Arguing for recruiting more male teachers in Canada as a way to counter increasingly female-dominated classrooms, one recent editorial suggested that "many perfectly normal little boys are spending their days in school surrounded by adults who struggle to comprehend them and have nowhere to turn for another perspective in a single-gender workplace." See Paula Dunning, "Closing the Gender Gap," *Canada Education* 51, no. 1 (2010–2011): 3.

88 Ken Coates and Clive Keen, "Snail Males: Why Are Men Falling Behind in Universities While Women Speed Ahead," *The Walrus* (February 2007), 58–63.

89 Luvll, 19 February 2013 (12:35 p.m.), comment on Kate Hammer and Caroline Alphonso, "School Board's Hiring Policy Singles Out Men, Minorities," *Globe and Mail,* 19 February 2013.

90 Diogenes1, 18 December 2010 (4:36 p.m.), comment on Kenyon Wallace, "The Problem with 'Edu-Babble,'" *National Post,* 18 December 2010.

91 Christina Hoff Sommers, "The Boys at the Back," *New York Times,* 2 February 2013.

92 For a short history of the call for more male teachers in Canada, see Rebecca Coulter and Christopher Greig, "The Man Question in Teaching: An Historical Overview," *Alberta Journal of Educational Research* 54, no. 4 (2008): 420–30.

93 Christopher John Greig, "Boy-Only Classrooms: Gender Reform in Windsor, Ontario 1966–1972," *Educational Review* 63, no. 2 (2011): 127–41 at 136. See also Wayne Martino, "Male Teachers as Role Models: Addressing Issues of Masculinity, Pedagogy, and the Re-Masculinization of Schooling," *Curriculum Inquiry* 38, no. 2 (2008): 189–223.

94 Wayne Martino and Goli Rezai-Rashti, "'Failing Boys' and Evidence-Based Equity Policy: Masculinities, Equity, and Neoliberal Accountability in Ontario," in Greig and Martino, eds., *Canadian Men and Masculinities.*

95 Wayne Martino, Michael Kehler, and Marcus B. Weaver-Hightower, *The Problem with Boys' Education: Beyond the Backlash* (New York: Routledge, 2009).

96 Bob Lingard, Wayne Martino, and Martin Mills, *Boys and Schooling: Beyond Structural Reform* (New York: Palgrave, 2009).

97 Important to note, some areas of post-secondary education remain overwhelmingly male-dominated, such as mechanical and electrical engineering. This fact has led to some male students to puzzle over complaints of boys' disadvantage. As one online reader pointed out: "My mechanical engineering class is still mainly males so it's hard to identify with the [failing boys] statistics. I feel like males have every opportunity to succeed." Queensuniversitystudent3, 19 October 2010 (8:45 a.m.), comment on Carolyn Abraham's "Failing Boys and the Powder Keg of Sexual Politics," *Globe and Mail,* 18 October 2010.

98 Louis Christofides, Michael Hoy, and Ling Yang, "Participation in Canadian Universities: The Gender Imbalance (1977–2005)," *Economics of Education Review* 29 (2010): 400–10.

99 Lingard, Martino, and Mills, *Boys and Schooling.*

100 Glenn Harlan Reynolds, "Title IX for Our Boys," *USA Today,* 25 February 2013. Available at http://www.usatoday.com/story/opinion/2013/02/25/education-failing-boys-column/1942991.

101 Michael Katz, *Improving Poor People: The Welfare State, The Underclass, and Urban Schools as History* (Princeton: Princeton University Press, 1995).

102 Wayne Martino, "Boys' Underachievement: Which Boys Are We Talking About?", *What Works? Research Into Practice.* Research Monograph #12. Literacy and Numeracy Secretariat (2008).

103 Canada, Natural Science and Engineering Research Council of Canada, *Women in Science and Engineering in Canada* (Ottawa: 2010), 9.

104 Statistics Canada, *Women in Canada: A Gender-Based Statistical Report.* Cat. no. 89-503-XIE, 92.

105 Statistics Canada, *Women in Canada.*

106 Ontario Society of Professional Engineers, "Engineering and Technology Labour Market Study," http://www.ospe.on.ca/resource/resmgr/doc_advocacy/2009_doc_elms_summary.pdf?

107 Expert Panel on Women in University Research, *Strengthening Canada's Research Capacity: The Gender Dimension* (Ottawa: Council of Canadian Academies, 2012), 30.

108 For a recent critique of how university subjects are gendered in a way that continues to disadvantage some women, see Cordelia Fine, *Delusions of Gender* (New York: W.W. Norton, 2010), 27–54. See also Lise Eliot, *Pink Brain, Blue Brain* (New York: Mariner, 2010), Chapter 6.

109 K. Rushowy, "Now Men Aren't Teaching High School Either," *Toronto Star,* 24 August 1999.

110 M. Reynolds, "Where Have the Boys Gone?" *McGill Reporter* 36, no. 5 (13 November 2003).

111 J. Bradshaw, "Brains Alone Won't Get You into McMaster Medical School," *Globe and Mail,* 12 December 2010.

112 C. Abraham and K. Hammer, "Is Affirmative Action for Men the Answer to Enrolment Woes?", *Globe and Mail,* 21 October 2010. See also N. Gibbs, "Affirmative Action for Boys," *Time Magazine,* 3 April 2008.

113 C. Alphonso and K. Hammer, "Targeting Male, Minority Hires an Attempt to Diversify," *Globe and Mail,* 20 February 2013; Christopher J. Greig, "Boy-Only Classrooms: Gender Reform in Windsor, Ontario, 1966–1972," *Educational Review* 63 (2), 127–41.

114 K. Hammer and C. Alphonso, "School Board's Hiring Policy Singles Out Men, Minorities," *Globe and Mail*, 19 February 2013.

115 Ontario College of Teachers, *Narrowing the Gender Gap: Attracting Men to Teaching* (Toronto: 2004).

116 Ontario Public School Boards' Association, "Fast Reports: Are Schools Failing Boys?" OPSBA Fast Reports, 12, 24 (2000). http://www.opsba.org/pubs/fast/2000.

117 Martino and Pallotta-Chiarolli, *So What's a Boy?*

118 Ned Ludlum, 19 February 2013 (9:08 a.m.), online comment on K. Hammer and C. Alphonso, "School Board's Hiring Policy Singles Out Men, Minorities," *Globe and Mail*, 19 February 2013.

119 ThinkAboutIt42, 19 February 2013 (9:47 a.m.), online comment on K. Hammer and C. Alphonso, "School Board's Hiring Policy Singles Out Men, Minorities," *Globe and Mail*, 19 February 2013.

120 1ply, 19 February 2013 (11:29 a.m.), online comment on K. Hammer and C. Alphonso, "School Board's Hiring Policy Singles Out Men, Minorities," *Globe and Mail*, 19 February 2013.

121 Thinking3, 19 February 2013 (8:09 a.m.), online comment on K. Hammer and C. Alphonso, "School Board's Hiring Policy Singles Out Men, Minorities," *Globe and Mail*, 19 February 2013.

122 Connell, *The Big Picture*, 599.

123 Gurian, *A Fine Young Man*.

124 William Pollack, *Real Boys: Rescuing Our Sons from the Myths of Boyhood* (New York: Henry Holt, 1998).

125 Sommers, *The War Against Boys*.

126 Philip Zimbardo and Nikita Duncan, *The Demise of Guys: Why Boys Are Struggling and What We Can Do about It*. TED Conferences, 2012. e-Book, available at http://www.amazon.com.

127 Leonard Sax, *Boys Adrift: The Five Factors Driving the Growing Epidemic of Unmotivated Boys and Underachieving Young Men* (New York: Basic, 2007). For a critique of *Boys Adrift*, see Shaun Johnson's review of the book in *Men and Masculinities* 12 (2009): 260–61.

128 Tyre, *The Trouble with Boys*.

129 Rao, *The Way of Boys*.

130 Connell, *Gender*.

Notes to Conclusion

1 William Attwood and George B. Leonard, *The Decline of the American Male* (New York: Random House, 1969), 23.

2 Doug Owram, *Born at the Right Time: A History of the Baby-Boom Generation* (Toronto: University of Toronto Press, 1996), 136; M. Messner, *Politics of Masculinities: Men in Movements* (Thousand Oaks: Sage, 1997), 31. The 1970s began in Canada with two monumental events for women: the *Report of the Royal Commission on the Status of Women* and the abortion caravan. Judy Rebick has noted that the 1970s saw the "flowering of the women's movement in Canada and around the world." See Rebick, *Ten Thousand Roses: The Making of a Feminist Revolution* (Toronto: Penguin Canada, 2005), 18.

3 Sophie Drinker and Josephine Scheier, Patriarchal Values in Women's Education, *Journal of Higher Education* 25, no. 3 (1954): 115–21, 171.

4 Margaret Wente, "Boys Will Be Boys—Schools Need to Understand That," *Globe and Mail,* 14 February 2013.

5 See, for example, Linda Diebel, "Where Are the Men?", *Toronto Star,* 17 August 2007; "The Absence of Fathers," *Globe and Mail,* 31 July 2007.

6 Ruth Watts, "Whose Knowledge? Gender, Education, Science, and History," *History of Education* 36, no. 3 (2007): 302.

7 Reg Whitaker, "'We Know They're There': Canada and Its Others, With or Without the Cold War," in Richard Cavell, ed., *Love, Hate, and Fear in Canada's Cold War* (Toronto: University of Toronto Press, 2004), 35.

References and Sources

PRIMARY SOURCES
Reports and Government Documents

Canada. 1908. The Juvenile Delinquents Act, Statutes of Canada.

Canada. Dominion Bureau of Statistics. 1947. *Juvenile Delinquents for the Year Ended September 30, 1945*. Ottawa: Edmond Cloutier.

Canada. Expert Panel on Women in University Research. 2012. *Strengthening Canada's Research Capacity: The Gender Dimension*. Ottawa: Council of Canadian Academies.

Canada. 2010. Natural Science and Engineering Research Council of Canada. *Women in Sciences and Engineering in Canada*. Ottawa.

Canada. Parliament. House of Commons. 1882. *Official Reports of the Debates of the House of Commons of the Dominion of Canada*. Ottawa: Queen's Printer.

Canada. Parliament. Senate. Special Committee on Mass Media. 1970. *The Uncertain Mirror: Report of the Special Senate Committee on Mass Media*. Ottawa: Information Canada.

Canada. Parliament. House of Commons. 2000. Parliamentary Debates, 36th Parliament, 2nd Session, vol. 83.

Canada. Truth and Reconciliation Commission of Canada. 2012. *Interim Report*. Winnipeg.

Canada. Statistics Canada. *2006. Measuring Violence Against Women: Statistical Trends, 2006*. Cat. no. 85-570-XIE.

Ontario. Bureau of Statistics and Research Department of the Provincial Treasurer. 1947. *A Conspectus of the Province of Ontario*. Toronto: Baptist Johnston.

Ontario. Ontario College of Teachers. 2004. *Narrowing the Gender Gap: Attracting Men to Teaching*. Toronto: Ontario College of Teachers.

Ontario. Department of Treasury and Economics. 1947. Budget Statement. Toronto: Baptist Johnston.

Ontario. Department of Treasury and Economics. 1970. *Corporation Growth in Ontario, 1946–1969*. Toronto: Ontario Statistical Centre.

Ontario. Royal Commission on Education in Ontario. 1950. *Report*. Toronto: Baptist Johnston, King's Printer.

Ontario. *Report of the Select Committee Appointed by the Legislative Assemble of the Province of Ontario, To Study and Report upon Problems of Delinquent Individuals and Custodial Questions, and the Place of Reform Institutions Therein.* 8 March 1954.

United Nations. United Nations Entity for Gender Equality and the Empowerment of Women. 2011. *In Pursuit of Justice: 2011–2012 Progress of the World's Women.* UNWOMEN.

Popular and Semi-Popular Periodicals

Canadian Forum
Chatelaine
Maclean's
Parents' Magazine
Saturday Night

Popular Religious Publications

The Canadian Baptist
The Canadian Register
Church Times
The United Church Observer

Key Professional Periodicals

Canadian Home and School
Canadian Journal of Psychology
Canadian Welfare
Education and Psychological Assessment
Educational Review
Journal of Educational Psychology
Journal of Educational Sociology
Journal of Education
Journal of Genetic Psychology
Journal of Higher Education

Newspapers

Acton Free Press
Essex County Reporter
Essex Free Press
Georgetown Herald
Globe and Mail
Kingsville Reporter
Leamington Post and News
London Free Press
Newmarket Era and Express
Toronto Daily Star
Toronto Telegram
Stouffville Tribune
Windsor Star

PRINTED PRIMARY SOURCES

A Mother. "Was Our Boy a Sissy?" *Parents' Magazine*, April 1951.

Allen, R.T. "Children Are Monsters." *Maclean's*, 1 August 1954.

———. "Children are So Annoying." *Maclean's*, 15 March 1947.

Alt, Herschel. "In Defense of Mothers." *Parents' Magazine*, 1 February 1950.

Althouse, John George. *Addresses: A Selection, Covering the Years 1936–1956*. Toronto: W.J. Gage, 1958.

Anderson, James C. "Father Was a Gambler." *Maclean's*, 1 January 1949.

Armour, Anobel. "Woods Were His." *Journal of Education* 5, no. 3 (1956): 11.

Arnold, Patrick M. *Wildmen, Warriors, and Kings: Masculine Spirituality and the Bible*. New York: Crossroad, 1991.

Attwood, W., and G.B. Leonard. *The Decline of the American Male*. New York: Random House, 1969.

B.E.N. Review of *Safe on Second Base* by Ed Winfield. *Saturday Night*, 2 May 1953.

Baber, Ray E. "Sociological Differences in Family Stability." *Annals of the American Academy of Political and Social Science* 272 (November 1950): 30–38.

Baden-Powell of Gilwell, Robert Stephenson Smyth Baden-Powell. *The Canadian Boy Scout*. CIHM/ICMH microfiche series, Toronto: Morang, 1911.

Baker, Louise. *Snips and Snails*. Toronto: McGraw-Hill, 1953.

Bannerman, James. "Our Men Are Mice." *Maclean's*, 1 January 1948.

Barman, Jean. *Growing Up British Columbia: Boys in Private School*. Vancouver: UBC Press, 1984.

Baumeister, Roy F. *Is There Anything Good about Men? How Cultures Flourish by Exploiting Men*. New York: Oxford University Press, 2010.

Benatar, David. *The Second Sexism: Discrimination Against Men and Boys*. London: Wiley-Blackwell, 2012.

Bergler, Edmund. *Homosexuality: Disease or Way of Life?* New York: Hill and Wang, 1957.

Berton, Pierre, and C.G. Gifford. "The Beanery Gang." *Maclean's*, 15 December 1948.

Blatz, W.E. "Your Child Can Go Wrong." *Maclean's*, 1 March 1946.

Bloch, Herbert Aaron, and Arthur Niederhoffer. *The Gang: A Study in Adolescent Behavior*. New York: Philosophical Library, 1958.

The Bookshelf. *Saturday Night*, 22 May 1948.

Borchardt, Henry G. "A Teacher Looks at His Job." *Life*, 6 January 1947, 77–80, 82, 84.

Boucher, Anthony, ed. *A Treasury of Great Science Fiction*. Garden City: Doubleday, 1959.

Breckenridge, Marian E., and Elizabeth Lee Vincent. *Child Development: Physical and Psychological Growth Through the School Years*. Philadelphia: W.B. Saunders, 1949.

Brown, Daniel G. "Psychosexual Disturbances: Transvestism and Sex-Role Inversion." *Marriage and Family Living 22*, no. 3 (August 1960): 218–27.

Brown, Fred. "Review: Maternal Overprotection by David M. Levy." *Scientific Monthly* 58, no. 4 (1944): 325–26.

Burkhardt, Eve. "The Soda Set." *Maclean's*, 15 December 1946.

Cahill, Brian. "Backfire of the Neighbourhood Spirit." *Saturday Night*, 1 September 1956.

Callaghan, Morley. *Luke Baldwin's Vow*. Toronto: Macmillan of Canada, 1948.

Callwood, June. "Will Your Youngster Turn to Crime?" *Maclean's*, 15 September 1954.

Campbell, Harold L. *Curriculum Trends in Canadian Education*. Quance lectures in Canadian education. Toronto: W.J. Gage, 1952.

Canadian Council on Social Development. *The Progress of Canada's Children, 2002*. Ottawa: Canadian Council on Social Development, 2002.

Canada. Department of National Health and Welfare. Child and Maternal Health Division. *Canadian Mother and Child*. Ottawa: 1953.

Canadian Research Committee on Practical Education. 1950. *Your Child Leaves School: A Study of 12124 Graduates and 14219 Drop-Outs from Canadian Schools during 1948*. Report, volume 2. Toronto: Canadian Research Committee on Practical Education.

Chapin, Miriam. "Boys Clubs Run by Police Cut Down Delinquency." *Saturday Night*, 5 April 1949.

Charlesworth, J.L. Review of *Scrubs on Skates* by Scott Young. *Saturday Night*, 22 November 1952.

Clark, Catherine. *The Golden Pine Cone*. Toronto: Macmillan of Canada, 1950.

Clarke, S.C.T. "The Effect of Teachers' Adjustments on Teachers' Attitudes." *Canadian Journal of Psychology* 7, no. 2 (1953): 49–59.

Coates, Ken, and Clive Keen. "Snail Males: Why Are Men Falling Behind in Universities While Women Speed Ahead." *The Walrus*, February 2007.

Cohen, Albert. *Delinquent Boys: The Culture of the Gang*. Glencoe: Free Press, 1955.

Corfield, William E., and Boy Scouts of Canada. *Keen for Adventure!* London: Boy Scouts of Canada, London District Council, 1967.

Corner, Horace C., ed. *Canadian Almanac and Legal and Court Directory for the Year 1945*. Toronto: Copp Clark, 1945.

Coughlan, Robert. "Changing Roles in Modern Marriage." *Life*, 24 December 1956, 109–18.

Crane, A.R. "Pre-Adolescent Gangs: A Topological Interpretation." *Journal of Genetic Psychology* 81, no. 1 (1952): 113–23.

Creighton, William Black. *Round 'bout Sun-Up: Some Memories That Live*. Toronto: Ryerson, 1946.

Cronin, A.J. *The Green Years*. Toronto: Little, Brown, 1972.

D'Amico, Lousie A., and Beeman N. Phillips. "Problem Behaviour in School." *Journal of Educational Psychology* 47 (1956): 350.

Derstine, C.F. *Paths to Noble Manhood*. Grand Rapids: Zondervan, 1944, 1954.

Doyle, Richard. "Save the Males." Lulu.com, 2006.

Dick, Philip K. *Voices from the Street*. New York: Tom Doherty, 2007.

Drinker, Sophie, and Josephine Schreier. "Patriarchal Values in Women's Education." *Journal of Higher Education* 25, no. 3 (1954): 115–21, 171.

Duncan, Ray O. "The Contribution of School Athletics to the Growing Boy." *Journal of Educational Sociology* 28, no. 6 (February 1955): 271–74.

Eby, Kermit. "Families. Our First Line of Defense." *Marriage and Family* 10, no. 3 (1948): 57.

Elkin, Frederick. *The Child and Society: The Process of Socialization*. New York: Random House, 1960.

English, Spurgeon. "How to Be a Good Father." *Parents' Magazine*, June 1950.

Fenichel, Otto. *The Psychoanalytical Theory of Neurosis*. New York: W.W. Norton, 1945.

Fenwick, Roy, Hollis Dann, and Robert Foresman. *The New High Road of Song, 6*. Toronto: W.J. Gage, 195?.

Forbush, William Byron. *The Boy Problem*. New York: Pilgrim, 1901.

Franklin, Adele, and Agnes E. Benedict. "Must Children Fight?" *Parents' Magazine*, April 1951.

Friedan, Betty. *The Feminine Mystique*. New York: W.W. Norton, 1963.

Gale, Valerie. *100 Ideas for Pack Meetings*. New York: Boy Scouts Association, 1953.

Garcia, Guy. *The Decline of Men*. Toronto: Harper Perennial, 2008.

Gibson, W.H. *Boyology or Boy Analysis*. New York: Association Press, 1922.

Glueck, Sheldon, and Eleanor Glueck. *Delinquents in the Making: Paths to Prevention*. New York, Harper, 1952.

Goldenson, Robert M. "Why Girls and Boys Go Wrong or Right." *Parents' Magazine*, May 1951.

Gray, S.W. "Masculinity–Femininity in Relation to Anxiety and Social Acceptance." *Child Development* 28, no. 2 (1957): 203–13.

Gurian, Michael. *A Fine Young Man: What Parents, Mentors, and Educators Can Do to Shape Adolescent Boys into Exceptional Men*. New York: Putnam, 1999.

———. *What Could He Be Thinking?: How a Man's Mind Really Works*. New York: St. Martin's, 2003.

Gurian, Michael, Patricia Henley, and Terry Trueman. *Boys and Girls Learn Differently!: A Guide for Teachers and Parents*. San Francisco: Jossey-Bass, 2001.

Hacker, Helen M. "The New Burden of Masculinity." *Marriage and Family* (1957): 227–33.

Hartley, Ruth E. "Some Implications of Current Changes in Sex Role Patterns." *Merrill-Palmer Quarterly of Behaviour and Development* 6, no. 3 (April 1960): 153–64.

Hartmann, H. "Managers and Entrepreneurs: A Useful Distinction?" *Administrative Science Quarterly* 3, no. 4 (1959): 429–51.

Hambleton, Jack. *Cub Reporter*. Toronto: Longmans, Green, 1951.

———. *Charter Pilot: A Bill Hanson Story*. Toronto: Longmans, Green, 1952.

———. *Fisherman's Paradise*. Toronto: Longmans, Green, 1946.

Hambleton, Jack, and Thoreau MacDonald. *Abitibi Adventure*. Toronto: Longmans, Green, 1950.

Heath, Clark Wright. *What People Are: A Study of Normal Young Men*. Cambridge, MA: Harvard University Press, 1945.

Hendry, Charles E. "Adolescence." *The School* (June 1948): 558.

Hewitt, Foster. *Along Olympic Road*. Toronto: Ryerson, 1951.

Hoff Sommers, Christina. *The War Against Boys: How Misguided Feminism Is Harming Our Young Men*. New York: Simon and Schuster, 2000.

Holliday, Joe. *Dale of the Mounted Dew Line Duty*. Toronto: Thomas Allen, 1957.

Hoogstraten, V. "Empty Saddles in the Old Bassinet." *Maclean's*, 15 October 1948.

Hopkins, Charles Howard. *History of the Y.M.C.A. in North America*. New York: Association Press, 1951.

Hymowitz, Kay. *Manning Up: How The Rise of Women Has Turned Men into Boys*. New York: Basic, 2011.

Iggulden, C., and H. Iggulden. *The Dangerous Book for Boys*. London: HarperCollins, 2006.

Ilg, Frances L., and Lousie Bates Ames. *The Gesell Institute's Child Behaviour from Birth to Ten*. New York: Perennial Library, 1955.

Intini, John. "Are We Raising Our Boys to Be Underachieving Men?" *Maclean's*, 25 October 2010.

Jones, Frank E., and Wallace E. Lambert. "Attitudes Toward Immigrants in a Canadian Community." *Public Opinion Quarterly* 23, no. 4 (1959–60): 537–46.

Kahn, Fritz. "Let Your Child Grow Up." *Maclean's*, 1 July 1949.

Katz, Sydney. "It's a Tough Time to Be a Kid." *Maclean's*, 15 January 1951.

Kelman, Norman. "Father's Part in Sex Education." *Parents' Magazine*, 1 March 1949.

———. "Social and Psychoanalytical Reflections on the Father." *American Scholar* 29, no. 3 (Summer 1960): 335–58.

Kinsey, Alfred C., Wardell B. Pomeroy, and Clyde E. Martin. *Sexual Behavior in the Human Male*. Philadelphia: W.B. Saunders, 1948.

Kisker, George. "Men Are Men—or Are They?" *Maclean's*, 1 April 1948.

Knowles, Joyce W. "Some Personality Characteristics of Fatherless Boys." *Educational Review* 9, no. 3 (1957): 197–204.

Lanski, Lois. *Davy and His Dog*. Oxford: Oxford University Press, 1956.

Lauchie, R. "The Rich 100 List: Canada's 100 Wealthiest People." *Canadian Business* (Winter 2010–11): 39–55.

Laycock, Samuel. "Educating the Six-to-Twelve-Year-Old for Family Living." *Canadian Home and School* 10 (March 1951): 20–23.

———. "Homosexuality: A Mental Hygiene Problem." *Canadian Medical Association Journal* 63 (September 1950): 245–50.

———. "How to Protect Your Child from Sex Deviates." *Chatelaine*, April 1956.

———. "You Can't Get Away from Discipline." *Educational Review of the New Brunswick Teachers' Federation* 60, no. 7 (1946): 4–7.

———. "Your Child's Love Life." *Maclean's*, 15 November 1946.

Layton, Irving. *A Red Carpet for the Sun*. Toronto: McClelland and Stewart, 1959.

Leacock, Stephen. *The Boy I Left Behind Me*. Garden City: Doubleday, 1946.

Letter to the Editor. *American Journal of Nursing* 60, no. 3 (1960): 288.

Leznoff, Maurice, and William A. Westley. "The Homosexual Community." *Social Problems* 3, no. 4 (1956): 257–63.

Lewin, H.S. "The Way of the Boy Scout." *Journal of Educational Sociology* 21, no. 3 (1947): 169–76.

Lewis, David, and F.R. Scott. *Make This Your Canada: A Review of C.C.F. History and Policy*. Toronto: Central Canada Publishing, 1943.

Lower, Arthur, R.M. "The Survival of a Soft Nation." *Saturday Night*, 31 October 1952.

Lundberg, Ferdinand, and Marynia L. Foot Farnham. *Modern Woman: The Lost Sex*. New York: Harper, 1947.

MacDonald, David. "Why Have the Boy Scouts Survived?" *Maclean's*, 20 August 1955.

MacLennan, Hugh. "It's the U.S. or Us." *Maclean's*, 5 November 1960.

———. "The Years Ahead." *Maclean's*, 31 October 1955.

MacLennan, Hugh. *Each Man's Son*. Toronto: Macmillan, 1951.

Maek, Pauline Beery. "Do Children Need Sweets?" *Parents' Magazine*, March 1950.

Mansfield, Harvey. *Manliness*. New Haven: Yale University Press, 2006.

Massey, Vincent. *Speaking of Canada: Addresses*. Toronto: Macmillan of Canada, 1959.

———. *On Being Canadian*. Toronto: J.M. Dent, 1948.

Mathews, Fred. "The Forgotten Child: The Declining Status of Boys in Canada." *Transition*, 2003.

Matthews, Louisa. "Review of *Boy on Defence* by Scott Young." *Saturday Night*, 28 November 1953.

Matthews, W.D.E. *100 Years of Public Education in London, 1855 to 1955*. The author, 1955.

Mays, John Barron. *Growing Up in the City: A Study of Juvenile Delinquency in an Urban Neighbourhood*. Liverpool: Liverpool University Press, 1964.

Meeker, Meg. *Boys Should Be Boys: 7 Secrets to Training Healthy Sons*. New York: Random House, 2009.

Meyer, William J., and George G. Thompson. "Sex Differences in the Distribution of Teacher Approval and Disapproval among Sixth Grade Children." *Journal of Educational Psychology* 47, no. 7 (1956): 385–96.

McAree, John V. *Cabbagetown Store*. Toronto: Ryerson, 1953.

McCreary, John K. "Psychopathia Homosexualis." *Canadian Journal of Psychology* 4 (June 1950): 63–74.

McIlroy, Kimball. "Shall I Let My Son Play Hockey?" *Saturday Night*, 18 January 1949.

McLuhan, Marshall. *The Mechanical Bride: Folklore of Industrial Man*. New York: Vanguard, 1951.

McKeown, James. "The Behavior of Mothers of Normals, Neurotics, and Schizophrenics." *American Catholic Sociological Review* 18, no. 1 (1957): 33–40.

Mills, C. Wright. *White Collar: The American Middle Classes*. New York: Oxford University Press, 1951.

Mirams, Gordon. "Drop That Gun!" *Quarterly of Film Radio and Television* 6, no. 1 (1951): 1–19.

Moore, Terrence O. "Wimps and Barbarians: The Sons of Murphy Brown." *Claremont Review of Books* 4, no. 1 (2003).

Morris, Joan. "Was the Victorian Father So Bad after All?" *Chatelaine*, April 1960.

Morton, G.F. *Highlands and Backwoods*. London: Christopher Johnson, 1957.

Mowat, Farley. *The Dog Who Wouldn't Be*. Boston: Little, Brown, 1957.

Mundy, Liza. The *Richer Sex: How the Majority of Female Breadwinners Is Transforming Sex, Love, and Family*. New York: Simon and Schuster, 2012.

Mussen, Paul, and Luther Distler. "Child-Rearing Antecedents of Masculine Identification in Kindergarten Boys." *Child Development* 31, no. 1 (1960): 89–100.

Neatby, Hilda. *So Little for the Mind*. Toronto: Clarke, Irwin, 1953.

"Need Top Efficiency to Compete." *Teamwork in Industry*, October 1960.

Newell, W. *The Code of Man: Love, Courage, Pride, Family, Country*. New York: HarperCollins, 2003.

———. *What Is a Man?: 3,000 Years of Wisdom on the Art of Manly Virtue*. New York: HarperCollins, 2000.

Park, Julian. *The Culture of Contemporary Canada*. Ithaca: Cornell University Press, 1957.

Phair, John Thomas, and Norman Raeburn Speirs. *Good Health*. Toronto: Ginn, 1945.

Pollack, William, *Real Boys: Rescuing Our Sons from the Myths of Boyhood*. New York: Henry Holt, 1998.

Powers, Janet. "Stan Was Too Cautious." *Chatelaine*, 1 May 1946.

Rao, Anthony. *The Way of Boys: Promoting the Social and Emotional Development of Young Boys*. New York: Harper, 2009.

Reist, Michael. *Raising Boys in a New Kind of World*. Toronto: Dundurn, 2011.

Reynolds, Laura C. "Calling All Fathers." *Parents' Magazine*, March 1945, 33, 102.

Robins, J.D. *A Pocketful of Canada*. Toronto: Collins, 1946.

Rogers, Kenneth H. *Boys Are Worth It*. Toronto: Ryerson, 1944.

Romano, A., and T. Dokoupil, "Men's Lib." *Newsweek*, 20 September 2010.

Rose, Albert. *Regent Park: A Study in Slum Clearance*. Toronto: University of Toronto Press, 1958.

Rosin, Hanna. *The End of Men and the Rise of Women*. New York: Riverhead, 2012.

———. "The End of Men: How Women Are Taking Control of Everything." *The Atlantic*, July–August 2010.

Ross, Mary Lowery. "Big, Rugged and Awkward." *Saturday Night*, 18 October 1949.

Rourke, Louise. *Lefty's Adventure*. Toronto: Thomas Nelson, 1945.

Sangster, D. "What Do Our Children Think About?" *Chatelaine*, March 1959.

Sargeant, Helen. "Review: *Maternal Overprotection* by David M. Levy." *Journal of Criminal Law and Criminology* 35, no. 3 (1945): 181–82.

Saul, Leon Joseph. *Emotional Maturity: The Development and Dynamics of Personality*. Philadelphia: Lippincott, 1947.

Sax, Leonard. *Boys Adrift: The Five Factors Driving the Growing Epidemic of Unmotivated Boys and Underachieving Young Men*. New York: Basic, 2007.

———. "Reclaiming Kindergarten: Making Kindergarten Less Harmful to Boys." *Pyschology of Men and Masculinity* 2, no. 1 (2001): 3–12.

Scarpitti, Frank R. "The 'Good' Boy in a High Delinquency Area: Four Years Later." *American Sociological Review* 25, no. 4 (1960): 555–58.

Schonfeld, William A. "Inadequate Masculine Physique." *Psychosomatic Medicine* 12 (1950): 49–54.

Schumpeter, Joseph Alois. *Business Cycles: A Theoretical, Historical, and Statistical Analysis of the Capitalist Process*. New York: McGraw-Hill, 1939.

———. *Capitalism, Socialism, and Democracy*. New York: Harper, 1950.

———. *The Theory of Economic Development: An Inquiry into Profits, Capital, Credit, Interest, and the Business Cycle*. New Brunswick: Transaction, 1983.

Sear, Robert. "Review: *Maternal Overprotection* by David M. Levy." *American Journal of Psychology* 58, no. 2 (1945): 282–84.

Seeley, John R., R. Alexander Sim, and Elizabeth Loosley. *Crestwood Heights: A Study of the Culture of Suburban Life*. Toronto: University of Toronto Press, 1956.

Senay, Emily. *From Boys to Men: A Woman's Guide to the Health of Husbands, Partners, Sons, Fathers, and Brothers*. New York: Simon and Schuster, 2005.

Service, Robert W. *Ploughman of the Moon: An Adventure into Memory*. New York: Dodd, Mead, 1945.

Sillman, Leland. *The Daredevil*. Philadelphia: John C. Winston, 1948.

Sinclair, Gordon. "Help! Equal Rights for Men." *Chatelaine*, July 1950.

Spock, Benjamin. *Dr. Spock Talks with Mothers: Growth and Guidance*. New York: Fawcett, 1961.

———. *Baby and Child Care*. Montreal: Pocket Books of Canada, 1946, 1965.

Stemo, Johanne, L. "Guns Are for Men." *Maclean's*, 1 September 1952.

Steyn, M. "Excusing the Men Who Ran Away." *Maclean's*, 22 March 2009.

Stoddard, G. "Is the Alpha Male in Danger of Extinction?" *Women's Health*, September 2009.

Stone, L. Joseph, and Joseph Church. *Childhood and Adolescence: A Psychology of the Growing Person*. New York: Random House, 1973.

Strecker, Edward A. *Their Mothers' Sons*. New York: J.B. Lippincott, 1947.

Terman, Lewis M., and Catherine C. Miles. *Sex and Personality: Studies in Masculinity and Femininity*. New York: McGraw Hill, 1936.

Strecker, Edward A. "Pops and Popism." *Parents' Magazine*, May 1947.

Tiller, Stanley C. *Stormswept*. Toronto: Ryerson, 1950.

Toth, Tihamer. *Youth and Chastity*. Toronto: Garden City, 1936, 1946.

Tyre. Peg. *The Trouble with Boys: A Surprising Report Card on Our Sons, Their Problems at School, and What Parents and Educators Must Do*. New York: Three Rivers, 2008.

Ullman, Paul S. "Parental Participation in Childrearing as Evaluated by Male Social Deviates." *Pacific Sociological Review* 3, no. 2 (1960): 89–95.

Vaz, Edmund W. "Delinquency and the Youth Culture: Upper and Middle-Class Boys." *Journal of Criminal Law and Police Science* 60, no. 1 (1969): 33–46.

Walker, Hiram. Advertisement. *Maclean's*, 15 April 1946.

Wallace, Archer. *The Field of Honour: Another Hundred Stories for Boys*. Toronto: Ryerson, 1949.

Webster, M. "Where the Guys Aren't." *United Church Observer*, March 2007.

Whyte, William H. *The Organization Man*. New York: Doubleday Anchor Books, 1956.

Wylie, Philip. *Generation of Vipers*. Toronto: Farrar and Rinehart, 1942.

Yablonsky, Lewis. "The Delinquent Gang as a Near-Group." *Social Problems* 17, no. 2 (1959): 108–17.

Index

100 Huntley Street (television program), 110

A

Aariak, Eva, 108
Aboriginal women, 108
Acton Free Press, xv, xviii, xx, 29, 40, 84
Adlow, Elijah, 1
Administrative Science Quarterly, 56
Adventures of Ozzie and Harriet, The, 6
Africa, eastern, 115
Albert Medal, 57
Albert, Prince (Albert of Saxe-Coburg and Gotha), 57
alcoholism, 2
Alexander, Judy, 59
Alexander, Mrs. Louis, 59
Along Olympic Road (Hewitt), 40
Alt, Herschel, 11
American Association of Motor Vehicle Administrators, 21
American Federation of Labour, 28
American Psychological Association Task Force, 107
American Scholar (magazine), 15
Ames, Louise Bates, 11, 20, 21, 24
Anderson, James C., 14
Anderson, Jim (*Father Knows Best* character), 6
Anglo-Protestant, xxvi, 4, 25, 92, 121, 122. *See also* Protestant
Anglo-Saxon, 66, 97

Apple, Michael, 106
Atlantic, The (magazine), 103
Atlas Shrugged (Rand), 110
atom bomb, xxiv, 30; atomic annihilation, x; atomic attack, xxi; atomic war, xviii
"atomic age," ix, xxvii, 29

B

Baby and Child Care (Spock), 4, 7, 9, 12
baby boom, ix
Baker, Louise, 85
Baltimore, 2
Bank of Montreal, 3, 108
Bank of Nova Scotia, 69
Barrie (Ontario), 69
baseball, xiv, 2, 31, 37, 90, 94
basketball, 32, 37, 90, 92, 95, 96
Bates, Gordon, xxii
Baugh, Charles, 72
Baumeister, Roy, 102
Beanery Boys (Toronto gang), 94. *See also* gangs
Belle River (Ontario), 77
Benatar, David, 102, 111
Berton, Pierre, 6
Big Brothers, 80, 82–83, 91, 92, 98, 137n35, 150n43
billiards, 50
Bingham, Adrian, 37, 39
Biscuit Eater, The (film), 61, 146n41
Blair, Gerald, 60
Blatchford, Christie, 103

Blatz, W.E., 76, 77
Bloch, Herbert, 50
Bly, Robert, 104
Bodsworth, Fred, xxiii
Boniface, Ted, 56
Booth, David, 116
Bothwell, Robert, 48
boxing, 32, 89, 90, 91
Boy and His Dog, A (film), 61
Boy on Defense (Young), 35
Boy Scouts, Boy Scout Movement, xix, xxvii, 4, 27, 46, 52, 68–73, 83, 88, 112, 153n150; "Boys Land," 71–72; Wolves, 77
Boys Adrift (Sax), 119
Boys Life–Dodd Mead Prize, xv
Boys Should Be Boys (Meeker), 119
boys clubs, xvii, xviii, xxviii, 46, 75, 76, 83, 86, 87–94, 95, 96, 97, 98, 99, 124
"Boys Land." *See under* Boy Scouts, Boy Scout Movement
"Boys Village" (London, Ontario), 96
Brampton (Ontario), 93,
Brantford (Ontario), 85
Breckenridge, Marian E., xi, 43, 44, 49, 50, 52
Brennan, Harry, 196
Britain, 39
British Army, 18, 41
Brozo, William, 110
Burstyn, Varda, 38
Business Cycles: A Theoretical, Historical, and Statistical Analysis of the Capitalist Process (Schumpeter), 5
Butler, Judith, 118

C

Cahill, Brian, 36
Callaghan, Morley, 61
Callwood, June, 78
Campbell, Wallace R., 153n150
Canadian Baptist, xv
Canadian Comstock, 141n53
Canadian Council on Learning, 116
Canadian Feminist Alliance for International Action (CFAIA), 107, 108

Canadian Forum (magazine), xv
Canadian General Electric Co., 30
Canadian Home and School, xvi
Canadian International Development Agency (CIDA), 107
Canadian Journal of Psychology, xvi, 43
Canadian Labour Congress (CLC), xvii, 96, 107
Canadian Motion Picture Distributors Association, 146n41
Canadian Natural Sciences and Engineering Research Council, 115
Canadian Oil Companies, 88
Canadian Penal Association, 80
Canadian Savings Bond (Canada Savings Bond), 59
Canadian Social Science Research Council, 14
"Canadian Way, The" (Hiram Walker advertisement, 1946), 40
capitalism, capitalist, xx, xxii, 16, 29, 31, 32, 34, 36, 42, 43, 54, 55, 56, 61, 66, 123, 134n75
Cappon, Paul, 116
Caribbean, 115
Carrigan, D. Owen, 75
Central America, 115
Chapin, Miriam, 89
Charlesworth, J.L., 36
Chatelaine (magazine), xv, xxiii, xxiv, 5, 11, 17, 21
Chemical Institute of Canada, 60
Chenier, Elise, xxv
Chesley Avenue Public School (London, Ontario), 91
Chicago Black Hawks, 95
Child and Society, The (Elkin), 10, 21
Child Development (Breckenridge and Vincent), 43, 49
Child Development (magazine), 10–11
Child Guidance Clinic. *See under* Toronto Board of Education
Chisholm, Brock, 17, 18
Chomsky, Noam, 106
Christian, Christianity, xii, 68, 110
Chrysler Corporation of Canada, 33
Church Times, xv, 83

citizenship, xii, xix, 52, 53, 68, 73, 82, 88, 89, 90, 92; corporate, 40; girls and, x; nature of, x–xi
Claremont Review of Books, 113
Clark, Catherine Anthony, 61
Clark, Christy, 108
class, xi, xiii, xv, xvii, xx, xxi, xxvii, 4, 25, 27, 36, 38, 48, 50, 54, 69, 82, 94, 106, 108, 115, 119; working-class, xii, xvii, xxviii, 50, 76, 77, 79, 81, 82, 87, 88, 89, 90, 92, 93, 94, 95, 96, 115, 124, 134n94, 149n9; middle-class, xii, xv, xvii, xxi, xxiii, xxvi, xxviii, 1, 2, 4, 6, 25, 75, 79, 82, 83, 92, 95, 96, 108, 109, 115, 119, 121, 122, 134–35n94, 136n24, 148n3; upper-class, 4
Cleaver, Nancy, 5, 23, 150n56
Cleaver, Ward (*Leave It to Beaver* character), 6
Cohen, Albert, 50
Cold War, ix, x, xviii, xix, xxiii, xxiv, xxvii, 14, 16, 29, 34, 38, 74, 80, 81, 85, 88, 98, 121, 123
Collingwood (Ontario), 17
Columbus Boys Club (Toronto), 89, 93. *See also* boys clubs
communist, communism, x, xix, xx, xxi, xxii, xxiv, 27, 29, 31, 39, 54, 123
Connell, Raewyn, xiii, 55, 106, 118
Cooper, Gary, 145n9
Cooper, Sherry, 108
crafts, 103
Crane, A.R., 58
Cratchit, Bob (*A Christmas Carol*), 42
Crisp, William G., xv

D

Dale of the Mounted: Dew Line Duty (Holiday), xviii
Daly, Tom, 40
Dangerous Book for Boys, The (Iggulden brothers), 101
Daredevil, The (Sillman), 61
Davy and His Dog (Lanski), 70
Deacon, William Arthur, 45
delinquency, delinquents, xii, xxv, xxviii, 6, 15, 16, 17, 50, 53, 75, 76, 77, 78, 80, 81, 82, 83, 84, 86, 87, 88, 89, 92, 93, 94, 97, 98, 124, 149n8, 149–50n34
Delinquent Boys: The Culture of the Gang (Cohen), 59
Delinquents in the Making (Glueck and Glueck), 89
Demise of Guys, The (Zimbardo and Duncan), 119
democracy, x, xix, xx, xxii, 4, 25, 29, 54, 60, 68, 97
Department of Foreign Affairs, 107
depression (economic). *See* Great Depression
Derstine, Clayton, xi
Dick, Philip K., 133n69
disability, 108, 109, 115, 119, 156n54
divorce, 2, 12, 21, 29, 30, 112
Dog Who Wouldn't Be, The (Mowat), 61, 65
dogs, 61–66, 67
Dovercourt Park (Toronto), 88
Dow Awards, 59, 60, 146n34
Dow Brewery, 59, 146n34
Drew, George, 68
Drinker, Sophie, 24, 25, 125
Duke of Edinburgh, 76
Dummitt, Christopher, xvi
Duncan, Nikita, 119
Dundas (Ontario), 89, 90
Dundas Street West (Toronto), 94
Dunderdale, Kathy, 108
Dyhouse, Carol, 37

E

Ealing (London, Ontario district), 88
École Polytechnique (Montreal), 105
Education and Psychological Assessment, xvi
education, xiv, xvii, xviii, xx, xxv, 3, 16, 38, 42, 46, 49, 50, 60, 71, 80, 84, 86, 89, 91, 92, 96, 102, 106, 108, 113, 114, 115, 116, 117, 118, 119, 122, 137n35, 144n132, 159n97
Educational Review (journal), xvi, 12
Edwards, Catherine Conrad, xv
Elizabeth II (monarch), 76
Elkin, Frederick, 10, 21

Emotional Maturity (Saul), xi

End of Men and the Rise of Women, The (Rosin), 102

England, 83

Enright, Michael, 131n21

entrepreneurs, entrepreneurship, xxvii, 27, 54, 55–61, 62, 64, 65, 66, 67, 73, 74, 145n9

Essex County Reporter, xv, xviii, xx

Essex Free Press, 29, 80

ethnicity, xiii, 25, 50, 115, 119

eugenics, 76, 77,

F

Faludi, Susan, xvii

family, nuclear, 1, 4, 13, 14, 24, 25, 83, 122

Farnham, Marynia, 89, 135n3 (chap. 1), 139n90

"Father Was a Gambler" (Anderson), 14

Father's Day, 9, 97

fathers, fatherhood, xxiii, 1, 3, 4–16, 20, 21, 22, 23, 24, 25, 40, 43, 44, 48, 59, 62, 64, 76, 80, 82, 84, 94, 96, 97, 98, 104, 122, 126, 136n15

Feminine Mystique, The (Friedan), 125

femininity, xiii, xiv, 8, 13, 22, 23, 33, 43, 44, 45, 46, 48, 57, 59, 74, 118, 122, 126

feminism, 101, 105, 107, 112, 113, 115, 126

Fenichel, Otto, 14

Fine Young Man, A (Gurian), 111, 119

Finlay, Fred, 69

First National Conference on the Status of Male Children in Canada, 156n59

Flannigan, Father, 31

Flood, R.G., 30

football, 4, 37, 51

Ford Motor Company, 153n150; Ford of Canada, 69

Ford of Canada. *See* Ford Motor Company

Fortune (magazine), 42

Fountainhead, The (Rand), 145n9

French (language), 117

Friedan, Betty, 125

G

Gang, The (Bloch and Neiderhoffer), 59

gangs, 28, 48–53, 65, 87, 123, 144n132, 148n3 (chap. 4); Beanery Boys (Toronto gang), 94

gay, gays. *See* homosexuals, homosexuality

George Medal, 57

Georgetown Herald, xv

Germany, 29, 41

Gibson, H.W., 48, 49

Gifford, C.G., 6

Girl Guides, 68, 73

girlhood, 56, 111, 113, 122, 125, 126; nature of in postwar era, xviii

girls: citizenship and, x; postwar gender identity and, 22

globalization, 101, 106

Globe and Mail, ix, xiv, xv, xx, xxiv, xxvi, 4, 6, 9, 13, 16, 17, 18, 19, 36, 37, 38, 39, 49, 52, 56, 58, 59, 62, 64, 65, 69, 70, 71, 77, 78, 79, 84, 91, 94, 95, 96, 98, 101, 109, 111, 114, 117, 137n35, 141n53

Glueck, Eleanor, 79, 80

Glueck, Sheldon, 78, 79, 80

Good Bye, My Lady (Street), 62; film, 61

Good Health (elementary school textbook, 1955), xxii, 42

Gouzenko, Igor, xix, xx

Governor General's Award for juvenile fiction, xv

Gramsci, Antonio, xiii

Grant, Julia, 51, 137n35

Great Depression, ix, x, xvi, xxvi, 1, 25, 50, 121

Great War, 87

Green, Amy Susan, 144n132

Griffin, John, 18, 19

Guelph (Ontario), 83

Gurian, Michael, 111, 119

Guttmacher, Manfred, xxv

gyms, 50, 89, 96

H

Hagedorn, John, 50

Halcrow, John, 92

Haliburton County, 72
Haliburton Scout Reserve. *See* "Boys
    Land" *under* Boy Scouts, Boy Scout
    Movement
Hall, G. Stanley, 137n35, 144n132
Hambleton, Jack, xv, 62
Hamilton Spectator, 103
Hargrave, Joe (character in Baker's *Snips
    and Snails*), 85
Harvey, George Isaac, 132n32
Hayes, John F., xv
H-bomb, xxii
Health League of Canada, xxii
Hendry, Charles E., 49
heteronormativity, xxiv, xxvi, 102, 105,
    106, 120, 121, 127
heterosexuality, 15, 118, 126
Hewitt, Foster, 40
hiking, 95
Hiram Walker, 40
Hitler, Adolf, 18, 41, 52, 124
hockey, xiv, 4, 31, 32, 34, 35, 37, 38, 40,
    41, 51, 89, 90, 92, 94, 112, 131n21,
    137n35
Hoff Sommers, Christina, 111, 114, 119
Hogeveen, Bryan, 77
Holliday, Joe, xviii
Holman, Charles, 76
homophobia, 14, 112, 118, 124, 126
homosexuals, homosexuality, xx, xxiii,
    xxiv, xxv, 1, 6, 12, 14, 15, 17, 19, 20,
    21, 25, 31 (gay men), 43, 45, 112
    (gay men and women), 122 (gay and
    lesbian liberation), 123, 124; queer
    identities, 101, 134n75
Hope Report, The, xi, 46, 75, 76
House of Commons (Canada), xx
Howard Roark (character in *The
    Fountainhood*), 145n9
Howden, Reginald, 69
Hudson's Bay, 76
Hymowitz, Kay, 102

I

Iacovetta, Franca, xiii, 2, 149n9
Iggulden brothers, 101
Ilg, Frances L., 11, 19, 21, 24

immigrants, xii, xxvi, xxviii, 2, 3, 6,
    34, 50, 76, 77, 81, 92, 97, 108, 124,
    134n94
Immigration Act (1950), xxvi
immigration, x, xi, xxvi, 101
Indigenous boys, xii; Indigenous com-
    munities, 115; Indigenous popula-
    tions, 117
Industrial Age (1925–60), 50
Institute of Child Study. *See under*
    University of Toronto
Institute of Marriage and Family
    Canada, 109
*Is There Anything Good about Men? How
    Cultures Flourish by Exploiting Men*
    (Baumeister), 102
Italy, 39

J

Jack, Earl, 89
Jackson, Harvey, 137n35
Japan, xviii
John Innes Community Centre
    (Toronto), 91
Johns Hopkins (hospital), xxv
Journal of Education, xvi
Journal of Educational Psychology, xvi, 80
Journal of Educational Sociology, xvi, 33
Journal of Genetic Psychology, xvi, 49
Journal of Higher Education, xvi, 24, 125
Juvenile Delinquency Act, 75

K

Katz, Elliot, 112
Katz, Michael, 115
Katz, Sidney, 77
Kelman, Norman, 7, 15, 16
Kidd, Bruce, 39
Kimmel, Michael, xxiv, 40
King Edward Hotel (Toronto), 129n4
King, William Lyon Mackenzie, ix,
    xx, 28; postwar "Reconstruction"
    program, ix
Kingston (Ontario), 83
Kingston Whig-Standard, 103
Kingsville (Ontario), 141n53
Kingsville Reporter, xv, xx, xxv, 81
Kinsey Report, xxiv

Kitchener (Ontario), xi, 84; Kitchener-Waterloo, 59
Kiwanis Club, 92, 94, 95, 97

L

Labour Council of London, xvii, 96
labour market, xxi, xxiii, 47, 101, 121
labour organizations, xx, 106
labour relations, x, 25, 28, 38, 121
labour, xvi, xx, 5, 6, 29, 30, 46, 93, 106, 108, 116, 121, 134n75
Labour–Management Cooperation Service, 28; Tommy Teamwork, 28
Labour–Management Production Committees, 28
Lacelle, Roger, 66
lacrosse, 90
Ladd-Taylor, Molly, xiii
Lakeshore News, xv, xviii
Lakeshore-Etobicoke Neighbourhood Workers District Association, 83
Lanski, Lois, 61
LaPlante, Jerry, 56
Lassie (series), 61
Laurentian University, 116
Laycock, Samuel, 20, 21
Layton, Irving, xxiv
Leamington (Ontario), 141n53
Leamington Junior Chamber of Commerce, 33
Leamington Post and News, ix, xv, xvi
Lefty's Adventure (Rorke), 61
Lepine, Marc (Marc Gharbi), 105
lesbian. *See* homosexual, homosexuality
Liberal government (King), ix, xxvi
Life (magazine), xv, xxiv, 13, 15, 19
Lions Club, 95 (Scarborough), 141n53
London (Ontario), xviii, 18, 21, 88, 89, 91, 95, 96
London Free Press, xv, 96
London Police Boys Club, 96. *See also* boys clubs
Longmans, Green (publishers), 62
Lower, Arthur, xix
Luke Baldwin's Vow (Callaghan), 61
Lundberg, Ferdinand, 89, 135n3 (chap. 1)
Luxton, Meg, 107

M

Maclean's (magazine), xv, xxiii, 6, 14, 19, 20, 22, 59, 60, 76, 77, 78, 105, 110, 131n22, 146n35
MacLennan, Hugh, 12
Macleod, Alastair, 13
Macleod, David, 143n110
Making a Mountie (film), 97
Man in the Gray Flannel Suit, The (film), 33
Manhood in America (Kimmel), xxiv
Manliness (Mansfield), 102
Manning Up: How the Rise of Women Has Turned Men into Boys (Hymowitz), 102
Mansfield, Harvey, 102
Marcuse, Gary, 11, 14
Marois, Pauline, 108
Martin, Franz, 33, 34
Martino, Wayne, 114, 115
Massey, Vincent, xviii, 70
Mathews, Fred, 156n59
McAdam, Vernon F., 89
McCarthy, Joseph, xx
McCleary, Ray, 151n69
McCreary, John, 43
McEwen, Nelson, 96
McGarvey, Albert, 96
McGill University, 13, 116
McIlroy, Kimball, 31, 32, 37
McInnis, Peter S., 28
McMaster University, 116
McNeel, B.H, 18
Meeker, Meg, 111, 119
mental defect, deficiency, 2, 18; distress, 6
mental health issues, xxii, xxvi, 18, 42, 53, 57, 92; experts in, xxv, 124
Mental Hygiene Division (Toronto), xxvi
mental hygiene, xxv, xxvi, 6, 7, 25–26, 86
Merchant Bank, 3
Meredith, Henry Vincent, 3
Meredith, John S., 3
Meredith, Richard, 3
Meredith, William Cooles, 3
Merrill-Palmer Quarterly of Behavior and Development, 6

Metropolitan Church (Toronto), 88
Metropolitan Toronto Juvenile and
    Family Court, 83
middle-class, 135n94, 136n24, 148n2
    (chap. 4)
Miles, Catherine C., 43
Milligan, Lewis, xvi, xvii, 29
Mills, C. Wright, 55
Mimico (Ontario), 93, 95
Mimico Boys Hobbycrafts Club, 93, 95
Minister of Education (Ontario), 42
minorities, racial, 117; visible, xii;
    minority groups, 114
minority groups. *See* minorities
Modern Woman: The Lost Sex (Lundberg
    and Farnham), 135n3 (chap. 1)
Montreal Massacre, 105
Montreal, 59, 89, 105
Moore, Terrence O., 113
Morris, Joan, 1
Moscow, xx
mothers, motherhood, xvi, xxiii, 1, 2, 3,
    5, 7, 8, 9, 10, 11, 12, 13, 14, 15, 16–25,
    43, 44, 45, 46, 53, 59, 62, 66, 78, 80,
    81, 82, 84, 86, 95, 98, 112, 113, 122,
    125, 126, 139n90
Mowat, Farley, 61, 65, 66
Mundy, Liza, 102

N

Nanaimo-Cowichan (riding), 112
National Film Board, 89
National Hockey League. *See* NHL
National Humane Act Award, 65
National Post, 103, 105, 113
Nazis, 135n3
Neatby, Hilda, xviii
Neiderhoffer, Arthur, 50
Nelson, Ozzie, 6
neoliberalism, 106–7, 134n75, 155n35
"New age" (post–WW II), ix
New York City, 137n35
New York Times, 114
Newmarket (Ontario), 90
Newmarket Era and Express, xv, 20,
    69, 70
News (magazine), xviii

Newsboys Welfare Association, 96
NHL (National Hockey League), 31
Nicholson, David, 51
Nobel Peace Prize, 98
nuclear annihilation, 121; extinction,
    xviii; threat, xx
nuclear energy, xviii

O

Oakville Sports Association, 31
O'Keefe's Brewery Company, 141n53
Old Yeller (film), 61
Ontario College of Teachers, 117
Ontario Hospital, 18
Ontario legislature, 77, 132n32
Ontario Public School Board
    Association, 117
Ontario Royal Commission on
    Education (1950), 38; *Report of the
    Royal Commission on Education in
    Ontario (1950)* (see *Hope Report*)
Orangeville (Ontario), 105
Organization Man, The (Whyte), 56
Osler family, 3
Ottawa, 39, 97
Oxford Street Armoury (London,
    Ontario), 96

P

Pacific Sociological Review, 14
Parents' Magazine, xv, 2, 7, 8, 11, 20, 32,
    43, 44, 53
Parliament (Canada), 112
Paths to Noble Manhood (Clayton), xi
Patri, Angelo, 8, 63, 137n35
patriarchy, xiii, xiv, xvii, xxviii, 32, 48,
    54, 58, 95, 101, 126
Pearson, Lester B., 98
Peck, Gregory, 33
Pelletier, Ovila, 89
Pitcher, Noah, 82
Pleck, Joseph, 12, 135n99
Poile, Bud, 95
Police Club for Boys (NFB documentary),
    89
Pollack, William, 111, 119
Porter, John, xxvii
Portuguese (language), 115

Power, Janet, 19, 23–24
Preston (Ontario), 41
Protestant, xvii, xxvi, 4, 6, 25, 92, 121, 122
Psychoanalytical Theory of Neurosis, The (Fenichel), 14

Q

Queen's University, xix
queer identities, 101, 134n75. *See also under* homosexual

R

race, xi, xii, xiii, xv, xvii, xix, xx, xxi, xxvii, 25, 27, 36, 38, 54, 69, 106, 107, 108, 109, 110, 115, 118, 119
racism, xii, 118
Raising Boys in a New Kind of World (Reist), 112
Rand, Ayn, 110, 145n9
Rao, Anthony, 111, 119, 158n86
Rath, Thomas (Gregory Peck's character in *The Man in the Gray Flannel Suit*), 33
RCMP. *See* Royal Canadian Mounted Police
Rea, W. Harold, 88
Real Boys (Pollack), 119
Rebick, Judy, 161n2
Redford, Alison, 108
Regent Park (Toronto), 151n69
Reist, Michael, 112
Renison, R.J., 71
Report of the Royal Commission on Education in Ontario (1950). *See* Hope Report
Report of the Royal Commission on the Status of Women, 161n2. *See also under* Status of Women
Reynolds, Glenn, 115
Rezai-Rashti, Goli, 114
Richer Sex: How the New Majority of Female Breadwinners Is Transforming Sex, Love, and Family, The (Mundy), 102
Rogers, Kenneth, 80, 82, 87
Rogers, Roy, 59
Roman Catholic, 32, 86

Romantics, English (poetry), 148n102
Rorke, Louise, 61
Rosebery, Lord (British prime minister), 68
Rosin, Hanna, 102
Rousseau, Jean-Jacques, 148n102
Rowallan, Lord, xix, 68
Royal Canadian Mounted Police (RCMP), 14, 76, 97
Royal Humane Society Bronze Medal, 57
rugby, 31, 32
Russia, 29, 39, 98
Ruth, Babe, 2
Rutledge, W.F., 83

S

Safe on Second Base (Winfield), 35
Sale, Rhys M., 69
Salvation Army, 72, 96
Samson (Old Testament figure), 64
Sandals, Liz, 117
Sanderson, Derek, 131n21
Saskatchewan, 65
Saturday Night (magazine), xv, 31, 36, 37, 89
Saul, Leon, xi
Saunders, Robert, 86
Sax, Leonard, 110, 111, 119
Scarborough Township (Ontario), 98
Schreiber, Julius, ix
Schreier, Josephine, 24, 25, 125
Schumpeter, Joseph, 55, 56
Scott Mission (Toronto), 3
scouting, Scouts. *See* Boy Scouts, Boy Scout Movement
Scrooge (*A Christmas Carol*), 3
Scrubs on Skates (Young), 35, 36
Seagram's, 9
Sears, Alan, 106
Second Sexism: The Discrimination Against Men and Boys, The (Benatar), 111
Second World War, ix, x, xii, xiii, xvi, xviii, xxv, xxviii, 19, 27, 38, 47, 52, 68, 87, 94, 121, 123
Sergeant Preston of the Yukon (television character), 103

Sexual Behavior in the Human Male. See Kinsey Report

sexual orientation, xiii, 119

sexuality, xi, 107, 109, 115

Shaw, Robert, 88

Sillman, Leland, 61

Simpson's (department store), 69

Sinclair, Gordon, xxiv

Singleton, George, 50

skiing, 95

Smith, Adam, 106

Smith, Sidney, 69

Smythe, Conn, 137n35

Snips and Snails (Baker), 85,

Social Problems (journal), 14

softball, 37, 90, 92

Somali (language), 115

South America, 115

Soviets, xx, 38

Spanish (language), 115

Spock, Benjamin, xi, 4, 5, 7, 9, 12, 34, 35, 48

sports, xiv, 16, 19, 23, 28, 31–38, 39, 40, 41, 45, 47, 51, 66, 69, 86, 89, 90, 91, 92, 94, 95, 97, 107, 118, 122, 123, 125, 126. *See also individual sports*

Spry, Dan, xix, 68

Spurgeon English, O., 8, 10

Sputnik (satellite), 98

St. Albans Boys Club, 89. *See also* boys clubs

St. John's Training School, 32

St. Joseph's hospital (London, Ontario), 21

St. Lawrence River, 57

St. Michael's College (Toronto), 31

Statistics Canada, 108, 110

Status of Women (Canada), 107; *Report of the Royal Commission on the Status of Women*, 161n2

Steyn, Marc, 105

Stouffville Tribune, xv, 5, 23, 84, 150n56

Strain, Bob, 95

Straith, George, 95

Strecker, Edward, 7, 11

Street, James, 62

Strengthening Canada's Research Capacity: The Gender Dimension (report), 116

strikes, 28, 29, 30, 41, 139n8 (chap. 2)

swimming, 32, 50, 89, 90, 94, 96, 97

T

Tashman, Harry, 13

Tays, Randy, 58

teachers, 1, 10, 18, 32, 43, 53, 78, 85, 96, 110, 111, 113, 114, 115, 117; gender and, 113–17; 158n86, 158n87

Teamwork in Industry (bulletin), 28

Teamwork in Industry (journal), 42

Tender Years, The (film), 61

Terman, Lewis M., 43

The Golden Pine Cone (Catherine Anthony Clark), 61

Theory of Economic Development, The (Schumpeter), 55

tobogganing, 95

Tommy Teamwork. *See* Labour–Management Cooperation Service

Toronto Board of Education, xxv; Child Guidance Clinic, xxv

Toronto Board of Trade, 151n69

Toronto Boys Club, 96. *See also* boys clubs

Toronto Daily Star, xv, xvi, 3, 24, 49, 56, 57, 59, 63, 64, 94

Toronto District School Board, 114

Toronto Evening Telegram, 17, 64

Toronto Maple Leafs, 95, 137n35

Toronto Metropolitan boys band, 93

Toronto Metropolitan Optimists Boys' Club, 98. *See also* boys clubs

Toronto Star, xviii, xx, 1, 17, 51, 61, 62, 64

Toronto Telegram, xv, 59, 60

Toronto West End Fathers and Sons Club, 94

Toronto, xix, xxv, xxvi, 3, 28, 31, 34, 39, 50, 51, 68, 71, 77, 81, 82, 83, 84, 86, 88, 89, 90, 91, 92, 93, 94, 96, 97, 98, 103, 112, 114, 115, 117, 129n4, 156n59

Toronto's Ward Two Business Men's Association, 96
Transition (magazine), 109
Trinity K Club of Toronto, 88
Trouble with Boys, The (Tyre), 119
Tumpane, Frank, xxvi, 48
"TV Age," ix
Tyre, Peg, 111, 119

U

unions, xvii, xx, 29, 30, 52, 106, 139n8
Unionville (Ontario), 31
United Church Chaplain's Conference, 18
United Church Observer, xv, 131n25
United Church of Canada, 52
United States (US), xvi, xvii, xviii, xx, 143n110
United Suburban Gas Company, 141n53
University of Saskatchewan, xviii
University of Toronto, 49, 69; Faculty of Education, 116; Institute of Child Study, 11
UNO Security Council, 30
upper class. *See under* class

V

Vacation Church Schools (Toronto), 92
Valverde, Mariana, 148n102
Varsity Stadium (Toronto), xix, 68
Vincent Elizabeth Lee, xi, 43, 49, 50, 52
violence, xii, 19, 24, 29, 34, 35, 39, 40, 41, 50, 79, 90, 105, 106, 112, 123, 124, 156n54
Vipond, Jim, 39
Voices from the Street (Dick), 133n69
Von der Osten, Robert, 58

W

Walrus, The (magazine), 113
War Against Boys, The (Hoff Sommers), 119
Washington Post, 110
Waters, Robert Thomas, 57
Watts, Ruth, 127
Way of Boys, The (Rao), 111, 119, 158n86
Welland (Ontario), 72
Weltfish, Gene, 129n4
Wente, Margaret, 18, 101, 111
Western, David, 57
Whitaker, Reginald, 11, 14
Whitby (Ontario), 92
Whitby Minor Athletic Association, 92
White Gold in the Cassiar (Hambleton and Crisp), xv
Whitmire, Richard, 110, 111
Why Boys Fail (Brozo and Whitmire), 110
Whyte, William H., 46, 47, 56
Windsor (Ontario), 153n150
Winfield, Ed, 35
Wolves. *See under* Boy Scouts, Boy Scout Movement
working class. *See under* class
Wynne, Kathleen, 117

Y

YMCA, 32, 46, 50, 51, 90, 92, 96; Gold Merit Award, 92
Young, Scott, 35

Z

Zimbardo, Philip, 119

Books in the Studies in Childhood and Family in Canada Series
Published by Wilfrid Laurier University Press

Making Do: Women, Family, and Home in Montreal during the Great Depression by Denyse Baillargeon, translated by Yvonne Klein • 1999 / xii + 232 pp. / ISBN 0-88920-326-1 / ISBN-13: 978-0-88920-326-6

Children in English-Canadian Society: Framing the Twentieth-Century Consensus by Neil Sutherland with a new foreword by Cynthia Comacchio • 2000 / xxiv + 336 pp. / illus. / ISBN 0-88920-351-2 / ISBN-13: 978-0-88920-351-8

Love Strong as Death: Lucy Peel's Canadian Journal, 1833–1836 edited by J.I. Little • 2001 / x + 229 pp. / illus. / ISBN 0-88920-389-x / ISBN-13: 978-0-88920-389-230-x

The Challenge of Children's Rights for Canada by Katherine Covell and R. Brian Howe • 2001 / viii + 244 pp. / ISBN 0-88920-380-6 / ISBN-13: 978-0-88920-380-8

NFB Kids: Portrayals of Children by the National Film Board of Canada, 1939–1989 by Brian J. Low • 2002 / vi + 288 pp. / illus. / ISBN 0-88920-386-5 / ISBN-13: 978-0-88920-386-0

Something to Cry About: An Argument against Corporal Punishment of Children in Canada by Susan M. Turner • 2002 / xx + 317 pp. / ISBN 0-88920-382-2 / ISBN-13: 978-0-88920-382-2

Freedom to Play: We Made Our Own Fun edited by Norah L. Lewis • 2002 / xiv + 210 pp. / ISBN 0-88920-406-3 / ISBN-13: 978-0-88920-406-5

The Dominion of Youth: Adolescence and the Making of Modern Canada, 1920–1950 by Cynthia Comacchio • 2006 / x + 302 pp. / illus. / ISBN 0-88920-488-8 / ISBN-13: 978-0-88920-488-1

Evangelical Balance Sheet: Character, Family, and Business in Mid-Victorian Nova Scotia by B. Anne Wood • 2006 / xxx + 198 pp. / illus. / ISBN 0-88920-500-0 / ISBN-13: 978-0-88920-500-0

A Question of Commitment: Children's Rights in Canada edited by R. Brian Howe and Katherine Covell • 2007 / xiv + 442 pp. / ISBN 978-1-55458-003-3

Taking Responsibility for Children edited by Samantha Brennan and Robert Noggle • 2007 / xxii + 188 pp. / ISBN 978-1-55458-015-6

Home Words: Discourses of Children's Literature in Canada edited by Mavis Reimer • 2008 / xx + 280 pp. / illus. / ISBN 978-1-55458-016-3

Depicting Canada's Children edited by Loren Lerner • 2009 / xxvi + 442 pp. / illus. /ISBN 978-1-55458-050-7

Babies for the Nation: The Medicalization of Motherhood in Quebec, 1910–1970 by Denyse Baillargeon, translated by W. Donald Wilson • 2009 / xiv + 328 pp. / illus. / ISBN 978-1-5548-058-3

The One Best Way? Breastfeeding History, Politics, and Policy in Canada by Tasnim Nathoo and Aleck Ostry • 2009 / xvi + 262 pp. / illus. / ISBN 978-1-55458-147-4

Fostering Nation? Canada Confronts Its History of Childhood Disadvantage by Veronica Strong-Boag • 2011 / x + 302 pp. / ISBN 978-1-55458-337-9

Cold War Comforts: Maternalism, Child Safety, and Global Insecurity, 1945–1975 by Tarah Brookfield • 2012 / xiv + 292 pp. / illus. / ISBN 978-1-55458-623-3

Ontario Boys: Masculinity and the Idea of Boyhood in Postwar Ontario, 1945–1960 by Christopher J. Greig • 2014 / xxviii + 184 pp. / ISBN 978-1-55458-900-5

A Brief History of Women in Quebec by Denyse Baillargeon, translated by W. Donald Wilson • forthcoming 2014 / ISBN 978-1-55458-950-0